THE BRIGHT SIDE

"Anyone who has had their life completely gutted and rewired will adore this family story. Bradbury's dark humour and gloriously upbeat voice makes it the perfect antidote to a tough year. I loved it!" —Plum Johnson, author of *They Left Us Everything*

"One of the miracles of this funny and poignant book is that Bradbury makes growing up along the Niagara Escarpment sound as enchanting as Paris. And in this era of fractured relationships, *The Bright Side*'s magnificent depiction of her parents' steady love for one another will touch hearts.... Not a wasted word—I loved it." —Catherine Gildiner, author of *Good Morning, Monster* and *Too Close to the Falls*

"It is rare for a memoir to be very funny and unwaveringly honest. But Cathrin Bradbury's *The Bright Side* is brilliantly both. You could (quite correctly) call *The Bright Side* charming—but only if you also point out that it is smart, beautifully written, and mercilessly clear-eyed on the subject of what time has in store for us all." —David Macfarlane, author of *Likeness*

"*The Bright Side* is funny and wise and sparky and surprising and heartbreaking and weird and honest and smart and gutting and completely whole-hearted without ever veering into maudlin or precious or self-indulgent, which is an enormous feat." —Leah McLaren, author of *Where You End and I Begin*

"In a spirit reminiscent of the great Nora Ephron, Cathrin Bradbury finds the funny in her own failings and the humour in heartbreak with her razor-sharp prose. *The Bright Side* reminds us when things get messy and painful, laughter is as important as light." —Jessica Allen, *The Social*

"The year 2015 was not a good one for Cathrin Bradbury. . . . After divorcing her husband of 25 years, she was forced to navigate the loss of a new romance and the passing of both parents— all in one truly awful *annus horribilis*. The result is this warm, chatty memoir, which serves as both a meditation on family and friendship and a love letter to Toronto and its colourful media characters." —*The Globe and Mail*

"A beautifully written and unabashed family memoir focusing on one bummer of a year. A book that can evoke both laughter and tears on the same page." —*The Hamilton Spectator*

"*The Bright Side* . . . is a memoir of longing and loss as well as a lightness of being. . . . Its charm lies in its relatability, which is underscored by Bradbury's wry voice, black humour and frank assessment of the world and her place in it." —*Everything Zoomer*

CATHRIN BRADBURY

THE BRIGHT SIDE

A Happy Book About a Sad Year

PENGUIN

an imprint of Penguin Canada,
a division of Penguin Random House Canada Limited

First published in Viking Canada paperback, 2021

Published in this edition, 2022

1 2 3 4 5 6 7 8 9 10

LIBRARY AND ARCHIVES CANADA CATALOGUING IN PUBLICATION

Title: The bright side / Cathrin Bradbury.
Names: Bradbury, Cathrin, author.
Identifiers: Canadiana 20200234285 | ISBN 9780735239401 (softcover)
Subjects: LCSH: Bradbury, Cathrin. | LCSH: Life change events.
Classification: LCC BF637.L53 B73 2022 | DDC 158.1—dc23

Cover design: Terri Nimmo
Cover image: (toast) © Tara Moore / Getty Images

Printed in the United States of America

www.penguinrandomhouse.ca

Penguin
Random House
PENGUIN CANADA

For the siblings, Laura, Tim, David, and Ann

Love! Tenderness! Courage!

—CAROL SHIELDS, *The Stone Diaries*

CONTENTS

Holes

MY HOUSE IS SPITTING ON ME. This bright home with four sides of windows that bring light from every direction, my doted-on Number 9, has turned against me. I'd like to spit on it too.

I'm lying in bed watching the holes in my ceiling. I don't trust the holes. The way they yawn (up, into the ceiling, an unsettling sight) into what shouldn't be empty space. The way they pockmark my house. The way their existence creates the piles of rubble I live with, like lumpen dinner guests who won't go home.

A van rattles up the street, and the hole above my head drops mushroom clouds of plaster dust onto my face. The hole in my ceiling is spitting on my filthy, fuming face. I think I'll close my eyes and picture fields of blooming red poppies turning toward the sun, or maybe those metallic Alexander Wang shoes I feel I badly need, but decide not to risk it. The plaster dust that coats my bedroom might stick my eyelashes together if I close them for too long. Better to keep my eyes open.

I'm having the house rewired. It was necessary after I took out a massive mortgage on an uninsurable, knob-and-tube-wired fire hazard, and now the massacre that I've invited in provokes and frightens me. Sixty-three holes in the walls and ceilings, thirty heaps of plaster, and one narrow swept path, the kind you should never follow in a fairy tale, to a single connected light dangling from a long black cord over my bed. It's not only the damage the rewiring has done to the house I've wrested this past fall from my husband as part of our divorce settlement—he didn't want it, but he didn't think I should have it either—but because as Number 9 becomes rubble, so does my life.

I'm a masterful, multitasking woman; aren't we all. I book the kids' dentist appointments, plan a dinner party, rip out the front page of the newspaper I run—"Switch out Justin Trudeau for the stink bug invasion!"—while biking home from work in my sensible helmet and less sensible shoes. I'm too busy for much self-reflection, and not inclined that way anyway. ("Nothing good ever came of too much thinking," Mom said whenever she caught me staring into the middle distance, drifting toward some inward call. "Go out and play.") I prefer to do, rather than be; I'm with Sartre on that one. Except for the occasional 3 a.m. whir down a drain of non-specific dread, I hurtle forward. Or I did until 2015 began like a hammer to the head.

Fifty-nine is late for a divorce, and not the wisest time to become the sole owner of a 1940s house badly in need of a lift. And it's not just the house that's falling apart. My parents, both in their nineties, barely add up to one semi-competent person. My brother, lost to alcohol for thirty years, has come back from the dead, and we're panicked by his improbable return, my mother most of all. My oldest friend has been gone from my life for twenty years, and the absence feels final. I've met a

Promising New Man, but the plaster dust makes him sneeze, and suddenly he's become hard to find. My son has moved across the country to Banff to launch his postgraduate life, and his texts are as fleeting as trilliums; my daughter comes home less often than she might from her nearby photography school, and when she does, she finds me wanting. Mom's sister Helen, the aunt I most resemble, the one who was meant to go on forever, died a week before Christmas. Even Pierre, our fourteen-year-old family poodle, is on his last legs. I keep finding him staring into corners, trembling. It's as if everything in my orderly and familiar existence has crowded together at once, only to be smashed apart. The wrecking ball is working overtime, the walls are crumbling, and I don't have a new blueprint. The best I can do is lie in bed as the hours tock from 2 to 3 to 4 a.m. and keep my eye on those holes. Who knows what will come out of them next.

Number 9

IT WAS A RANDOM GIRL on a warm spring afternoon who made me realize I would never let go of Number 9. Falling for the house was easy, and happened all at once. Deciding to hold on to it, even as I left my marriage—that I might have pondered for a moment or two.

On the day of the random girl, John and I were in our living room, reading or doing not much. The iron casement windows were flung open to catch the first breeze of spring, so we heard the high excitement of the schoolkids before we saw them come around the corner, holding hands, double file. Not two straight Madeline lines, but two stumbling, messy rows of eight- or ten-year-old kids, dawdlers and dreamers, shovers and bossy talkers. The last girl in the row stopped abruptly in front of our house and tugged her partner back. "Oh!" she said, staring at Number 9. She had dark pigtails and a yellow knapsack, and she stood there until her classmate yanked her away, and even then she looked back with longing. It might have been sweet, except for the greedy hunger in her eyes. "It's mine!" I wanted to shout out the window as she lollygagged up the street.

The first time John and I saw the house was on a spring day like that one, and I was stopped in my tracks like that girl. I might have even said "Oh!" because seeing Number 9 felt like my future, and it looked bright. I loved the way the house sat back from the street with stolid determination, its white stucco facade and wide symmetrical windows letting you know it had no secrets until you filled it with your own. Its dependable squareness, so different from the stern Victorian houses that jutted into the street like the prow of a ship. Number 9's wide wooden door with its lion's head knocker had the gravitas of a great entry and seemed up to the purpose Edith Wharton described in *The Decoration of Houses*: front doors are to let people in, and also to keep them out.

We moved in with the kids a few months later, in 2000, the auspicious turn of the millennium. We had a big mortgage but good jobs, reliable friends, and, for me, the tugboat of the family, a determined and familiar forward momentum that didn't brook disagreement about where we were heading or why. We were on course, that was the important thing, and it had been steady as she goes for some time. Not everything was perfect. We were well into our second decade of marriage and had to navigate around the occasional boulder to have our morning coffee in peace. But moving into Number 9 gave us a project, and one we were good at together. We combined handed-down furniture with our own modern splurges in a way that suited us and the house. We knew how to make a place look and feel like home, to provide for ourselves, and to welcome friends and family. We painted the wide wooden door bright chartreuse, bought a piano so the kids could learn (they did not), and held martini-fuelled parties and smaller talky dinners with good pals. We were in our forties, "that itchy age," said a sexy Ellen Burstyn in *The Last Picture Show*, and we lived noisy, exciting lives.

"How does a woman know when a marriage is over?" asked Carol Shields in *The Stone Diaries*. "Because of the way her life suddenly shears off in just two directions: past and future." I can't say precisely when we began to unravel. It was gradual but also final. It started before we moved to Number 9 and picked up pace once we realized a change of place was not a remedy for a failing marriage. John began to sit alone in the living room with a tumbler of vodka and was mostly silent, which was better than when he was not silent. I stayed late at work. We had ugly arguments that were hard to come back from, and after a while, neither of us tried. Tolstoy's "each unhappy family is unhappy in its own way" gets a lot of pickup, but I'm not so sure. Unhappiness has a dreary, inescapable sameness, a day-by-day drudgery, and ours was no different. Without knowing it, we were heading for divorce with all the compromise of a high-speed train. Suddenly there were no small decisions, only big ones. Would I stay or would I go?

"You won't last five minutes without me," John said matter-of-factly one morning, sitting in the kitchen at Number 9, and I knew it was true. I would literally die without him. (Ask unhappy couples why they stay together and they'll say something similar—"I'll die without her," "I'm nothing without him"—even when the evidence is to the absolute contrary.) I'd spent half my life knowing whether John was breathing in or breathing out. "You bring a lot to this marriage, you know," Mom had said years earlier, but I didn't see it. John had the brains, he had the Google domination over facts, he had the privileged

WASP taste and discernment. We liked going to movies, where a film could easily be ruined for John by a small factual or aesthetic failure, a fake Noguchi lamp in a supposedly stylish home. When a Civil War soldier bit into an apple in *Dances with Wolves*, John hissed into my ear, "It's a McIntosh. They weren't in production yet," and nothing about the movie was believable for him after that. He stretched his long legs into the aisle and leaned his head back to watch the ceiling until the credits rolled. At some point, I became the one with the facts wrong. I didn't add up for him anymore.

It took a lot of energy to look away from our problems, but I got pretty good at it. I mostly blamed John. It required less self-reflection that way. That's the beauty of a marriage to someone difficult—you spend so much time managing that person that you let yourself off every hook in sight. There was a summer of hell, or was it a year or three? In 2009, almost ten years after we bought Number 9, John moved into an apartment around the corner so he could stay near the kids. We remained married in many ways: a shared bank account, Christmas and cottage holidays together, forced-march Sunday family dinners we imagined were good for the children (they were not). We went on like this, unmarried but not, lingering in the end days of our twenty-five-year marriage, for five years. It's hard to think why now. We couldn't let each other go, or let our marriage go, not all the way. It began to seem ridiculous, or at least indefensible, our halfway divorce, and in the flattened, humid summer of 2014, we started to navigate a legal and financial severing, spending long hours with a lawyer and an accountant who divided our life in two.

The first time I arrived at the door of the boardroom on the fourteenth floor of the accountant's office building, I couldn't step through it. It was like crossing the threshold of a church to mourn the death of someone you dearly loved. "Let's start by reviewing your joint assets," said our cheerful tennis-playing accountant. She might as well have poured boiling tar over us. Our aversion to any kind of financial conversation had bonded John and me right out of the gate. We'd merged our bank accounts the first time we slept together and didn't worry about what was whose, then or later. This was the first time we'd talked financially in twenty-five years, and it was about as comfortable as the Puritans talking about the sexual continuum. John put his head in his hands and didn't look up for the rest of the two-hour session. I became maniacally upbeat.

"I think I've worked out how I can afford to keep the house," I said as our first session ended, smiling around the room like a hyena. This was the subject I most feared, because it mattered the most. "It's important for the kids," I added. This was part of the truth, but not all of it. I wanted the house for me. It would be like losing a leg or an arm to be without it.

"You don't want to keep the house," John said, looking up at me finally. "You can't manage it." He held my eyes as he said this, and I could see he meant it literally and even kindly. "It's too much for you alone." I also knew this to be true. I didn't know how things worked. John could darn a sock, build a dock, and eyeball seventy-eight yards at a glance, a mysterious and useful skill I did not share. But I did know how to push through doubt, his and mine, and by the end of our third session with the lawyer and accountant, I owned Number 9. I alone owned it, at great expense and half furnished, once the spoils were divided.

It was as if the house itself disapproved. First the central vacuum system caught fire, then the pipes backed up and flooded the basement apartment we'd rented out for years. The messy Manitoba maple in the backyard came down in a winter storm, although I wasn't sorry to see it go. "Chop it up and take it away!" I shouted from my backyard stoop as the tree guys hauled it, branch by scrawny branch, to their truck. Most maddening of all, I was constantly barred from entering my solid front door; my keys kept getting stuck in the tricky German lock I kept meaning to replace. It felt personal, as if the thing I'd fought to hold close was rejecting me.

And then there was the full-on assault of the worn-out wiring. Wiring quirks weren't new at Number 9, if you want to call the minor electrocution of our son, Kelly, a quirk, which I'm afraid we did. Knob-and-tube wiring had made Number 9 uninsurable since the day we'd bought it, but John and I had resisted the expensive and intrusive job of rewiring the house, despite constant prodding from friends. And we'd kept resisting, even after Kelly came into the kitchen one morning—he might have been twelve then—looking pale and shaking his right arm.

"Dad, I just got electrocuted by the bathroom tap," he said.

"Don't be ridiculous, Kelly." John didn't like to be interrupted from his morning espresso. "You can't get shocked by plumbing." He dropped his newspaper on the kitchen table and headed for the bathroom to turn on the tap. "Don't do it, Dad!" said Kelly, as the muscle-clenching shock that ran up John's arm turned his face heart-attack grey. "I'm late for work," John said, and he left me to solve the problem. I spent the rest of the day begging emergency contractors to come and help. One wanted to rip out the entire north side of the house; several left baffled and defeated, no more useful than my husband. My emergency call to the city works department began with a standoff at my front door.

"Are you sure you want me to step through this door?" Mr. City Works said. I was pretty certain that he knew the correct answer to that question, but I did not.

"I think so, yes?"

"Because if I step through this door and find a dangerous situation, it will be be-HOOV-en on me. . ." He paused here to look me over, like a surgeon making sure I was taking in the complicated procedure he was about to perform on my brain. "As a city em-ploy-EE, I will be required to bar you and your family from further entry to this house. It will become a DANGER ZONE. Do you understand what I am telling you?" I shook my head no then yes as he walked backwards, away from the house, still holding my gaze.

In the end, a man named Eugene or Eric or Edward, his name was a blur after a dozen plumbers and electricians came and went, found the live wire that had been exposed to a leak at the faucet and fixed it in five minutes. Problem solved! Crisis averted! Onward ho! I suppose it was too much for John and me to rewire the house together, to turn it inside out, leaving it raw and exposed, when there was so much we couldn't face in the crossed wires of our marriage. The bathroom tap fixed, I put off thinking about the wiring, and my marriage, for another five years.

I wasn't being merely bloody-minded. My father did not approve of rewiring Number 9, for one thing, and I'd held on to his certainty for some time. He was my dad, after all; his mastery of all things mechanical ruled my well-functioning childhood domain. He was the person who knew how things worked and fixed them when they were broken.

"Mary," I said recently to my daughter. We were sitting at the round white kitchen table in Number 9, talking about love, as we sometimes did. "There are three things you want in a man: he needs to be handy, 1; cheerful, 2; and energetic, C."

"You mean 3," Mary said.

"What?"

"Never mind." Mary had long chestnut hair and a good laugh. "In other words, Granddad."

I hadn't realized I'd just described my father. "You could do worse."

"There's nothing wrong with knob and tube," Dad would say, although at ninety-three, he had his own wiring issues. Dad and Mom, ninety-one herself, were headed for oblivion, and it was not a smooth trip. They needed steady intervention. Confusion, falls, midnight ambulance runs to the emergency department, urgent calls at 6 a.m. "Cathrin, we're out of wet wipes!" Dad regularly escaped the locked floor of their retirement home in central Toronto to walk to the bank to pad his wallet with money. "You never want an empty wallet," he said, sadly, when he looked into mine. Now he gave away twenty-dollar bills to anyone with a smile: a grocery cashier, a street person, the bank teller who'd just handed him his own money (she gave it back). We limited the amount he could withdraw at one time. His workaround was to go banking several times a day. He didn't always make it back.

"I saw your dad on Avenue Road this morning," said a friend who liked to go on long walks through the city. "Looking dapper, as always. He asked me the way to the bank machine."

"Jesus, no! I hope you sent him home?"

"Not at all. I pointed the way. He seemed good to go, ready for a bit of adventure."

That time, Dad ended up at the five-star Hazelton Hotel instead of Hazelton Place, their retirement residence, insisting to the concierge that he was in room 208, until the nice woman at the reception desk walked him the few city blocks to the two small rooms he was living in with Mom. Unlike Dad, Mom was mostly in her right mind but frail as a blade of grass. She weighed nothing, wasn't able to swallow solid food without choking, and lived on puréed pork chops and thickened tea. Everything on her plate was the same shade of taupe. You could say she was the brains and he was the brawn of Operation Ancient Dotage, but that would be generous.

When we came up with the plan to move them from St. Catharines to Toronto, I drove with my sister Laura and brother Tim to the Niagara Peninsula to make the pitch. "We'll be five minutes away," Laura said. "We'll take drives to the Beach, where you grew up, Dad," said Tim. We didn't add that it was a two-hour trip to the St. Catharines emergency room and we couldn't take it anymore.

"Your father and I will discuss this and let you know our decision," said Mom with calm dignity.

We drove home trying to imagine that conversation. "He can't remember and she can't hear, so how will they discuss it?" But they did somehow, and a few days later, they said they wanted to be near us.

These wobbly people were the only ones left more or less standing between death and the next generation—namely, me and my four siblings. "Well, that's the last of them," said Mom, then in her sixties, when her final remaining aunt died. "There's no one ahead of us." I got what she meant now that I was bumping up against sixty myself. We'd be buffer-less, too, after our parents' generation was gone; the great beyond would be yowling for us next. It was galvanizing. Maybe that's why it took Aunt Helen's death to make me do something, finally, about my faulty wiring.

Like me, Aunt Helen was the middle sister, between Aunt Mary, the matriarch, and my mother, the youngest. She was a diligently bad cook for her husband and six sons, with a temper as sudden and unexpected as a summer hailstorm. She was funny, too; she could make a whole room laugh. Aunt Helen had my kind of forward momentum down to a hard science. Nothing stopped her, especially as she got older. When Uncle Jack died, she got an extra spring in her step as she organized her nineties precisely to her liking. She walked each day, first to the library and then to the butcher to buy a single slice of bacon to have with her burnt, unbuttered, cold crustless toast, the way she liked it. (She would insist on the same at a restaurant, which never went so well.) When walking got hard, she added a cane; when the cane wasn't steady enough, she got a walker; when a broken collarbone kept her home, she hired a neighbour to ease her in and out of her deep claw-foot tub and to do her hair, which was unfailingly chic. If you faltered or fretted, you didn't have guts (my mother fell into this category), and if someone spurned you, it was their loss, not yours. Helen was on the phone in minutes when I got fired from a good job. "I have two words: screw them." That Aunt Helen saw a soulmate in me mostly made me proud. In her, I saw a model for how to age with unflinching courage.

"I'm checking myself in with the Carmelites," she said when she turned ninety-six. "The nuns will see me out." The Carmelites had one of the last nunneries still standing and had stopped taking in roomers until Aunt Helen's son Paul (her sons were a devoted squad of middle-aged men she put to good use), a lawyer, offered to do their years of backed-up legal work gratis. Two months later, Aunt Helen moved into a sunny corner room.

"I want to go and see Helen with the nuns," Mom said as the days got short in November. We drove her to St. Catharines on one of those hopeful mornings when the sun goes in behind a puff of cloud and then comes out again. "Look, the sun's out!" you got to say, over and over. Aunt Helen's new room had two sides of bright windows, so even though it was small, it felt open. She hadn't kept much. A comfortable chair, some photos, a blanket crocheted by her sister Mary. She toured us around a small cafeteria filled with pictures of the baby Jesus and the Virgin Mary beaming at each other, flowers in their hair, and showed us the empty activity room.

"This is where we do nun crafts," said Aunt Helen, grinning, although there was not a nun to be seen. Most of them were older than she was and could barely get out of bed themselves. In the sparely furnished common room, I took a picture of Aunt Helen and Mom holding each other's arthritically twisted hands, looking in opposite directions. I like to think Mom got what she wanted that afternoon at the Carmelites', something more to hold on to than Helen's hand. A visual to remember her sister by while they were both still earthbound.

"So she's gone, then," Mom said, dry-eyed, when we told her Aunt Helen had died of a broken hip a month shy of her ninety-seventh birthday. The funeral was set for the week before Christmas. By then, Number 9 was a series of escalating provocations. Turning on a light switch gave off tiny shocks, using more than one appliance at a time plunged the house into blackness, and John wasn't there to do whatever you do with fuse boxes. "Don't toast, I'm doing laundry!" I'd text the basement tenant. He had a new girlfriend, a red-haired, long-legged toast lover. She'd moved in with her van-sized toaster oven—the least planet-friendly countertop appliance, at 1,700 watts a pop—and my Medusa fuse box had become a terrorist, zapping us into blackness with every slice of sourdough.

I was in the kitchen getting ready for the funeral, blow-drying my hair beside the fridge because the king-sized outlet was the least likely to flip the circuit breaker, when my sister Ann, who'd flown in from Vancouver, walked downstairs in her black funeral dress. Her black ankle boots were polished to a high sheen.

"What are you doing?" She put her hands on her hips and looked at the station of brushes and sprays I'd set up between the coffee grinder and the oils and vinegars. Her fresh eye gave me pause. Everyone else had gotten used to my kitchen salon, me included.

"What?" I said. I thought I'd play it nonchalant.

"This" —Ann swept her arm over my station— "situation."

"It's a wiring thing. Nothing to worry about," I said, hoping she didn't get a jolt when she turned on the blender. She liked a good breakfast, and grief makes you hungry. We had a long, sad day ahead of us.

"Perhaps it's time to address this, Cathrin?" Ann was a West Coast union activist and took a head-on approach to a crisis. She dressed in black, not only for funerals, and tended to stand with both feet equally weighted on the ground, like the Queen, especially in conversation. I have two sisters. Ann is eight years younger and Laura is eight years older, and which of us is the bossiest is a subject of constant debate. But it's not me. Ann would describe herself as direct, which works for her because she also has the kind of positive energy most people can only dream of. She sweeps you along. I'd never seen her in a flap—a quality thin on the ground in our family—and she was calm now as she looked left, then right. She rarely had an opinion she didn't express, and I watched her struggle not to share one as she surveyed my kitchen hair salon.

"I can't take on the chaos of fixing the wiring right now," I said. "I've got too much going on with work and the kids. The divorce. Now Aunt Helen. I need to maintain some order."

"Order." Ann checked her red lipstick in the mirror I'd propped on top of the cookbooks. "So that's what this is."

The funeral was an endlessly genuflecting Catholic High Mass in the cold and rattling cathedral in St. Catharines (our parents had already requested the same for themselves, to our irritation). The priest repeated so many times that Aunt Helen's body would ascend to heaven when the Resurrection happened that I half expected to see her rise before us, arms beatifically outstretched. I wouldn't have put it past her if she'd set her mind to it. At the end of the Mass, women of the St. Catharines Catholic Women's League, with whom Helen had been doing good works for seventy years, silently processed up the side aisles of the church. There weren't many of them left. They wore hats and jaunty red banners over their winter coats, and when they got to the front of the church, one woman draped Helen's red banner over her casket. They patted her casket as they walked by. We're here, we're here, goodbye, goodbye.

Outside, it had started to snow-rain, and we didn't linger in front of the cathedral. "Dad, you take the front seat," I said unnecessarily as we loaded our parents into the car to make the short trip to the graveyard; he hadn't sat in the back seat in eighty years, and he wasn't about to begin now as he manoeuvred his walker past Mom's to claim his primo spot. Getting our parents into the car was as dodgy as loading a pair of nuclear missiles: packing the walkers, easing the two of them into their seats, rummaging around to fasten their seat belts. "Scooch up, Mom. I think you're sitting on yours." They both looked straight ahead throughout the procedure, holding on to an idea of themselves that the physical facts no longer supported.

On the way to the graveyard, Mom, squeezed in the back with Laura and me, wanted to know about Helen's last moments.

"Describe it to me," she said.

Laura explained that the emergency room doctors had given Helen two choices: they could manage her pain as best they could, or they could perform surgery on her hip, with a 10 percent chance of success. Helen decided to have the operation and died on her way into surgery.

"So she chose life," said Mom. I hadn't thought of it that way, but Mom understood immediately that her sister remained her essential self, the go-forward Helen, even in the final moments of her life.

Back in Toronto after the funeral, channelling Aunt Helen, I finally acted decisively. The new year hove into view with all the promise of a new leaf. My divorce was done. The house was mine alone in which to incinerate dinner guests, and then I'd have nothing but a pit of ash and debt. It seemed too heavy a burden to bear by myself. No. I would stride into 2015. I would rewire the house. How bad could it be?

I hunted down Joe, a master electrician who could barely squeeze his NHL-sized shoulders through my front door.

"Knob-and-tube wiring?" he said. "A ticking time bomb."

"So rewiring?" I got up my nerve to ask. "It won't be too bad?"

Joe did not give me false hope. "It's going to look like Swiss cheese," he said. "It's going to be like a scene from *Dexter*. A psycho house."

Knob and tube was meant to plug in a lamp, not washing

machines and toaster ovens, Joe said as he drilled a few preliminary holes, his massive triceps popping. "So what happens is people keep upping the fuses, but the infrastructure becomes brittle. Once we take it apart, we can't put it back together again." Was he looking at my house or my brain?

Joe explained they'd start in the basement apartment—I felt toaster girlfriend deserved this—and also in the upstairs bedrooms, working their way up and down toward the heavily applianced centre of the house. "We'll try to come after you leave in the morning and be gone before you get back at night, and we'll always sweep a path for you." They were as good as their word, although I was usually in the shower when they arrived in the morning and would dodge the four-man work crew in my bath towel. "Oopsie! Excuse me." I dawdled over my mornings at home. I liked to see them banging and shouting. It felt like progress.

Nighttime was a different story. Alone in the dark in my debt-laden house, progress felt like an abstract idea. I'd wake up at 2 a.m. and reach out to pat the empty space where John would have been, an old impulse. Even at our worst, I used to touch my husband's face or shoulder in the night, sometimes shaking him awake to make sure he was alive and I wasn't alone with my fear. It would begin with a whoosh of dread-adrenaline and then one thought led to another. Would I die tonight? Would it matter? Death was an unwelcome prospect, but living with this floating middle-of-the-night anxiety, undefended by my steady daytime denial, was exhausting. The script didn't change much, but that didn't make it any easier to find my way out. John wasn't there to help, though, and hadn't been for some time.

I'd had my horoscope chart done, a fiftieth-birthday present from friends, and what was strange, if you go in for that kind of thing, was that this grim pandemonium was right there in the planets, laid out years before. Uranus and Mars conjuncted in 2015 to create intense vibrations. "There is a wild, pent-up energy. Things are bursting, faucets are opening," Georgia Nichols, the astrologer who did my chart, had said. "Uranus governs electricity. Frequencies we don't see but feel, things passing from one state to another. Unconscious patterns are brought to the surface and recharged during this time." There was a complicated diagram. Sadly, Venus was in Capricorn, at the bottom of the chart. It didn't bode well for love.

These disruptions could lead to beneficial change, Georgia went on, but it would be uncomfortable while it was happening. "It's not easy," she said. "You will become unusual to yourself."

Unusual to myself? That couldn't be right, I thought, as I glared at the holes in my bedroom ceiling. I'd lived with myself for fifty-nine years. I liked my Aunt Helen ability to keep going, toward what hadn't mattered as long as I was at the helm. St. Augustine worried about being a mystery to himself in his thirteenth confession: "For that darkness is lamentable in which the possibilities in me are hidden from myself: so that my mind, questioning itself upon its own powers, feels that it cannot lightly trust its own report." Were the energy and drive that made me who I was in fact making me unknowable to myself?

After a bad night like that, I'd fall into a deep sleep around 5 a.m. and be immediately pleased when I woke up a couple of hours later. The night of the terror of the falling dust turds was finally over. I'd got through it, and I'd get through it again. I knew how to do that. I'd muscled my way through plenty before.

There were more holes in that theory than in the walls of Number 9.

3.

Promising New Man

BEFORE AUNT HELEN DIED, and before Number 9 turned to rubble, back in the salad days of early 2014, I met Promising New Man. We'll call him that because that's what he was. A cheerful, energetic, uncomplicated man. The kind of man I told my daughter to marry, a granddad kind of man. My relationship with Promising New Man began, as did many things in my life, with a list.

"What are your three best qualities and your three worst qualities?" I asked Promising New Man one late-spring evening as we sat in his tidy condo living room. I get that asking someone to list himself out for you might not be how Anna Karenina flung it all away for a night with Vronsky; it's not what Lara likely whispered to Dr. Zhivago under the covers during their blindingly white winter of love. "Yuri, hold on a sec while I get down your flaws: married, bad ticker, that Russian bottomless-sorrow thing." But I liked my question's sensible ordering of emotion, its head-on, job-interview approach to love. He did not, if his deep frown across the coffee table was anything to go by.

Earlier that evening, he'd pointed out the kitchen's crown moulding, which he'd hammered in place to make his boilerplate condo feel more homey, and also the framed black-and-white photos of buildings and flowers that hung in an even row on the wall behind where he was sitting. A sliding glass door opened onto a brick patio with a gleaming barbecue the size of a small submarine, on which he had just made a stress-free dinner of grilled vegetables and salmon. He was a big man, outsized for his small condo, and the massive barbecue was on a better scale for him than the inside rooms, where he looked hemmed in. On the kitchen counter, he kept a large red horn that went off like a thunderclap whenever the Maple Leafs scored a goal, and except for the horn, which was so loud it gave me heart palpitations for the full minute it blasted, the evening so far had been convivial and comfortable. Like Promising New Man himself.

"Oh, brother," he said in answer to my question, which was about as bad as it got with PNM. We'd met at a work party in early 2014, and in the three months since, when we weren't exactly dating but weren't exactly not dating, I'd never seen him angry. This was a novel departure from my past fare of brainy, don't-fence-me-in reprobates, who warmed to their anger like a good friend. With those men, I'd swoon over their big brains, then we'd have sex, and then I'd be a basket case for the next six months to twenty-five years. Not this time. If I was going to get back into the whole love gauntlet at fifty-nine, I would dip my toe in until the temperature was right. I would wait for love to be reasonable and kind. I would go off-type.

"I can be impatient," PNM said reluctantly. I wanted to get out my pen and paper to write out his first fault before I forgot it, but even in the dimmed light that made everything prettier, I could make out the hard bead of his pale blue eyes as they fixed on me. He put his large hand on top of his head and held it there, soothing his brain. He had recently grown his hair, a very short blond brush cut, about an eighth of an inch longer, to please me. It was surprisingly soft to touch, I would soon find out. "I've never grown my hair for anyone. That's how much I love you." He talked easily about love like this, his love for me.

I thought my list-making would be fun—"I'll do mine too!"— but I'd forgotten how hard men can be on themselves, at least men of my generation raised by unpleasable mothers and uninterested fathers. Verbalizing their faults comes too close to revealing the inner asshole they hump around with. "I used to be a huge asshole," or "You didn't know me when I was an asshole," the nicest men will say, and I'm never sure whether they're awed or shamed by their old selves. I wasn't going to let small sympathies get in the way of my tally, though. I needed to decide whether PNM was right for me so I didn't get hurt or waste precious time or stab myself in the forehead with a dull pencil when I woke up beside him every morning for the rest of my life. If I'd dug a little deeper into my motivations, it might have saved me some suffering later on, but as we have established, self-reflection is not my strong suit. I was a long way from the self-actualizing Socratic sage I feared I was supposed to be but never could. Hence the list.

"Impatient," I said, nodding encouragement. "Interesting. I hadn't noticed that." I hadn't, which alarmed me. What else was I missing?

"Would you like me to do myself now?" I said, when Promising New Man had completed his answers and put out a dessert of strawberries and chocolate on the coffee table. "I can be jealous, for example."

Promising New Man didn't answer but moved around the table to sit beside me on the couch. I touched his hair and found it soft. He took my head in his hands and kissed me. A first kiss. I'm susceptible to kisses. The way they open you up to possibility, carnal and otherwise. My love for a man began in my mind, but my body clinched the deal. Tonight was no different, despite my resolve. The air around us wobbled gently in the candlelight—when had he lit candles?—and I swooned, just a little, but it was PNM who left it at one kiss. He drove me home in a big black car that was so high off the ground I needed to be lifted by the waist from behind, up into the air like a dancer, to get into the plush front seat. He navigated the night streets with confident ease, and when we got to my house, he came around to my side of the car to help me out, and then he took my keys and opened my front door and made sure my lights were on so there was nothing to be afraid of in the dark. You see what I mean? A lovely, thoughtful man.

Half an hour later, I was alone in my bed writing my list, propped up by several pillows, for gravity, so my ink kept flowing. Promising New Man had just sent me a long and tender email about our first kiss, which I'd skimmed and put aside so I could write down his strengths and weaknesses before I forgot what he'd said. "Impatient," I wrote, then paused, pen to mouth, to think what came next. Another *I* word. "Irritable"! I hadn't noticed that either. Yeesh. I wrote it down.

At work, I relied on lists for their physical evidence of my progress. Crossing things off is very satisfying, as everyone knows, or it was until the morning a younger colleague watched me and said, "Cathrin, those times are over now. Roll with the day. What matters will present itself." This caught me deeply off guard. I began to notice that younger people arrived at meetings with no pens or paper, just their squeaky-clean fresh brains and their listening faces. I decided to give it a whirl, and to my intense interest, I found I not only listened better but retained more *sans* list. I went with the flow, with where the energy of the day felt I needed to be, taking it all in with my benign-Zen-master slightly smiling face. I've never been so productive. It couldn't last, though. Ticking off my daily tasks made my lack of progress on more important things less obvious. I don't judge myself too harshly. It's not nothing to accomplish so many things in a day. It's just that they matter a lot in the moment, and then don't matter at all.

The Promising New Man list, the List of Love, was on a whole other scale than these work lists. I wrote it on my pro/con pad, which I kept in my bedside drawer and reserved for only the most life-changing decisions. Move to Number 9: six pros, four cons. Keep house after divorce: twelve pros, eight cons. Rewire house: three pros, one con. Done. Boom. Decision made.

As I tried, pen poised, to remember PNM's third flaw, I thought of the time I used the pro/con pad to weigh John's strengths and weaknesses while I'd struggled to decide whether to leave our marriage. On the pro side, First Husband List had qualities like smart, complicated, handsome, talented, observant, brave, uncompromising, aggressive, hidden depths. But over time, some of those pros had become cons. When I married John, I'd wanted a hard-won husband with unreachable corners. My own Mr. Darcy. Jane Austen leaves out the enormous difficulties of such a union, the sadness of never being able to reach corners that are closed not only to you but also to him.

I began Second (Potential) Husband List with three qualities carried over from First Husband List on the pro side—aggressive ("There's nothing you can do about wanting aggressive men; it's who you are," said horoscope-woman Georgia Nichols), observant, and smart. But mostly this list showed how Second Husband would puzzle piece into me, rather than me into him, with words like kind, good manners, social, self-aware, energetic, partner, loves me.

Note "loves me" comes last, as if it was unexpected or undeserved, or maybe even unwanted, and it was this aspect of Promising New Man that I found almost impossible to trust or believe. He fell in love with me at first sight, for starters. "I saw it happen," said the colleague who'd introduced us at the work party. "He stepped back from you, then forward. Everyone saw it." When he found out I'd come down with a cold later that week, he dropped off flowers, chicken soup, and homemade chocolate chip cookies at the front desk of the newspaper where I worked at the time. (Kind: tick. "It doesn't occur to us to be with someone kind until we are almost dead," Amy Schumer said in one of her stand-ups). The cookies and soup, once I got over my alarm at his eager delivery, were very good. "There's nothing better for a cold than homemade chocolate chip cookies," he said, which turned out to be a surprising new truth. My cold cleared up and we met for lunch at a loud downtown sports bar, where he seemed boyishly pleased to be sitting across from me. I said yes to dinner the next week, and this time, I chose the location and he drove the fast-paced conversation, politics and media, mostly.

And so it began. I've never been so ferociously wooed. It wasn't only that he kept track of my keys, although that alone made him an outstanding human being. It was the way he didn't falter, even in the face of my steady uncertainty. I'd open my door at Number 9 before a date and he'd be holding a bouquet of flowers, grinning. He fixed a bathroom shelf. He liked everything I wore. ("Now *that* is my favourite of all your dresses," he'd say every time I arrived in a different getup.) He handwrote love letters. It was corny, but also more and more welcome. A full-on pursuit. A quest, and I was the object. I began to feel that I deserved it. That after all this time, I was worthy not only of admiration but of adoration too. Being cherished made me feel protected, from what I wasn't sure. An unpartnered future with no one to find me drooling and half-dead on the bathroom floor, my walker upended in the hallway, something like that.

My pals rallied round PNM: "He's helpful and supportive; it's time to be on the receiving end." "Accept that you deserve this." "He loves you, and he's an affable man. What's not to like?" Promising New Man was his own best advocate. "You've spent your whole life with men-children," he said one day. We were sitting across from each other at my white kitchen table, round and bright as a happy face. It was early spring, and the backyard birds were shrieking their heads off. We'd just taken a long walk along a white-capped Lake Ontario, and his vivid orange gloves, the kind construction workers wear, sat stiffly in the middle of the table like a warning beacon. He had stubborn fashion quirks. Between the gloves and the birds, it was hard to pay attention.

"Why construction gloves?" I'd asked on the walk.

"I like them," he said. "My former wife hated them, but I don't care what people think about how I dress."

I felt a sudden fondness for his ex-wife. "Although maybe a small thing to give up for someone else's happiness?"

"Babies, all of them," he said now in the kitchen, about the men in my life. I pulled my gaze away from the gloves to look into his pale blue eyes as he spoke. He was trying to help me; I could see that. Help me let go of old patterns and be brave about new ones. To be brave about him.

"What you want is a grown man to love and appreciate you, and look after you." This was the kind of thing that would have had me running for the hills when I was twenty, but at a battered fifty-nine, it was a spray of catnip. He was leaving to take a new job that would divide his time among Houston, New York, and Toronto, and he'd just given me a small silver heart on a chain, "So that you know you have my heart wherever I am." He'd described his conversation with the Tiffany sales clerk about the length of the chain. "I eliminated long right away, but I couldn't decide between medium and short."

I found this earnest exchange between him and the clerk more endearing than the gift, and the medium chain was exactly the right length. One of the things I liked early about Promising New Man was his ability to quickly observe what people were most interested in and play to it. He won over an initially skeptical sports mad friend with his complex football minutiae; my sister Laura with his left-wing political savvy (he was a right-leaning liberal); Mary, the youngest and least heard of the family, by listening at length to whatever she had to say. When someone—my son, Kelly, or sister-in-law, Nancy—remained unconvinced, he plotted how to win them: "I've got Laura, but Nancy needs work." I didn't see this as manipulation or sociopathy, but as the thoughtful effort of someone who cared enough about me to want my friends and family on his side. It felt smart and attentive; it ticked the "observant" box on Second Husband List. It didn't occur to me that he was doing the same thing with me, carefully curating what I most wanted to hear. And what if he was? Because he had it right: I'd never been looked after, or not for a long time, and I badly wanted to be. It wasn't anti-feminist; it was just my turn. Promising New Man had the sympathy and the wit to understand that.

There was no sex. PNM let me set the pace. "For Christ's sake, Cathrin, isn't that your first clue?" said my friend Matt, who wrote thrillers about blood diamonds from his Manhattan condo while his wife wrangled a huge TV news job. "If you don't want to have sex with the man, you don't want the man." It was true Promising New Man needed some reforming. ("It is possible to *trans*form so long as we do not harbour ambitions to *re*form our partner," said the bishop of London at the marriage of Prince William and Kate Middleton, and I noted and then forgot my own reformist tendencies with men.) There was that brush cut that made him look as if his hair had been moulded in a doll factory; I chalked it up as a win when he added the extra eighth of an inch. He was not trim, although there was nothing wrong with a man with girth. It felt solid and dependable, like a sturdy hatchback. What else? Bad speller. Couldn't ride a bike to save his life. He liked baseball caps and Paddington Bear movies, enthusiastically shared his favourite books about media, and had an excellent eye for British TV police procedurals. Looked smart in a good suit, didn't suffer fools, enjoyed doing complicated math, was a good talker, and had a full and sexy laugh. But it was the barbecue that turned it around.

House ownership comes with two defined jobs: outside maintenance and inside maintenance. I was inside, John was outside. One morning when we were still married, he walked through the kitchen wordlessly, went into the backyard, rattled the gate, then came in and sat down for his coffee. "I had a dream that the back gate was unlocked." This was the second and last dream John remembered in my twenty-five years with him (the first was trying to strangle a portrait of his great-great-great-grandfather), but I got how deep the unlocked gate went. Securing the perimeter was his job. Now John was gone, taking the Weber barbecue and his knowledge of how to use it with him, and I felt more and more that the one thing missing from my life was the ability to grill meat outdoors. My sister Laura barbecued constantly on a gas grill bigger than she was, and I decided I badly needed something similar.

"Start with installing the gas line, then we'll choose the barbecue," said Promising New Man. I did as I was told, thrillingly, and a couple of weeks later, we were at Home Depot lifting the lids off dozens of floor models and talking about side burners, angled flame tamers, and cooking boxes. Promising New Man and the sales clerk talked about each of these things for many minutes. I wasn't convinced.

"I want something that will turn on, grill a leg of lamb to perfection, and carve it up for guests while I put on my lipstick."

"We've got that," said the clerk.

"I want just one button. On or off. It needs to be attractive and not too big. Plus, I don't like black. Do they come in colours? Maybe red or white?"

They didn't have that at the first store, so we moved on to another across town. This detail, going to a second store in search of a barbecue in Saturday afternoon gridlock, resonated with every woman in the western hemisphere: Promising New Man drove us miles to another store in terrible traffic to look for a white or red barbecue with one button, and he never got mad or complained about his life leaking away between his fingers. "Wow!" my women friends said with awe. Not only that, but when we finally found the perfect small white number with one button—"R2-D2," I said—it came in a box. "But how does it get put together?" It turned out that would cost another $150, which was when Promising New Man said, "I'll assemble it." And he did, as I served him homemade lemonade to quench his virile barbecue-building thirst, and after he built it, he connected it to the new gas line, and after he connected it to the new gas line, he cooked chicken for dinner, and as he cooked chicken for dinner, he calmly quelled the occasional flame and showed me how to turn the breasts as they cooked to get the pretty criss-crossed grill marks on the skin.

"Cathrin, any man can put a barbecue together, for Christ's sake," Matt said, sitting in my backyard on a visit to Toronto as I pointed out R2-D2's satisfyingly few features while grilling a pair of turkey burgers with criss-crosses.

"Yes, but do you actually do it, Matt?"

My women friends saw Promising New Man in a haloed light after the barbecue episode, and so did I. A couple of nights after the barbecue building, we kissed in his kitchen and he slipped off my shift dress with one hand and lifted me to his bedroom with the other, a deft and decisive move I greatly admired. "I'm not sure I'm ready to have sex," I said. "Cathrin," he said, stating the obvious, "we are having sex. That's what we're doing right now."

And so began phase two of our relationship. We took trips to London and New York, living the life of energy and ease he offered. He liked to iron his shirts when he travelled, and then he would iron mine too, and this small kindness seemed to make him happy. More often, I wanted him to be happy too. I began to cook ambitious dinners and dress up for our evening FaceTime calls when he was out of town. I bought tickets to plays and art exhibits that I thought he might enjoy, or that I wanted him to enjoy. In Houston, I took him to the Rothko Chapel, where we a spent a long time enveloped by the fourteen massive black canvasses with their muted hues of purple and brown, painted not long before the artist committed suicide. They were hard to look at, speaking of unreachable corners.

"What did you think?" I asked PNM once we were back in the light-filled park after an hour of quiet contemplation in the chapel.

"I liked it very much, although I'm colour-blind, so I couldn't really tell the difference between the paintings." (Good manners: tick. His, not mine.)

Somewhere that fall, my early reservations about PNM left me. The more I loved the idea of what he offered, and the force with which he offered it, the smaller the step became to loving the man himself. What was so wrong with a man who was on my side? Who saw me and what I wanted now, which was a solid, conventional man, "so thoroughly square," the kind of man Professor Higgins pretended to be? A man who relished opening utility bills. A man who was there, to take it down to its most basic level.

"I miss partnership," I said to my good friend Ellen, a writer and also separated, who lived up the street in an elegant condo with a sweeping balcony where we often talked over wine. Before PNM, Ellen and I had taken a couple of stabs at online dating. One of her dates showed up in arm gaiters. "Not only that, he talked to me about his arm gaiters for some time." When she declined to see him again, he said a woman her age (that is, his age) would be lucky to find anyone. After that, we made up imaginary boyfriends whom we occasionally fought over. "Peter the Architect just asked me to go to Oaxaca," I said. "That's odd," Ellen replied. "Peter and I just got engaged in Paris." It was funny until it wasn't. "I miss partnership too," Ellen said on the phone. There was a pause. "As if either of us had that."

But now I had a shot at it, a second chance. I began to picture a life in the country, with Promising New Man barbecuing and me writing and reading; a quiet, partnered life of mutual respect. Leaning into his bulwark of a body, just leaning there, being safe. Waking up in the night and patting his face; walking into a party on his reliable arm. Finally, after months of getting to know this man, I did something I hadn't done for a long time. I fell in love. I hadn't been swept off my feet. I'd come to this love slowly and carefully, until it felt not just believable but reliable. I trusted him and the life he offered us, together. I gave him the gift of myself, all in; it was what he'd said he wanted.

This was also more or less when, as winter snowbanked the city and 2015 approached, Promising New Man began to cancel things: a weekend in New York because of a sudden work meeting; a night at Number 9 after the dust from the rewiring made him sneeze. But none of that mattered because he had a plan, one that I loved: to take me to Sicily for my birthday in February. Laura had wanted to throw a bash for my sixtieth, but Promising New Man said no. "I've got Cathrin's birthday covered." Instead, Laura shared her hiking maps of Sicily and her favourite place to stay, and I stayed out of the rest because it was a birthday present and not for me to boss my way into. I'd long since forgotten about the pro/con pad in the bedside drawer. Now I began work on an equally complex and possibly more important list: What to pack for Italy?

4.

Shakespeare on Love

"MOM, I HAVE A QUESTION," said Mary. We were watching a romantic comedy at Number 9 on a late-winter evening between Christmas and New Year's, the time of year when people begin to feel hopeless about the loss of light. John and the kids and I had managed to survive another fuming fractured faux family Christmas. Number 9 was by now a slaughter of holes. But the New Year's Eve party, when PNM would meet my friends for the first time, was just ahead, and Sicily, lovely Sicily, was on the near horizon after that. My suitcase was pulled out and open on the bedroom floor. I liked to get a jump on packing. Laura, who travels carry-on only, suggested I pack and repack three times in order to cull, which I did. But every time I repacked, I added instead of subtracting. "Oh, an empty shoe. Let's stuff it with three underpants."

Mary tugged the too-small blanket we were sharing until I had none, but the movie was on her laptop (TV out of commission due to the wiring situation), so I kept my mouth shut. You never know when one of your grown kids is going to get fed up with you, shake her head sadly at your fathomless flaws, and pack off for the night to her own place. It kept me on my best behaviour. I wanted to finish the movie, for one thing. The two stars' eyes had just locked across a flock of fat sheep, and knowing exactly what would happen next only made it more satisfying when love came out on top. And I was greedy to have these couple of hours with Mary to myself. When the commercial break started, she poked me under the blanket with her long leg.

"Do you believe in love at first sight?" she asked. This was manna from heaven, a question like this from Mary, who listened intently and gratifyingly to my answers on this one subject only. Up until a few months ago, I would have been ready with one. "Oh yes. I remember the precise moment I first saw your father," I would have said. And I did. I've met thousands of people, I couldn't tell you where or when. But John was the single tap on the triangle when the rest of the orchestra went quiet. Science says it takes 0.13 seconds to determine our attraction to someone, and I came in under that with John. He strode into the Trent University coffee shop with his flapping dark overcoat, undone wool scarf, and deep scowl and sat beside me at my small table. I was terrified but took him in. He was self-absorbed but not self-satisfied. Handsome, substantial, angry. Like someone to unlock, if you dared. "I haven't slept all night," he said, and looked it; he was the editor of the student newspaper and had just made the overnight press run. I might have been pretending to read Sartre's *Being and Nothingness* at the tiny cafe table that John's legs struggled to get out from under, and I might have tossed out some bon mot I imagined was mysterious yet alluring: "Nothingness lies coiled at the heart of every being—like a worm." Not surprisingly, our first date was a long, long way off. (John told me later that before this cafe meeting, he used to check out books from the university library where I worked so he could stare through my gauzy black peasant dress. That didn't jibe with my memory, which was me the hound and him the fox.)

Before Promising New Man, I might have said all this to Mary about love. I'd have trotted out Shakespeare. "Who ever loved that loved not at first sight?" he wrote in *As You Like It*, and he knew more about love than anybody, in words, at least. For most of my life, I'd agreed with him. Before this reasoned love that was about to wing me to Sicily with a suitcase full of shoes for every possible occasion, I'd thought Shakespeare was spot-on. I'd have told Mary that love at first sight wasn't the feeling you noticed so much as the pacing. "A bracket in time. Things slow down. Pay attention, something is happening here, it says." And Mary would have loved that answer.

But I couldn't say it, not anymore. That kind of love had ended badly for me. True, I'd been married for twenty-five years, but divorcing after all that time made the failure more colossal. Not a mere mistake, but an epic, lifelong fail. I hadn't paid enough attention, certainly not during the trying middle of marriage, when there was a lot that might have been mended with some serious conversations. Or even just silently glossed over for a decade or two. I'd seen that work in more than one marriage: people who'd quietly hated each other for twenty years retired or had a grandchild and suddenly started making googly eyes again.

"Oh no, Cathrin, you're wrong," said a friend with three little kids and a hard marriage she was on the doorstep of leaving. We were sitting in a packed hotel bar, and she was on her second badly needed martini. "You've just forgotten. You can't say, 'Let's talk about this or that, honey,' to an angry man. They hurl insults at you. There's no talking it out."

I remembered the rage in my marriage then, the speed with which it could get to "fuck you" over a morning espresso. A friend whose husband fumed around the house over minor infractions confided that she would tiptoe behind him giving him both fingers, and it turned out many of us did the same, jabbing our fingers in the air and making faces behind our husbands' backs, then smiling sweetly when they turned around.

"You're right, it's not so simple," I'd said to my friend at the bar. I couldn't decide if she should stay in or leave her frayed marriage; she wanted my advice. Neither was the wrong choice. And neither was the right one either.

It's not just the middle of a marriage that can veer. I didn't pay enough attention at the start, the early blurred heights with John. Who doesn't lope through the beginning of love, the glorious bigness of it? Except that maybe if I'd thought more about the man I was in love with, and the way we fit (love of family, devotion and attention to home, the joy of paddling a canoe together on a bending river) and didn't fit (temperament), then I might have avoided the unreasonable, indifferent, cold ending of love.

"How do our hearts survive?" a friend asked me recently, and I considered her question for some time. She'd had her share of heartbreak when she was younger, but in the end she made a great success of love and was now celebrating her thirtieth wedding anniversary. A doctor friend explained that a broken heart often leads to a literal broken heart, that people who have endured a terrible loss or sorrow are more likely to have a heart attack. That added up, I thought; it was the perfect kicker to the story. Love wasn't soft and pretty but frightening and painful, and if my doctor friend was right, even fatal. And it wasn't as if the wisdom of experience let you skip over the mess. "When you're in love, you're always young and always vulnerable," my friend said as she described the misery of her own friend in her eighties, betrayed by her lover. "She is utterly heartbroken."

I didn't want any of that, for my daughter especially. Not the pain and not even the head-turning thrills, which she was susceptible to. "I believe in love," Mary said on the couch at Number 9 that night. She adored her father but had got on side with PNM pretty quickly. ("Mom, he bought me a toaster oven for my birthday. What's not to like?") Now she looked at me fiercely. "One hundred percent, unconditional love." Ay yi yi, I thought.

This was nothing new coming from Mary. Even when she was a tiny girl, things had a way of breaking when she was in the room. The real danger, though, wasn't to a smashed glass of milk (37, John counted) but to Mary's tender heart. Mary loved the baby Jesus for years simply because one of her nannies told her that the baby Jesus loved her. When Mary was five, a bunch of us took our kids to a Good Friday parade, which was as cheerful as you might imagine. Men playing Jesus wore crowns of fake thorns that dripped with fake blood as they dragged fake crucifixes along the grey-skied street. A crew from the local TV station, desperate for a sound bite so they could wrap and go home, landed on our ragtag group. The kids mumbled answers about not knowing why they were at this desultory parade until the camera landed on Mary.

"I'm here because I love the baby Jesus and I pray for him every day," she said.

"And what's your name, little girl?" The camerawoman's eyes glistened. If she could nail this interview, a tumbler of Chardonnay was in her near future.

"Mary," said my daughter, eyes heavenward.

The clip led the local news that night.

Mary coped with her susceptible heart by demanding happy endings to her storybooks and movies. "It's sad," she would cry, as she threw a book at my feet. She was eighteen when her first love broke up with her, and she cried for three days. Not teenage tears, but big, wrenching sobs. She howled in the shower, when she opened her eyes in the morning, between mouthfuls of toast and jam. On the third day, I gave her a Gravol and took her to see *Gravity*. I wanted to distract her and I needed a break. She watched silently as a so-sad Sandra Bullock revealed that her daughter was dead, an untethered George Clooney drifted to certain death, and Bullock subsequently ran out of fuel and oxygen, attempted suicide, and caught fire. The credits came up and Mary let loose, her tears spurting sideways.

"Mom, seriously?"

"But Sandra Bullock lived!"

I didn't regret that Mary's first love was seismic, and neither did she; after the pain let up, it made her bigger too. Or so we told ourselves. But I couldn't remember anymore why I'd thought our hearts needed to be mauled for us to understand love. My dad hadn't thought so. His love story came right out of the romantic comedy playbook, minus the dark night of the soul at the bottom of the second act. He saw Mom across the room at a wartime YMCA dance. The air blurred. He asked her to dance. He missed the last bus and had to walk miles back to the army base. "It was the best walk of my life," he said every time he told the story.

Mom accepted this story but didn't tell it herself, because unlike Mary, Dad, and me, she was clear-headed, love-wise. She married at the baby age of twenty, choosing a man who adored her and could look after her, my dependable, never-say-no dad, and she was well married for seventy-two years. I used to feel sorry for Mom and her obvious need to be cherished up there on her poncy pedestal. How certain and dull love must have been for her. When I was a young woman, emotionally available men seemed to lack outline; they'd lose themselves in you. So judged my scary young heart, a difficult place to enter. Hard-hearted Hannah, Mom would say. But now, closing out my fifties, I felt Mom had been onto something. Maybe it wasn't so much the devotion that couldn't be trusted as my own stubborn habit of resisting the pull of a smooth romance.

"I don't think it happens too often that two people fall in love at the exact same moment," I said to Mary on the couch at Number 9. "Maybe you love him, maybe he loves you. Whatever it is, when love lands near you, pay attention. Who knows where it might take you." I sounded like a corny advice column, but I could see that Mary was listening by the way her green eyes looked not at me but just past me, following my words. I thought some more about PNM and me. We wouldn't really be like my parents; we weren't a start-up with our children and first house and careers ahead of us. A union in later life is about *your* future, no one else's. That's all you've got left. It can be a sobering place to begin.

When the romantic comedy was over, Mary took an Uber home in the bitter December night, wiser about love, thanks to me, and I climbed into my sooty bed, where I read my book with one of those camping flashlights strapped to my forehead. I'd never finished my list of Promising New Man's strengths and weaknesses, the one I'd started in this very spot when the lights were still on, almost ten months ago. I couldn't remember his third fault after "Impatient" and "Irritable." It had started with an *F*. "Fearful"? That might have added up, but I was pretty sure not. It might have been "Fretful"—I had noticed him fretting in the months since.

My iPhone pinged on the pillow next to me. It was a text from PNM: *cant make new years party will call first thing and explain.*

I stared at it for a while, my mind whirring between disappointment and a sickening suspicion that he wasn't telling the truth. He'd cancelled that New York trip at the last minute too, but he'd been eager to join the New Year's Eve party. It was a big moment for us, a public outing. We were both excited about it.

I beamed my headlamp into the bedside table, its light darting crazily as I rummaged for the pro/con pad. I shook my pen and wrote on the con side: *Big Fat Liar.* I finally had his third fault, there, on my list. He was lying; I was sure of it. He wasn't a dependable man but the mere guise of one, a bluff, one of those boys I was suspicious of as a young woman because they seemed too unknown to themselves. My God, when he'd warned me about boy-men, he was warning me against himself!

You are a Big Fat Liar, I wrote again, this time in a text. I knew he was watching the three dots as I hovered there, waiting to hit Send. I couldn't believe I'd fallen for this. At the exact moment I began to want a life with him, he abandoned me. It was sad. If PNM was a liar, that meant there was no reasoning my way to a partnered life in the dodgy back quarter I was about to enter. No buoy against randomness.

It was thoughtful of him to text in the middle of the night, though; he didn't need to do that. He knew how badly I slept, and he'd had the decency to send a note right away. I read his text again. He said he'd "explain." So there was an explanation. Flights that time of year were a nightmare. And his work was crazy busy, the usual year-end scramble. Maybe his father was sick, didn't he have something or other? Maybe *he* was sick. Maybe he had Ebola, they'd found a case of that in Texas. Maybe texting was all he could manage with his last working finger as he bled out on the linoleum floor through his pores and eyeballs. God, what was wrong with me? Why did I have to go all the way to *Big Fat Liar*, just like that? Why load up the nuclear arsenal before we'd even had a simple conversation, as he reasonably suggested, that would clear it all up? I was sick of my unwillingness to trust. My exhausting capacity for self-doubt. My thrill at every opportunity to feel aggrieved. It was a miracle he'd stayed with someone this crazy, actually. It was only a New Year's Eve party, for Christ's sake.

"Get a grip," I said out loud as my rage seeped up and out into the night. I deleted my *Big Fat Liar* text, click click click, and wrote, *yes talk tomorrow*.

Neutral, not needy. Open to possibility. Then I picked up my pen and crossed out *Big Fat Liar* on my pro/con pad. The only thing I needed to fix was myself.

5.

The Joy of Socks

I AM A MISLAYER. I put my phone down and—poof!—it disappears. The glass of milk I just poured myself will turn up in the front flower planter, I don't know why. I went to a new local bakery to buy a croissant. It ended up in the garbage before I could eat it. "Who did that!" I said to my empty house after I found the still-warm croissant sitting in its brown paper bag inside the kitchen waste bin. If I was going to take on the mostly hopeless job of self-improvement, fixing my propensity to lose things seemed like an easy enough place to start. I saw big payback, even. I wouldn't lose Promising New Man, for one thing, and I'd maybe hold on to a cellphone for more than a few months, for another. If I'd known the plan would force me to think about what was really lost, my stuff, me, or something more ineffable than either of those, I'd have chosen a simpler path to self-improvement. I'd have become totally open to everything: "So you're a misogynist, interesting. Please tell me more."

The leafy summer afternoon when I first realized I lost things more than most people was a pleasantly domestic day so ordinary it hardly seemed worth remembering. The kids were little and tearing around in a repeating loop, speeding by us the same way everything sped by in our warp-drive forties—front hall, dining room, living room, *SHRIEK!*, front hall, dining room, living room, *SHRIEK!* The shriek was for the moms, my friends and me, who sat in the living room at Number 9 and talked about socks, a satisfyingly expansive subject. "John shouts from three rooms away, 'Cathrin, where are my striped black-and-brown socks?' Not 'Do you know where they are,' or 'Have you seen,'" I said to get us going. "Yes, honey, upper right drawer, left side," someone else said, rolling her eyes. We knew where the socks were, but like all self-respecting women, we refused to answer the question on principle. "My brain is a shelf and has room for only so much; the rest falls off." That might have been Johanna, except that you couldn't choose what fell off your brain shelf, you couldn't select what mattered and what didn't, and the whereabouts of a husband's socks were like the twenty-volume *Oxford English Dictionary*—nothing could budge them. John's socks stayed put on my brain shelf so his had room for Spinoza's laws of the universe.

Like everyone, I often lost them—socks, not men, though I was well down that road too. "I keep my single socks in a special basket in hopes that the match will turn up one day," I said to my friends, pleased with my system. I didn't think my basket was any different from anyone else's until I fetched it from the laundry room and Tecca started to laugh so hard all she could get out was "Whaaaa?" and then Johanna was laughing too. Which was when I realized that I had more lost socks than the average household. My hamper was the size of a Whirlpool dryer, not the modern compact dryer but the full-on, energy-swilling monster cube.

"But why are there so many?" This was Tecca; she barely had her breath back. The truth was I never threw out a single sock. "Do you pack them with you when you move?" Tecca was not going to let this go anytime soon. John and I had been at Number 9 for only a couple of years at this point, and it was obvious my Mount Vesuvius of single socks predated that move.

"Yes."

"Do you ever find a pair?"

"Oh yes. It's great when that happens, sometimes even years later." I saw immediately that I'd answered with too much enthusiasm, which set them off again. It wasn't only socks that went missing, but wallets, bags, phones, rings, earrings. ("You've taken the most important step and called me," said Pam the jeweller when I lost a gold hoop, and then took me through the stages of earring loss and retrieval with the skill of an air traffic controller landing a damaged plane.) While I looked for lost things I wasn't here or there, two places I was very fond of, but suspended in that in-between space that modern sci-fi writers go gaga for. If I had a superpower it would be teleportation, not to Jupiter or Honolulu but from the grocery aisles to my kitchen, to avoid transitions, where things were liable to disappear. I began to wonder if I spent so much time in that in-between place because I wasn't paying attention in some more fundamental way. I worried that I was careless not only in the way I lost socks and earrings but also in the way Fitzgerald called Daisy Buchanan and her husband careless, that I wasn't paying attention to the things that mattered most. It felt important to know what I should no longer be careless about.

Gloves and mitts vanished faster than I could put them on my hands. The ones that stayed behind had their own box, a medium-sized wicker one I kept in my closet. So far all of them, including my much-loved red leather driving glove from Milan, remained single. Hats and scarves, too, nothing unusual there. But that's not all I lost. After the slight snag with Promising New Man, when I went to the swanky New Year's Eve party, solo, and clanged my cowbell at midnight, solo, and kissed whoever was randomly standing beside me, solo, I made a list of the things I'd lost or had stolen from me, not once but repeatedly:

> socks, mitts and gloves, hats and scarves (too many to count)
> passports (6)
> wallets (7)
> bags (5)
> cellphones (12)
> words (50 pages)
> house robbed (7 times)
> jewellery cleaned out (3 times)

"Keys, Cathrin! For God's sake, don't forget keys." I showed my list of lost things to Laura.

"Do you ever lose anything?" I asked her, unnecessarily.

Laura was a lawyer, married to a lawyer, and she had that ordered clarity of mind that kept things in place. Not everything was shipshape about my sister. She liked to wear my clothes, "so I don't have to worry about what to buy," and she arrived fifteen minutes early to dinner parties to be sure she wasn't late. Mom could send her on a trajectory too. But Laura was the go-to for everyone in our extended family when they were in trouble (a full-time job right there), not only because she was excellent in a crisis but also because she was on your side. She was on my side; she introduced me to most of my formative influences, including the pill, Margaret Atwood, and coq au vin.

"I did lose something once," she said. "A box of mementoes and notes from work; it meant a lot to me, but I was distracted." She blamed her husband, who was a worry to her at the time. "I still think about it. It was very upsetting."

We were strolling down my street after dinner, and people were out on the sidewalk, laughing and talking, bits of conversation floating past us like leaves in the breeze. When we got to my door, I couldn't find my key. I tried to pat myself down surreptitiously so Laura wouldn't notice. She could get irked about this key thing. I casually slipped my hands into my pants pockets, then my jacket, while I held her gaze and pretended to be supremely interested in whatever she was saying.

"What are you doing, Cathrin?" said Laura, nobody's fool.

"Um, I think it's, ah, my key, I—"

"Omigod, Cathrin. You can't be serious." Laura quickly took her spare from the inside pocket of her sleek black bag to let me in. It was the same key I'd given her nine years earlier as part of my backup system, still on the same chain. In those nine years, I'd lost thirty keys, at a conservative count. She opened the front door and there was my key, on a long, bright yellow cord for easy visibility, draped over my bike carrier.

"Ta-da," I said, holding it over my head.

"Well, thank God for that, at least," Laura said as she returned her key to its spot in her bag and headed home to her fluffy white dog, Buddy.

The key situation at Number 9 became epic after John moved out. He was the one who had the keys in our marriage, so I was often at a loss now that he was gone. But really, I blamed the house. Like a disobliging Tolkien gate, the large wooden front door with the lion's head knocker decided whether to let me pass. More and more, my keys became recalcitrant in the lock, which was no small thing because Number 9 had an Assa Abloy lock-and-key system, "a high-security lock that provided increased resistance to compromise." And also to my own entry, it turned out.

The Assa Abloy system involved a key ID: each crisply cut key had its own one-of-a-kind, ten-digit ID code that could be replicated only on an Abloy cutting machine to decrypt the microelectronic blah-diddy-blah. My particular key, small and elfin, was an Abloy Classic, created in 1920 and the graceful parent of a good-looking Abloy family, including the Abloy Sentry, the Abloy Protec2, and the Abloy Novel. They were all made from nickel silver, and so cost twenty dollars apiece. The place in Toronto that kept my key ID on file, Lock Clinic Inc., ESTABLISHED SINCE 1968, *A. & E. Sintnicolaas & Son*, Locks & Safes, was an hour's trek from where I lived. I had to go in person, to present not only my key ID but also my own ID, to guarantee I was the one and true owner of my Assa Abloy. The family business kept eccentric hours, so even when I made the journey to the dark coven of a store on a homely street that mixed homes and businesses, Mr. and Mrs. Sintnicolaas & Son might or might not be in. I'd ring the bell, peer through the darkened window, rattle the no-doubt-impenetrable lock, and then leave, defeated and keyless.

"Get new locks," Laura said, and she meant not only to let me into my house more reliably but also to keep John out. Since our separation, he'd wander into Number 9, unhindered by his own always-willing key, to rifle through the fridge or rattle the grate in the fireplace. "Grate's open, you're heating the wide outdoors," he'd say and leave, chowing down on my provolone and mortadella on a fresh baguette.

But I was disinclined to change the locks. I liked that my stubborn house was well defended. And I liked my queer, strong key most of the time, too, although I sometimes spat "Asshole Abloy," as I fiddled it in the lock. "Get twenty made at once," said Laura, which I did and kept in a blue tin, but soon the tin was empty again. One hectic day just before Christmas, as Aunt Helen was dying and the house was pitch-black, my Assa Abloy went above and beyond and got firmly stuck in my front door lock, and Mr. Sintnicolaas, who did look like St. Nicholas and was also very jolly, made an emergency home visit to replace the entire lock and bring new keys. I asked Mr. Sintnicolaas how many keys he had replicated for me since I'd moved to Number 9 in late 2000 and told him my thirty-key estimate. "Ho, ho, ho," he laughed (no wonder, at twenty bucks a key). "We don't keep that kind of paperwork. It goes in the basement for a while and then we throw it out."

There was no point in simply not losing my keys, as some friends counselled. Whatever was going on, key-wise, was not in my control, I decided. I had workarounds. Laura, who lived a couple of blocks south, was step one in my backup system, and Ellen, up the street, step two. Ellen had a system she called SWIK for keeping track of "specs-wallet-iPhone-keys", so I figured she was a good bet for not losing my key, although she sometimes forgot her code word.

Passports belonged in this category. I tended to discover that my passport had gone missing days before leaving on a trip, which meant finding three friends to vouch for me as part of the emergency passport procurement process. I've had to do this for friends as well, and the passport officials ask you so many details about how the person looks that you resort to describing things like their misshapen toes and touching cowlicks. When I picked up one of my emergency passports, the two guys behind the counter stared intently at my chest. "What the hell did you tell them?" I asked the friends who'd vouched for me. "There were so many questions, I finally had to mention your big breasts," said one. "Really?" said the other. "I started with the breasts."

I'd prefer to leave the twelve cellphones off this list, but so many had vanished that they were hard to ignore. At this point, I was running a Canada-wide chain of local newspapers, and I'd had other big media jobs before that. I won't go so far as to blame the jobs for my lost phones, although I'd like to. They took up a lot of mental energy. Fortunately, my employers also replaced the phones, which is as much as we need to know. I'll just mention the once, when cellphone #8 rang, or rather buzzed, on my bedside table, and before I reached for it, half asleep, it vibrated off the edge and plopped into my glass of water on the floor. My phone committed suicide rather than spend another moment in my gentle hands. I tried not to feel aggrieved. But seriously? Could those socks not stand another minute under warm, hospitable roof before they marched out, a Terracotta Army of socks on the move?

"So you feel aggrieved when you lose things?" This was Tim the Jungian, an analyst I'd begun to see recently, who was helping me understand this losing streak of mine, among other things. His office was on the ground floor of a large brick house, and to enter it, I had to go through not one but two doors, mysteriously; they were only a foot apart. It felt like entering a magic portal, and in a way it was. We talked about dreams and other things impossible to remember or write down; it would be like trying to describe sex. Tim was fit and energetic, and sessions with him had a physicality. He'd jump up suddenly to follow a thought to his bookshelf, or toss a book he'd been reading aloud from to the floor, or lean back and stretch his legs when he was thinking something over. Sometimes, rarely, he'd fling his head back and laugh at what I'd said.

When Tim and I talked about prescriptive things, he passed over them quickly and efficiently. I told him about a time-consuming ritual I repeated in my head when I got on an airplane so it didn't crash in a burning ball to the ground. "Please, God"— an old habit to start with God—"don't let there be bombs or broken wings or faulty landing gear or gas leaks or exploding aerosol cans, fires in bathrooms, poison food trays, pilots committing suicide-while-flying, anyone dying for any reason," I began. My checklist had to be perfectly timed for just after the plane started to taxi but before lift-off, and it always ended with

"Nothing bad whatsoever," in case I missed something. I didn't tell Tim the details, I'm not an idiot. "It's time to move on from that now," he said. "It will free up space in your head for other things." When my work was stressful, he sat up straight in his black leather chair and directed me. "Hands on the chair, bum on the seat, feet on the floor. Grounded. Try it next time. It will calm you down." I imagined him waving his hand like Obi-Wan Kenobi when he said this; the few imperatives he spoke had that kind of unadorned power. And not only that but when I did as he suggested, I found out he was right. Letting go of unnecessary rituals did make room in my head for other things, and planting my feet on the floor made me a still pond of calmness at work. Also: even without my incantations to keep them safe, the planes stay in the air. So far.

But my losing things, Tim did not pass over quickly. That, he wanted to talk about, especially after I lost my phone coming and going from his office, twice. I told him how all-consuming it was to lose something, how the rush of panic whooshed me down to a frightened place far inside myself. The worst was when losing things clustered, when everything fled at once. It made me feel personally targeted, and yes, aggrieved. "More to think about there," Tim would say, eyebrows raised, as he firmly shook my hand at the two doors he'd opened for me to leave through, the parting ritual.

In one four-day cluster I lost my credit card, my keys, my wallet, and fifty pages of a manuscript after hitting Save, a less and less trustworthy word, you may have noticed. The Apple guy, Justin, a laconic Midwesterner, gently guided me to the realization that the words were irretrievably gone.

"So you are saying it's lost?" I said, after twenty minutes of doing almost all the talking.

"Cathrin, I never use that word," said Justin sagely.

The Microsoft guy I tried next was chattier. "Every minute of every day, work vanishes from computers all over the world and is never found again," he said.

"But where does it go?" I wanted to know.

"Empty data space," he said, and I pictured my words floating calmly in a vast and still void, maybe bumping into some physicist's quantum equation and, who knows, getting together to solve the mystery of the universe.

I didn't only lose things. They got stolen from me. Wallets and bags were grabbed in restaurants and sometimes from my house. One afternoon at Number 9, I was sorting bills at the dining room table. My bag was on the window ledge, and a bald-headed thief hoisted himself halfway through the open window before he saw me sitting there. He paused, calculated his timing, and grabbed the bag before I could lunge from my chair. Window Thief brought the total tally of break-ins at various houses to seven, and in three of those robberies, all my jewellery was ferreted out. For a long time, I pictured seeing someone in the unmistakable combination of my Florentine ring and fringed suede jacket and punching them in the head, growling "Thief!" at their dull-eyed face. Yes, it was personal. At a country bungalow we owned for a while, the thieves stole only tools and beer; even the wine got left behind. I thought of leaving a sign saying, "I like your style! Come back any time." Which they did, a couple of months later.

I developed a theory that my losing things, or their losing me, had to do with patterns. I'm not talking about pattern theory, the way mathematical patterns repeat in zebra stripes, sunflowers, weather systems, and galaxies—deeply interesting though that is—but simple repetitions in people's lives. Life patterns. Freud wrote about repetition compulsion, a psychological Groundhog Day in which a person repeats a traumatic event going all the way back to infancy, when Mom, say, walked off distracted with the rattle she was meant to give back. That feeling of childhood abandonment created a destiny neurosis, Freud said, which compelled us to repeat the experience of Mommy being an untrustworthy trickster with every subsequent love partner for the rest of our lives.

Freud, no ray of sunshine, could get pretty dark on the subject of repetition compulsion. He talked about patients being pursued by a malignant or demonic force. But there was no need to get that black here. Because mostly if you asked people if their lives had a repetition pattern, it was remarkable how quickly they answered, and devil compulsions didn't come up. One friend said his pattern was that he had a good year every four years. "What year are you in now?" "My good year was last year, so I have three more to go." A work colleague said her pattern was to put out fires in people's hair. "The first time I did it with my hands, which was unwise. The second time I grabbed a glass of water from a man's hands. I had to wrench it with both my hands; he didn't want to let it go because he didn't know about the burning hair." What did hair on fire look like, I wanted to know. "It looked like a golden halo of light." How did the hair catch fire? I couldn't get enough. As patterns go, this was a hell of a good one. Both times, a tendril of a woman's hair caught fire in a tea light, she said, and seconds later . . . *whoosh*.

Ann's mother-in-law, Ruby, told the story of a family diamond that escaped its setting three times and was found three times, hidden in the crack of a wooden floor or tucked inside a car seat. "That's a diamond that wanted to be lost," I said. "I'd call it a diamond that wanted to be found," said Ruby.

My son's repetition pattern involved being in life-and-death situations, which I didn't love. Kelly, like Laura, still had the same key to Number 9 that we'd given him twelve years earlier. A grounded man in his twenties who had a hyperawareness of what was going on around him, he saw everything that was visible to see, often at a glance. "Sensate," said Tim the Jungian. When he was twenty-one, Kelly hitchhiked to Banff. He and a kid from Lyon, France, had thumbed a lift with a driver who suddenly veered off the highway and onto a dirt field, where he got out of the car, opened his trunk, and pulled out a long hunting spear. The French kid started to run down the field, but not Kelly.

"I went to the trunk and stood as close to the spear holder as I could get."

"Kelly. No. Why?" I was aghast.

"The closer I got to him, the less traction he'd have when he threw the spear."

This would never have occurred to me, although I could see it was the smarter move. The driver used the spear to draw a map in the dirt of where they should go next. An odd man, but not a murderer.

Kelly's second brush with life and death was at a party on Toronto Island, where he strode down to people gathered at the shore of Lake Ontario and jumped straight into the water to pull out a kid who was flailing, face down. The other kids thought the boy was horsing around, pretending to swim badly, but Kelly saw at a glance that it was all wrong, and he was right: the kid had hit his head on a rock and his forehead was split wide open.

Recently I discovered that Kelly also kept me out of danger; he walked behind me in the kitchen, quietly moving things in my wake.

"Kelly, what the hell?" I said one day, bumping into him as he moved a ten-inch chef's knife dangling from the countertop to the drawer.

"Mom, you leave everything on the edge: knives, bowls, wine glasses, your computer."

"How long has this been going on?" I was irked.

"Years," he said.

I started to watch Kelly after that: the way he quietly rechopped my already chopped sweet potatoes to make them evenly sized for better roasting, how he'd slide my iPhone further back on the windowsill. The pas de deux he made of our movements through the kitchen, mine precarious, his careful and ordered. I hadn't noticed it before. How sweet it was. How he kept watch on the edge of things, a place I seemed to be overly familiar with.

I loved limbo as a kid, when I took the Catholic catechism as my gospel. The word comes from the Latin *limbus*, meaning "border" or "edge." Limbo itself was a kind of pleasant void, like empty data space, and home to the lost souls of the unbaptized dead, newborn babies, mostly. You couldn't get out of limbo; it wasn't a way station to heaven like purgatory, there was no aspiration to be somewhere better. In limbo you just were. I longed to end up there, but could not since (a) I was baptized and (b) Pope Benedict in 2007 booted limbo out of the Catholic real estate pool. He said banning the faultless from heaven reflected an "unduly restrictive view of salvation." "First no fish on Fridays, now no limbo," said Mom, fed up.

So limbo was off the list for my eternal digs, but I was beginning to understand that I'd created a kind of limbo here on earth. There was something unresolved or neglected about a place like limbo, I thought now, and it began to seem less benign than when I was a child. Some longing for oblivion, perhaps. It felt dangerous.

I traced my own repetition pattern of losing things not to losing my stuff—in a family of five you held on to your meagre possessions, and if your siblings robbed you, Mom would say, "That will teach you to look after your things"—but to being lost myself. There was an early family video shot on a Kodak Super 8 of Laura twirling with her pincurled hair and my brothers and cousins roughhousing, a quaint term for pummelling each other into a trip to the hospital for stitches. After a long while, the silent camera panned down the backyard, where I'd been forgotten in a baby swing that hadn't been pushed for some time. As I grew a bit older, Mom constantly lost me in the racks at Reitmans or Eaton's. "Where'd you get to?" she'd say blandly to my panicked face as she fondled skirts and tops. One Sunday I got fully lost at a family picnic at Queenston Heights, a hilltop park for kids to run free with pools, a bandstand where my uncle Jack played the sax, and a statue of General Brock, vanquisher of the invading Americans. You could climb inside the general himself, to the broad-viewed height at the top, although the dark and twirling staircase made more than one kid vomit, not just me. On this picnic, I followed the wrong family from the parking lot; they all looked the same, with their half dozen brushed-cut and pig-tailed kids, their giant food hampers and stacks of brightly striped folding chairs. My parents were angry when I was finally located, which was puzzling. Didn't they want me to be found? I wasn't sure of the answer to that as a child, and maybe that's where the panic started.

As an adult, I was often in the wrong place at the wrong time, which could get hairy. In another cluster of losing my phone, credit card, and transit pass, I muscled through each loss and made it to the airport in time for a work trip. My shoes, belt, and sweater were already in the plastic bin—"I get more action here than I do in my bedroom," said the woman ahead of me—when the security officer looked at my boarding pass.

"You're at the wrong terminal."

"How did I get this far?" It wasn't my fault that I'd breezed through two boarding checks. I furiously laced up my runners as the security man listed the odds of me making my flight.

"If the airport shuttle is right there. If you run all the way from the train. If your gate is not too far. Then you might make your flight."

And I did, miraculously, and was just settled into seat 2B when a trim suited man said, smiling, "That's my seat."

I got out my boarding pass to show him he was wrong, and the flight attendant said to me, "You're on the wrong plane."

"Maybe being lost is a place you want to get to," said Tim the Jungian, not surprisingly in the face of the evidence. I often commented on the mystery of the double-door entry to his office, expecting some kind of psychological explanation, to which he would say, "Yes, this seems to interest you." For a long time, I didn't notice that there was also a third door, until he went through it one day to retrieve a book he wanted to share. It bothered me that I could be that unobservant; I prided myself on taking it all in. But he was unsurprised.

"Years ago with my supervisor, I commented on a new, very large ceramic urn in the room, and he said it had been there for five years." He smiled at me and then nodded at the wall to my right, which was entirely taken up by a massive oil painting of two fish, one pink and one blue, swimming in opposite directions. "Yesterday, a patient noticed that painting for the first time." The painting I had noticed; I was relieved I wasn't as far gone as that poor sap, but I wasn't consoled.

What else was I missing that was right under my nose? As I struggled to answer Tim's question about how it felt to lose things, my eyes darted crazily around the room to memorize his seal carving and moose antlers and water glasses so I wouldn't get caught by surprise again. He looked at me kindly. "Being lost is okay, you know. It's a place where most of us end up spending a lot of time." I thought about how the sock-losing husbands often went into the deep backcountry in canoes and on skis, and how the best and funniest stories from their trips were about the times they got hopelessly turned around. "We don't like following directions. We like being lost so we can find ourselves," said Johanna's husband, Ian, who could offer a master class on the subject, so vast was his experience.

"The tricky thing about being lost is that you don't want to get stuck there, like the Lost Boys," Tim said in his office with the three doors. Or like those babies I once loved to think about in limbo. "It's a place you want to move in and out of." He took off his glasses, and we sat in comfortable silence before he spoke again. "Hermes was the messenger god, moving between the immortals and the humans," he said. "He was the god of a lot of things, like alchemy, a kind of magical transformation where things move from one state to another, and thieves too." Tim liked Hermes, he'd come up before, and I listened carefully when he talked about him, because there was usually something. "When you think about it, what's thieving but lifting things from one place and taking them to another? A transactional profession."

I thought about what was shifting in my life, what was moving from one place to another, like my black bag with the brown straps that Window Thief had nabbed. Not my stuff—that didn't matter, not really—but more important things. My once bright house now dark, its invisible electrical frequencies passing from one state to another. I thought about John, back when we were happy, and how that had passed too. And PNM, was he coming or going? I wasn't sure. My fading mom and dad, the centre of everything for so long and now not. They didn't know where they were headed, and neither did I. And maybe it didn't matter. Maybe it wasn't where any of it was going that was important, but the uneventful moments that connected here and there. I thought about that sunny day at Number 9, when my friends and I had talked about lost socks as our kids hurtled by us. The ordinary beauty of that afternoon was what I remembered now. The way the slanting sun fanned into the living room, a seashell of light. How the kids were happy as clams. Maybe the in-between wasn't a place of neglect but a place to be found, a place where *I* might be found. A place to figure out what was worth holding on to and what was not.

"Remember," Tim said as our session ended and he opened the double doors for me to leave through, "being lost is an interesting place to reside."

It had better be because I was about to spend a whole lot of time there. I've learned to let go of things like single socks, but that high dale with the rolling views was a long way off. I was now and for some time to come in the low valley of the lost socks.

6.

Would You Stand Up
and Walk Out on Me?

HELD UP IN THE CITY, Promising New Man had to drive alone to the country cabin where I was staying with friends. He was a day late but still in time for the birthday dinner they were throwing for me. Alone in the dark with no one to help navigate, he lost his way on the snowy, bending, unlit country road. Not bad as metaphors go.

Every February, a dozen good friends and almost as many yipping dogs came to this converted fishing cabin on a lively river with its two long wings of nun-like rooms—or I suppose they were fisherman-like rooms, which meant small, spare, and thin-walled; there were enough of them to sleep ten or twelve people with ease. The weekend was organized around the convergence of three Aquarian birthdays, and most especially that year, my own. It was my sixtieth, after all, a landmark event. Dinner was the beginning of a celebration I hoped would span days and weeks, capped by the trip to Sicily, because two things were true about my birthday. One was that nothing was too much. Parties! Trips! Presents! "No, not another one!" I'd say, adding more ripped paper to the mountain of wrapping on the floor beside me. The second was that I was convinced everyone would forget, which wouldn't be the case this year either. Not precisely.

My pals and I had spent the day in the fresh snow, some of us on cross-country skis, where the trail was snug and fast, and some on snowshoes, and now, as we waited for PNM, we were pleasantly sapped, flopped here and there doing not much. Someone strummed a guitar in front of the massive stone fireplace; a few others played Scrabble in the wide sunroom overlooking the river. "Close game," said Sue, our host, as she grabbed a beer from the overstuffed fridge, looking grim. We were big on games at this cabin and ruthlessly competitive. The night before, we'd played the man in the hat. I've never excelled less at any game; it required the mental pace of a child prodigy on amphetamines—there was an obnoxious egg timer—as well as a broad base of knowledge of famous names. If you don't know the game, and I pray you don't, the basics are that everyone writes down a dozen or so names of supposedly well-known individuals, from Gandhi to Beyoncé, and then puts the names in a hat. When you're *it*, you give your team members clues, like "Indian proponent of nonviolent resistance," and the faster they're able to guess the identity of the secret person, the more names you draw and points you score. "I don't know who this is," I'd said the night before as I stared in cold fear at the name I'd drawn, which turned out to be the author of *The Compleat Angler*. The egg timer sifted away and I earned zero points, a new low. But seriously, Izaak Walton? What normal person would know that name? Mostly, though, it was my own malfunctioning brain that made me the worst at the man in the hat. "She's the Queen of England, for fuck's sake!" my team members reminded me.

"I can't find you," PNM said, when he phoned to let me know he was close. He sounded tense. Sue and I bundled up and walked out onto the road, so bright with snow it felt like the sun had come up in the middle of the night. We waved our flashlights in the air so he could find his way, and after a while we saw the headlights of his big black car come around the corner. I hugged him out in the thick snowfall.

"You made it! Well done." I brushed the fat white flakes off his car coat.

"I feel like an idiot getting lost like that." He looked at me, irritated, with me or himself, I wasn't sure.

"Not at all," said Sue. "Everyone gets lost on this road."

We brought him into the warm kitchen to meet everybody. "Hello!" "Let me take that coat." "You must want a drink." I'd worried they'd judge his brush-cut squareness, but they didn't. They were my friends, we shored each other up; that was our job, one of the most important left. They wanted this shot at happiness for me. Once PNM got settled, they asked him about himself and his work, and about the trip he had planned for us. Tecca, a hiker who preferred to be lightly shod, commented on his construction-style yellow boots.

"Maybe a bit heavy?"

"I like them," he said, smiling sheepishly.

At the trifecta birthday dinner that night, PNM was his usual talkative self, and I relaxed into the evening. We could be a lot, loud and opinionated, but he held his own. For birthday presents, I gave one of the Aquarian men a package of stick-on moustaches, which the women immediately put under their own noses. "I am deeply alarmed by how good I look in this moustache," said Johanna, and she did; she looked like Johnny Depp. Mine was silver and straight across, and I looked like Walter Cronkite. My cake had a big red heart made up of smaller red cinnamon hearts, the way Mom made my birthday cakes when I was a kid. Not that my friends knew this, or maybe they did. Maybe I'd hinted, I wouldn't put it past me. After the cake, someone brought out a dreadful new game (at least it wasn't the man in the hat), where you had to answer "Would you rather" questions. Would you rather fart every time you kissed for the rest of your life or dive into a pool of snot? "Oh, brother," said PNM, but he played in good sport, as I knew he would, and that night in our thin-walled, chilly room we had under-the-covers sex, quietly.

Back in town, there was a lot to do before we flew out to Sicily in five days. Promising New Man headed to Houston to tie up loose ends at work, and I ticked the chores off my travel list: prescriptions, repack, pedicure, repack, dry cleaning, repack. "I'm off to buy my travel-size shampoo!" I said to a friend as I headed out for the final pit stops.

"Ha ha." This was how Lynne at Knob Hill Cleaners greeted me when I hurried in to pick up my clothes for the trip, as she did every time I entered her store. It wasn't mean, but it wasn't like I'd said something funny either. I wasn't cracking jokes whenever I picked up my dry cleaning.

"Does Lynne laugh at you when you get your cleaning?" I asked Laura, needlessly, because of course she didn't.

"Why would she?" Laura said, my point precisely.

"I need these because I'm off to Sicily in three days," I said to Lynne as I paid up, draping two sagging bags of cellophane-wrapped holiday clothes on my arms. "For my birthday. Two weeks!" I really wanted to impress her.

"Have fun," she said, waving and laughing as I left, because the news of my trip did perk her up, and perhaps also because she was contributing to its success with her beautifully pressed and mended handiwork. Earlier that day, my work gang at Metro News had baked a cake with "Bon Voyage!" written gaily across the top; they were big cake bakers for any occasion, and those two details—the farewell cake and Lynne at Knob Hill, happy about my trip—were the things I couldn't get out of my head when Promising New Man called that night to cancel.

"But I told the woman at my dry cleaner," I said, as if this would change the direction of the tide.

He said it was a work crisis. "Cathrin, no one is more disappointed than I am."

I replied with stone-cold silence. I knew immediately that I'd never speak to him again. "Goodbye," I said, and hung up.

And that was all I said until I called back, and then back, and back. "But why?" I couldn't understand, even though part of me had known that this final cancellation was coming; that for months, I'd been hearing the faintest warning bell ringing far in the distance, as across a mountain village. Even at the fishing cabin, I saw his cold feet in his late arrival. You'd think having your suspicions realized would end the need to deny them, but the opposite was true: I was a superstorm system of denial, a blinding downburst of denial.

His explanation was loose. A sudden big merger at work that would take all his time. "Nonsense," said Laura when I phoned her. "Massive mergers aren't sudden."

I was lying on my sooty bed in my house of holes with a Kleenex box on my stomach, my mostly packed suitcase on the floor. Laura listened while I talked on a repeating loop, going over the story. "I knew it," I said. And seconds later, "I can't believe it." White Kleenex bobbed on my bed like sails on a lake. I grabbed a fresh one from the box and blew my nose loudly into the phone. "I told Lynne at Knob Hill Cleaners. Now what will she think of me?"

"Oh, dear," said Laura. She was really upset by the whole debacle. She'd put aside her own plans for my sixtieth to make room for PNM's bigger, better plan. "I'm going to throw the party after all," she said.

"I don't want a party. Everyone standing around feeling sorry for me." I honked into the phone again with my Kleenex.

After an hour of this, she got the idea to look up the hotel rooms in Sicily, the ones Promising New Man told her he'd booked for us. She gasped, almost choking. "Cathrin, nothing's been booked." Laura was calm in her outrage. "Your dates are open. I'm checking your flights next," she said. "I'll call you back."

"You never booked the hotel," I snarled at PNM on my fourth or fifth call. "You are a liar."

"I'm not, I promise you," he said, and he sounded really broken up. "It's just work, that's all."

I wanted to believe him. The alternative was humiliation and misery. I was beginning to be lulled by his suggestion that I come to Houston for a visit when his work settled down; or maybe Florida in the spring? I liked the idea of Florida, and I decided I'd see him again after all, because it wasn't adding up, this rejection from him. The more we talked, the more my heart softened, which was when he became colder.

"That time I came to Toronto last September, you weren't happy to see me," he said. "You wished I hadn't come."

This was new, PNM pretending it was my fault he'd cancelled Sicily. I quickly tamped down a hazy, unwelcome memory of being mildly put out by his unexpected arrival back in September, before I'd gone all in with him. "I can fly to you now and we'll sort it all out," I said. Which was when he started to cry about all the work he had to do, and I recognized something that anyone over the age of three can recognize in another human being: crocodile tears. He wasn't sad, he was relieved to be out of it, to be back to his life before me. That's what I heard on the phone.

I composed a letter. I'd like to say it was a letter with high purpose that made its way to clarity and forgiveness, but it was nothing close. It listed every lie I'd imagined he'd ever told me. "The super-soft sheets at Target that you said you bought for me. *Lie!*" "You had to work at New Year's. *Lie!*" "You had a cold that time. *Lie!*" By the fifteenth or thirtieth draft, I was adding long expositions that ended with exclamations like "Paddington Bear! Clues everywhere, Cathrin!" I emailed the letter to my brother Tim, for a man's opinion. It was long, I warned him.

"If someone sent this letter to me, I'd have to commit suicide," he called to tell me.

"Really," I said, impressed. "Which parts?" I hung up and hit Send.

———

A loose gang of friends and acquaintances were heading to Quebec on a cross-country ski trip the day after the Sicily cancellation, and they swept me up at the last minute, adding me to their mishmashed group. The trip was meant as a rally around a good friend, who was in the midst of his own divorce. He was in a rough way, and I was added to the stunned and wounded. After a few hours of stunted conversation on the road, our cars pulled up to our pitch-dark "villa," rented by my newly separated friend from Goblins Getaways. I couldn't figure out where else he might have found it; he normally had a good eye for a winning inn. A red pickup truck parked out front ran ominously for half an hour with no sign of a person, like a Stephen King set-up for the horror to come, and when we finally found someone to let us in, we were shown into two off-kilter rooms. "The owner built it all himself," said our guide, in the least surprising statement of the weekend. The common rooms were connected to the bedrooms by rounded underground tunnels, and the walls of the tunnels featured glass-encased dioramas of incomprehensibly dull and meaningless scenes. Some tunnels, like mine to my crazy-ceilinged bedroom, curled up, and some, to the men's bedrooms below ground, curled terrifyingly down. It was like travelling through someone's large intestine to get to bed.

The skiing was cold, −30°C Canadian cold, the kind of cold that made us proud to survive and bound us as a nation. We were skiing the Canadian Ski Marathon, in fact, at 160 kilometres the longest ski marathon in the world. It wasn't a race but more a personal endurance test, and the keeners in our group, which was most of them, racked up 50k a day. My lonely friend and I skied behind at our own sorrowful pace. I'd done part of this circuit before, and so had he, although then it was with our spouses and kids. I skied it the first couple of times on my wooden Asnes; it felt authentically Canadian backwoods. I smartened up the year I was constantly passed by the Coureur des Bois skiers, the men and women who started before dawn to ski the entire distance, their huge backpacks stuffed with overnight camping gear. The real deal. Being passed by them was nothing new, it was the "Wow, wooden skis—haven't seen those in years" comments that finally turned my head as they sailed by wearing their hand-knit woollen toques and fresh-off-the-rack fibreglass skis. On this trip, I skied on my own fibreglass pair, light as flower petals under my feet, although I knew little about the varying states of preparation and readiness that went with my new skis, the wax and scrapers and corks, the pack pockets and jacket layers and hydration systems. I do now. But on this trip to the ski marathon in Montebello, I didn't have a system or even a pack of my own, so I stuffed my pockets with wax and corks and an orange, and my friend carried my water bottle. Our goal was 25k a day. We lagged along and talked about our cracked hearts.

"I don't get it," he said of the end of his long marriage as we skied the widest, flattest part of the Montebello trail. He'd stopped to light a cigarette, an old habit returned, and I wondered if our frozen blue bodies would be found that night under the blank cataract eye of a moon. Pausing was unwise in this cold when we were so far behind the others. "Was it so bad?" he asked of his marriage. "Was I so terrible as a husband?"

I wasn't sure if I got to stack the pain of my failed one-year romance against the end of my friend's twenty-five-year marriage, but my wound was fresh, so I did. "I mean, you met him that night at my place," I began. "He barbecued salmon and I forgot to put out the dill sauce? Did you see it coming then? Was it me or was it him?"

I don't think we answered each other's questions. We were too wrapped up in our own stories, although my friend's idea of his situation might have been instructive for me. Because I was sad about his divorce, but I wasn't surprised by it. He hadn't been paying attention to his marriage when he needed to most, that's how it seemed to me. I wasn't going to say that to my wounded friend, and I didn't stop to wonder about the things people weren't saying to me about my role in the PNM split. "You had a lot of improvements for the guy, didn't you." "A little humiliating to make him wait for six months before you had sex." Nobody said that to me, any more than I talked frankly to my friend. But they might have, and they might have been right. Sue, our host at the fishing cabin, came closest.

"We landed like a thud that weekend," she said, long after it was over.

"What, us? We brought out our best selves for him." I was surprised. It hadn't occurred to me that being force-marched through a chummy weekend with my tight circle of friends might not have been a barrel of laughs for PNM.

"We were great," Sue said. "That was part of the problem. I've never seen someone in such a hurry to leave."

On day two at Goblins Getaways, my friend returned from his second trip to the grocery store, lugging bags of unnecessary food. "Shoring up the supplies," he said, and laid out a massive post-ski spread. He ate nothing himself, only chain-smoked out on the balcony. "Dig in, dig in!" he called to us, his cold breath mixing with the smoke from his cigarette. None of us were hungry. It wasn't only the house that was lopsided. The usual couples were there without their partners and seemed off balance on their own, and the new people I'd barely met talked too much about things that didn't register. It was a *Cabinet of Dr. Caligari* weekend, you didn't know what was sane and what was crazy. The harrowing passageways, the pointless dioramas, the piles of uneaten food. The whole weekend was like walking through the horror movie of my new life curving on and on without purpose. I wondered if my newly single friend felt the same way.

Back in the city, I showed up at work, embarrassed to be behind my desk so soon after my "Bon Voyage!" cake, but no one said much and I was quiet too. I considered never going to the dry cleaners again, but the prospect of handwashing and pressing everything for the rest of my life was too daunting. I headed out early the next Saturday morning. It was well below zero and the fat snow didn't melt but stayed put on the ground. I loved the city on a winter day like this, when the usual February slush was replaced by mounds of snow so soft you might lie down and rest your head on it. Just stare up at the white sky while the snow slowly covered you. It was fresh and deep enough for snow boots, which didn't happen often in the city anymore; you could sometimes get through a whole winter in sneakers.

"Ha ha," said Lynne when I walked into Knob Hill with a new bag of cleaning. Not the summer clothes I'd picked up for Sicily but my winter workwear of jackets and skirts and pants. "How was Sicily? Back so soon?" she asked, suddenly confused.

"Oh, it got cancelled," I said.

"Oh?" she said.

She looked at me with concern. I shrugged and smiled.

"Ha ha," I said.

Lynne smiled back. "Oh, okay. Ha ha ha."

The Doomed Trip to Sicily became a recurring subject, even more giving than socks. My friends weighed in for years afterward. It wasn't that it was such a tragedy. There were worse things, way worse. It was that it had no answer. The mystery drew us back.

Recently a group of us had dinner at Tecca's place. She had managed her divorce much differently than I. Her paperwork was finished in a year instead of my ten, and it didn't take Tecca too long to sell her house and buy a condo in a groovy 1960s low-rise that backed onto a treed ravine. Many of the people in the building were older than she'd expected—she was our pioneer on downsizing, so we watched her every move for clues to our own future—and she'd quickly charmed her way onto the condo's design committee and chosen new paint colours for the hallways. Her own apartment, too, had much that was new: Inuit art, sculptural lights, sleek couches, a welcoming wooden dining room table. "The pine is reclaimed," Tecca said, like her life.

Tecca, pretty in a tailored navy summer tunic, got it into her head that we would have cocktails in the fading summer light on the green lawn below. She'd loaded a butler trolley with wine, ice, and asparagus wrapped in prosciutto, and we all trooped down on the elevator with our drinks and high spirits, loudly dragging the co-op's lawn furniture out of storage.

"Should we be quiet?" I asked, not wanting to disturb the

early-to-bed crowd. Tecca was a busy television executive and lived full on.

"Of course not," she said.

This was the kind of thing we used to do when we were all still married and went on holidays to cottages together, when the kids couldn't get enough of us and we'd finally push them off our laps. Dinner on the rocks! Dinner on the porch! Drinks on the dock! We'd make ambitious cocktails and meals on a summer evening like this one and then drag tables here or there, to the perfect setting with the perfect light, at this or that cottage on this or that northern lake. The kids would strew flowers on the table, and the tablecloths would flap in the lake breezes. It was full and also fleeting, like all happiness. Because none of it was as perfect as it looked, but it had the appearance of perfection, which carried us over a lot, for a long time. We banded together to distract ourselves from difficult marriages, lost jobs, sick children. We glided together over the frightening depths the same way we sidestroked over the deep northern lakes.

At this dinner, twenty years after those summer days and four years after the Sicily no-go, the subject of Promising New Man came up again. Almost all of us there on Tecca's sloping lawn had been together at the fishing cabin for my sixtieth birthday. Lots had gone on since that weekend. We'd shambled our way through divorces, heart attacks, cancer, abdominal fissures, and pyelonephritis (the *–phritis* was there to terrify you). We'd endured the loss of parents, friends, and most terribly, children. We'd gathered around to pull each other out of the sinkholes that threatened to swallow us whole. In the early cottage days, when the kids were little, we mostly kept our troubles to ourselves, but the older we got, the more we talked about the big stuff without fear or shame. No one was going to stand up and walk out on us; we'd proven that to one another. The Beatles at their sappiest were sounding less mawkish; like gods of truth, even. PNM's coming up again was natural, because it wasn't just my story—it was all of ours.

"I still think it was because of the head injury," said Johanna, recycling her favourite theory, and we were off. PNM had been beaten up by random strangers that fall of 2014, a frightening and painful event. "It all changed after that, remember? He'd been so great up until then. I'm sure that was it."

"He probably did love you, and then he messed up the trip and he got trapped," said one of the men, taking a puff on a lime-green vape pen. Pot had become a feature of these dinners now that it was legal and half of us had health issues the dope eased. And now that it was fun as hell again to get stoned.

"It wasn't love or a kick in the head or good or bad intention." This was Ellen, who had strong opinions on the subject. "He pursued you because you represented something he thought he wanted; it doesn't matter what. None of it was real, because he wasn't real."

The conversation might have veered to Trump or Netflix or Me Too, but Tecca had the kicker. She'd been goofing around on dating sites and had perfected a comic routine, with visuals, of the various men she'd been matched with. Most looked like a cross between Santa Claus and Jesus Christ. Jesus if he had lived to be a hairy old man, but with the same expression of pain for the terrible betrayals he had endured. Some of these dating-site men posed themselves with props, like Gary,

"Owner at Consulting," with his eight-foot-tall plastic lobster. "Is that a hospital bed Kurt is lying on?" I asked of Match #3. "Looks like it," said Tecca, delighted.

"So the other day, I took a look around the site and guess whose name came up?"

It was Promising New Man, of course. I was surprised by how bad I felt, after all this time. Some part of me had thought that PNM's love for me was so frightening and big that he could never take a shot again, as if that was the real untold story. But now that wasn't it either. I couldn't figure any of it out, and it bothered me.

We drove home from dinner in one overloaded car, our voices spilling out the open car windows and drifting into the open windows of the unlit houses as we motored slowly by in the warm summer night.

At Number 9 in my pajamas, I remembered what had been tugging at me. I paid $4.99 to rent *Terms of Endearment* from iTunes and fast-forwarded to the scene where Jack Nicholson, the philandering astronaut next door, brings Shirley MacLaine to her mid-life realization that sex is "fan-fucking-tastic!" and then breaks up with her after her grandkids spend the weekend at her house. The too-present fact of her family terrified him. Nicholson and MacLaine sit across from each other in her claustrophobic gazebo in the back of her over-manicured garden.

Him: "You're some kind of woman. But I'm the wrong kind of man, and it doesn't look like my shot at being the right kind is as good as I was hoping for."

James Brooks's brilliantly empathetic camera is by now on MacLaine's face, framed by a hilariously frilly dress from the closet of hilariously frilly dresses that she has worn throughout the movie. But there is nothing funny or flouncy about her expression, which has moved from apprehension to a kind of resigned boredom. She does a little bounce before she speaks.

Her: "You don't even know how much you're going to miss me."

He says something about not wanting to feel obligated, especially living next door, but she interrupts with an ugly face.

Her: "*Blah blah blah blah blah blah blah blah.*" She stops, then makes an even worse face than she had been making up until then. "*Blah,*" she mouths silently one last time. That was nine blahs. My memory was of Nicholson leaving at that point, but—and this changed everything—he doesn't. He sits still and looks at her.

Him: "I am going to miss you. And I do feel bad."

Her: "You're lucky. I feel humiliated."

Nicholson sits for a moment longer and then gets up slowly and exits the gazebo. Cut to car driving in town.

My memory of the scene had been pretty good, although I'd forgotten how many "blahs" and also how long Nicholson stayed put in that demented gazebo. What was different in this viewing, forty years after the first one, was the way I felt about the breakup. The first time I'd thought Nicholson was a good-for-nothing cad, quickly mumbling his excuses before he slunk back to his house full of pictures of himself. But now he seemed like a decent man. There was no crying or obfuscation. No ghosting, no hiding behind texts and emails. Just a respectful face-to-face goodbye. He took all nine of her "blahs" on the chin without looking away. She got to hear why he was leaving, stupid as it was, spelled out with reasons. She got to say to his face what she thought of that and how he had humiliated her.

At the end of the movie, Jack the reprobate comes back to Shirley when she's at her lowest. "Who would have expected you to be a nice guy?" she says. "Who would have expected PNM not to be?" I said to Shirley on the screen as I lay in my bed (alone, it doesn't need saying). I felt like I was the one who wasn't a real person. PNM hadn't even taken me seriously enough to properly end things, and now my love life was the kicker to a joke at a dinner party. "I want my gazebo breakup scene," I told the TV. But Shirley didn't answer me.

7.

What If

KELLY AND HIS GIRLFRIEND, VONNIE, played "What if" when they marvelled at their new love. "What if you had left Guatemala a week earlier?" Vonnie would say, because they met in the northern mountains of Guatemala, where Kelly was studying Spanish, and he really was meant to have left a week earlier. "What if you hadn't been in the cafe that afternoon?" Kelly said back. They looked into each other's eyes as they said these things, so I imagined, telling their story to each other. "What if my girlfriend hadn't asked you to sit with us?" said Vonnie. "We do this over and over," said Kelly-in-love, and the respect and even awe in my son's voice surprised and moved me. I thought about the random purposefulness of life as I listened to him from three thousand miles away, how everything could teem toward one point and one place, one metamorphic moment. What if you had sex the next week instead of this one, which baby would or wouldn't have been born. What if Dad had stayed in at the army base playing cards instead of going to the YMCA, where he saw Mom across the dance floor. What if I had gone to Sicily for my birthday and not had this chance tonight to talk with Mom. It wasn't good when my birthday trip was cancelled

82

at the last minute. But I'm grateful that it kept me in the city on February 11, 2015, the day of my sixtieth birthday, so I could be with Mom and not far away across the ocean. It wasn't the only gift I'd be given before the night was through.

"What are you two troublemakers up to?" I said to my parents as I came through the unlocked door of their apartment at Hazelton Place. The precision plan for the evening was to get them to the lounge for a birthday celebration with the sibs, then back upstairs and into bed—they were past restaurants at this point—in time for the rest of us to head out for a hastily thrown together dinner in my honour. I'd worked on this breezy entrance. I'd crack a joke or two, it was my new style with Mom and Dad now that they were in their nineties. I'm not sure whose steady runnel of worry I was trying to divert, theirs or mine. The miasma of death seemed to hover around them, that "night air" sixteenth-century doctors believed you could catch, like a cold, and die from. And maybe I could. Today I turned sixty, after all. I wasn't that far off myself.

Mom and Dad didn't complain about or comment on their situation. Mom had already taken a couple of dry runs at death. This seems to be one of the things about living until you are very old; death becomes a practical joker, taking a scythe or two at you before it reaps you once and for all. John and I, years ago, were preparing for the end with his ninety-year-old father as he gradually stopped breathing for what seemed like minutes, when his devoted caregiver arrived. "He does this sometimes." She held his hand. "Don't worry." My friend Ian's dad, at ninety-seven, seemed to die more than once while doing his morning calisthenics, most alarmingly during a trip to the US. "Just get his body over the border into Canada or the costs will be astronomical," said Ian's brother, but after a minute or two, old Peter came to, bright as a robin.

Mom had a particular talent for ducking death. I thought of those Edgar Allan Poe stories of people buried alive and suspected that my mother's wilful ancestors were among them. When Mom coughed, she said, "It's not the cough that carries you off, but the coffin they carry you off in," although in her case I wasn't sure her coffin would be the last we saw of her. Mom liked us kids to fetch things for her when we were little. She could summon you from a floor away, where you were likely labouring over a chore she had assigned—scraping wax off the bathroom floor tiles with a spoon, say—to turn off a light just over her head so she could take a quick nap. I pictured her sitting up in her coffin with a last-minute request. "I could use a pillow, not too thick." A year earlier, when she'd begun to choke on things as harmless as a sip of water, she went stiff as a board after a particularly bad incident. Tim and Nancy lifted her rigid body to bed and sat vigil that night before calling the rest of us in the morning to tell us she was gone. "The next thing we know, she's in the kitchen asking for an English muffin for breakfast," said Tim. "Not too much butter."

The night of my birthday, Mom and Dad stared straight ahead in their side-by-side easy chairs like a pair of nesting hens. They spent their days this way, dozing and I wasn't sure what else. A bit of chatting, maybe. They often held books but were past reading. The TV might have been on, but they didn't watch it. For most of my life, they were the busiest people I knew; they rarely sat. Now this stillness, like waiting. It threw me every time.

"Here she is!" Mom said as I wisecracked through the door. For months, she'd had an expression that I struggled to recognize. It was obedience, a willingness to please. At her age, being pleasing was a survival skill, so your caregivers kept bringing you your lime-green Jell-O. But there was something else that made me look over my shoulder to see who she was beaming at. Mom smiled at me as if she no longer saw the contention and disapproval and love and devotion and shame and sadness that formed our relationship, our constant management of each other. The offspring that mother and child create between themselves, recalcitrant, impossible to please. For years, whenever I saw Mom, I saw not her but this whiny brat, MommyCathy. Even now, at her frail eighty-five pounds, I saw the complications of pleasing her and deflecting her worry about me. The necessity to make time for her. The way she needled around in my brain when I didn't.

But at ninety-one, Mom had stopped lugging around the heavy suitcase of our relationship and just saw me. I was Cathrin to her, my simplest self, from the rashy, excitable baby she'd rocked in her white rocking chair fifty-nine years ago to this knobby, slightly battered woman approaching her own old age who was standing in front of her now. She seemed to just love me, that's what I saw in her uncomplicated smile. It was disconcerting as hell. I mean, she'd taken a long time to show it. It took me a long time to get to undiluted Mom, too, to put down my own heavy suitcase. I wish it hadn't because I missed a lot in that final year. I think of the conversations we might have had. I would have been the one doing most of the talking because she'd become too anxious to sustain the steady haul of a conversation. But that would have been fine too.

"Here's our birthday girl," said Mom again, still smiling. This time I did take a quick look over my shoulder, just to be sure. "You look great!" I said, and she did; they both did. Dad was in his usual snappy coordinated look, tan pants, striped cardigan, brown suspenders, and Mom had put on pearls and a smart black jacket. I was briefly embarrassed that I'd forced her into the jewellery. Once I'd dropped by the residence's spiffy public dining room to join Mom for lunch, and her hair was lank and her shirt was stained. "Mom, people dress for lunch," I said less kindly than I might have as I combed her hair off her face and found her a fresh shirt back in her room. "Why are you in this baggy old top?" I secretly chucked it and other ratty things I found squirrelled here and there, likely her most comfortable clothes. I'm not sure which part of my pride was hurt, mine in her or mine in myself, to see her so unkempt, but after that she spruced up.

"Snazzy pearls," I said now. "Let's get this show on the road." I clung to my everything-is-all-right-here, game-show-host personality like a life raft. What else could I do in the face of my mother's lassitude, her preternatural stillness? Their walkers were ready at the door; Dad had taken to his like a kid to a tricycle, but Mom resisted until she fell checking herself out in a gilded hallway mirror. "A little sideways peek and I went flying," she said. "Pride goeth..."

"Mrs. Bradbury," the geriatrician began when Laura and I took her for a full workup after the fall. "Do you know why so many women break their hips on Sundays? Because they put on their heels for church."

"These aren't heels," Mom said defensively of her one-inch wedges, reluctant to lose this final small vanity. This was a woman who'd worn high-heeled slippers around the house.

"Flat like a pancake," said the doctor, wagging her finger at her.

Mom did resign herself after that to a pair of flat-soled black shoes. Her ceaseless anxiety was harder to fix. The geriatrician gave her a list of three tasks to ease it: meditate twenty minutes a day; exercise daily, "even a walk around the block"; and go to talk therapy. (I rolled my eyes at that last one. Mom believed self-reflection was a mortal sin.)

"How many of those do you think Mom will do?" Laura said, irked, because Mom refused to comply with anything meant for her own good.

"Your father and I just walked around the block," Mom reported the next day to prove us wrong, an experience not to be repeated.

I'm a dauntless self-improver. I had quite a lengthy list, still, at sixty. Avoid touching face (fewer colds and plagues); practise micro-frugality (stave off financial doom); consume less TV and wine, more sleep and books (*ha ha ha ha*). If I stopped believing I could fix every bad habit, I worried I'd give up on myself, like Mom had done. Because what did walking around the block get her, ten minutes off the roller coaster of her loop-the-loop anxiety? Does that count as an improvement?

In the hallway, Dad entered the secret elevator code meant to keep residents from leaving their locked floors, then held the elevator open for another man with a walker, who pointedly banged into Dad's for taking up too much space. Dad stared straight ahead until the man got off and then said, "I don't go in for that kind of nonsense," which was as bad as it got with Dad. That and "jeez," close enough to taking God's name in vain to let you know you were on the knife edge of . . . what? Certainly not his anger. It wasn't Dad's temper you had to worry about, it was his disappointment.

"Here's Laura!" Dad said, all smiles, as we paraded single file into the expansive lounge. The gas fire glowed in the fireplace, and Laura had secured our own area of chintz couches and chairs. Our brother David, reliably early, sat next to her. "Hello, David," Dad said, so carefully it sounded tactical. Mom and Dad couldn't get used to David's being there; none of us could. It wasn't just that he was sober. He was seraphic. He gave off the scent of delicate roses—instead of tobacco and beer and failure. It had been a long time, thirty years or more, since he was a clear-headed member of the family, and we were wired for sorrow when David was in the room. He had a way to go to prove that we could relax and even rely on him as the steady keeper of Mom and Dad in the months to come.

"I have a story," Mom said after we got her and Dad settled into chairs. This was unexpected. She hadn't taken command of a room in years. A photograph of Mom in her eighties, before the anxiety took hold, suddenly filled my mind. She was holding forth at Tim's cottage, her hands waving wildly in the air in front of her, and her grown children were laughing at whatever she was on about. When I was younger, I loved Mom's trips with her sisters, Mary and Helen, by bus from St. Catharines to Toronto for the stories they brought back. It didn't matter that they'd only been a hundred miles. They were Jane Austen characters going to visit an aunt two villages over, they could make a chapter out of a small event. Aunt Helen had the timing around a story—she sat back on the beat and waited for her moment—and Aunt Mary was good on the dramatic summary: "And that's what I think of that service, I said as I put a nickel in his hand." Mom, as the youngest, could be outshone, but she had an eye for detail that kept her in the running.

"Your father and I were sitting in our easy chairs yesterday," she began, pausing to stop the side talk. "We'd just woken up from a mid-morning nap, and he reached out to take my hand and say, 'I love you,' the way he does, and I decided to make a dramatic gesture." She rocked back and forth in her chair to show how she'd built the momentum to stand up. "I went over and sat on his lap and kissed him. I was about to say, 'I love you too,' but before I could, I slid slowly off his lap toward the floor. Your dad tried to stop me, and then he started to slide too."

"Right onto the floor!" Dad shouted.

Mom gave him a steely look and continued. "Neither of us could get up. We wiggled until your dad could get ahold of my button." Her button? What were they getting up to in their retirement digs?

"The emergency assist necklace we wear when we're in our room," Mom said. "And that's how they found us: your dad on top of me on the floor. I called it Necking in the Nineties." She stopped on the punchline, and we all laughed. It wasn't the story so much as Mom's pleasure in telling it.

My brother Tim arrived, shaking the cold off him. I hadn't spoken to him since his "I'd have to commit suicide if you sent me this letter" call, and he hugged me a little harder than usual. "Happy birthday, Sis."

Have I told you about Tim? Second-born, and first boy, with all the confidence that bestowed. He would decide he wanted to learn the sax, write a detective novel, build a cottage, master bridge, and then he did. When Tim dreamed, he was always flying, on top of the world. (Nancy dreamed of flying just once, and then it was through the grocery shelves, buying food for their three boys.) Tim would say of himself that he was racked with insecurities, but if that was true, he kept it extremely well hidden.

"Hello, family!" he said now, and we all perked up, Mom especially.

"Timmy!" she said, and it didn't take any prodding for her to tell her story again. "This is how I always imagined it," Mom said.

"Imagined what?" I said, but I pretty much knew.

"How it would be when we moved here to Toronto. All together like this."

She shot me that smile again, but this time I heard the guilt. Guilt that we hadn't made good on our promise to visit as a family together; guilt that we parcelled out our visits to share their needs across our busy days. *How could you have abandoned me?* was what Mom meant. Or did she? When I was on a recent hiking trip with friends, one man told a story of his mom writing to him while he was travelling in his twenties. "I'm glad *you're* having fun," she wrote. There was a pause before someone said, "But it was a letter, so the inflection might have been 'I'm *glad* you're having fun,' or 'I'm glad you're having *fun.*'" "You didn't know my mother," he said. None of us do.

In her short story "Soon," Alice Munro wrote about mothers the way only she could: terrifyingly. Her character Juliet, a new mother herself, travelled across the country to visit her own ailing mother, Sara. "A useless piece of goods," Sara described herself, reminding me of something Mom might have said. ("Look at this face, just hanging there," was one of Mom's standard lines as she stared at her aging reflection in the mirror.) In the Munro story, Sara was dying, and Juliet's rage, whether because her mother was dying or because she was still living, was unrelenting. At one point, there was an angry argument between Juliet and a visiting minister about religion and faith, and when the minister left, this exchange between mother and daughter followed:

"My faith isn't so simple," said Sara, her voice all shaky (and seeming to Juliet, at this moment, strategically pathetic). "I can't describe it. But it's—all I can say—it's *something*. It's a— wonderful—*something*. When it gets really bad for me—when it gets so bad I—you know what I think then? I think, all right. I think—Soon. *Soon I'll see Juliet.*"

Juliet didn't reply that day, and not long after, her mother died. Years later she asked herself why she had turned away without a word.

"Could it have not been managed?"
"Why should it have been so difficult? Just to say *Yes*. To Sara it would have meant so much—to herself, surely, so little."

Likely, Mom wasn't dealing in guilt as we sat in the lounge at Hazelton Place. I was the one looking for the guilt. I was missing the more complex relationship with my mother. But at ninety-one, she'd pulled in her ambitions; she was at the constantly grateful stage of life, like Alice Munro's Sara. Or like Dad, who talked mostly about love in his final months. When Mom said, "This is how I always imagined it," she was stating a simple truth. She really had imagined all of us together in Toronto, laughing and telling stories. It was the way we'd imagined it too.

We lingered in the lounge, noisily—we're loud talkers—and when a woman seated nearby sighed dramatically, Mom's anxiety started to overtake her happiness. "Shhh," she said to us, worried about what the woman thought. "It's okay, Mom." I held her hand. "We're allowed to make noise." Mom's lifelong fear of what people, any people—strangers, friends, family—thought of us had worn us out when we were kids, but this advanced-age anxiety was something more powerful. It took hold of her like an imminent danger. We started to head out for dinner and to get Mom and Dad back to their rooms and into bed. It wasn't just that they were beyond navigating restaurants. Mom could barely eat food. She had what was known medically as an esophageal stricture, which made it difficult for her to swallow. Even her tea was thickened so a stray drop didn't wander down her windpipe. None of this made me think she was close to death. How could she be? She was my indomitable mom.

"Night-night, bye-bye, see you soon," we said as we hugged and kissed goodbye, and it was the last time Mom would fully know she was being kissed by any of her children.

I don't remember much about the birthday dinner my siblings had hastily put together for me in lieu of my trip to Sicily. They'd rallied to help me through; that was important. It was the beginning of becoming a family without our parents, feeling our way toward that new way of being together. We were going to need one another to get through whatever came next—not as the children we were a lifetime ago, bound by bitter rivalries, petty grievances, and our parents' hierarchical idea of us, but as the people we had become. There would be setbacks.

The other important thing about this dinner was that I got the best birthday gift ever. My second gift of the night.

"I have a present for you," said Tim. As we have established, I love presents. But Tim didn't have anything for me to unwrap. I scanned him greedily for a bit of ribbon or a glint of shiny paper and came up empty. Instead, he took his phone from his jacket pocket and showed me a text. It was from Meryl, my first and longest friend. Meryl, Mom, and I had a big connection—life-saving, even—that had begun fifty-four years earlier. But Meryl and I hadn't spoken for the last twenty of those years, and the silence had become too deep to breach. Now, on the eve of Mom's death and my sixtieth-first year, Tim showed me the note from Meryl: *I would love to talk to Cathrin.*

Kelly and I had an earlier "What if" conversation, long before Guatemala. He would have been about three, and he came into the house wearing a wide-brimmed straw hat on an early spring day. "My hat!" I said, because it had become my favourite gardening hat, and I thought I'd lost it until Kelly found it under the newly melted snow. He was puzzled. He was a backyard explorer, and the hat was a fresh discovery. It had no past as far as he was concerned. So I showed him a picture of me in the hat when it was new, at a country wedding with his father years earlier. Bright streamers floated over a still pond from a trellis behind us, and the hat was more fetching than I'd remembered.

Kelly was sitting on my lap staring at the photograph. "Where am I?" he asked.

"You aren't born yet."

"Am I inside the house?"

"No, you aren't. You still haven't been born."

"Am I playing in that barn?"

I began to see I was in heavy waters. It was the most existential conversation I've ever had, and three-year-old Kelly's distress was intense. How could we have existed without him? He had never had the heartlessness to exist without us. Finally, desperate, I said, "You were waiting up in the sky to come down to make us the happiest mommy and daddy ever."

He slid off my lap then and went back outside to play, without the hat. Maybe he knew it was as good as it was going to get, and there was still an hour of playtime waiting for him outside.

I worried at the time that my answer was a cop-out, but now I think the hat was a small damp gift to help us puzzle through how life had brought us together. The same way the cancelled Sicily trip meant that we were all together with Mom. Soon, I'd have to exist without her for the first time. It was as baffling to me as it had been for Kelly to think of me existing without him.

8.

Mom's Last Room

TO UNDERSTAND WHY I ORDERED a clubhouse sandwich from room service at my Vancouver hotel immediately after I got the call that Mom had stopped breathing for several minutes and was not expected to last long at the hospital where she'd been taken, let me explain something about my family. We live in denial. (And that's enough on that subject.) Don't knock denial. It comes in handy sometimes.

When Dad had a heart attack in his seventies, I was the one who called the siblings. "I'm just driving up north and I'll call when I get there," said Tim, cool as an ice pack. "I'm getting cookies out of the oven; I'll get back to you," Ann said, mildly harassed, from her kitchen in Vancouver. Only Laura reacted the way people do in movies. "Oh, my God! Where is he? Is he okay?" She cried and then I did too. I was pretty sure this was the more suitable response to the imminent death of a loved parent. Within half an hour, Tim had called to say he'd turned around and was driving back to Toronto, and Ann had called, crying (but at least her cookies weren't burnt).

"Maybe it's not denial, more just human nature," I said to Tim the Jungian. "We have our forward momentum, our busy lives getting here or there, and it's hard to stop and turn around and go in the opposite direction, isn't it?"

"Possibly," he said. "Although possibly your family is very good at this."

Also, I like to order a clubhouse from room service when I travel. I was in Vancouver for work and had only just checked into the hotel. I'd been thinking about this sandwich for much of the plane ride. Hoping they didn't do anything fancy with it, like make it on artisanal bread instead of thin, plain white, or use turkey bacon instead of regular bacon. I had a lot of important work meetings set up for the next day, too, so I decided to get through them and then fly back home in about twenty-four hours.

I can't say when I thought better of this plan. I know I ate the clubhouse, which was on focaccia, so much too bready. My room was terrific, and I remember the high blue view with seagulls yelling in the sunshine. What happened next wasn't dim; it was a blank sheet until I was standing at the front door of Toronto General Hospital at 2 a.m.

Hospitals lock their doors in the middle of the night, did you know that? I banged for a long time until a cleaning man arrived and silently unlocked the middle revolving door. Pushing myself forward inside that tight, round shell with my too-big suitcase was only my first hurdle in getting to Mom. I got stuck, twice, pressed against the glass as the cleaning man watched and shrugged until I was burped into the lobby. David had given me Mom's room number—by now they'd moved her out of emergency—and I heard my brother say, "Eleventh floor, room 14," which I repeated in my head. That useless trick.

Eleven pipers piping—floor 11; *fourteen days in a fortnight*—room 14. On the eleventh floor, I rolled my bulging suitcase alone along a gleaming, slowly curving hall, its wheels repeating on the shiny floor like a skipping record. In the background was the faint whir of . . . drills? Were they renovating at this hour? I didn't see another person or even a room for some time, just the endlessly curving hall. When I finally arrived at a desk, it wasn't a typical hospital desk, with nurses and doctors and whiteboards and bustle, but a large, serene, uncluttered counter, like at a corporate hotel. I rang the bell on the counter, and a woman came out from behind an almost invisible door in the wall.

"I'm here to see my mother," I said. The woman was well put together, and I was glad she couldn't see my unseemly suitcase over the tall counter.

"You are? Here?" She looked at me with alarm. I was too late, Mom was gone. I saw it in her concerned face.

"Yes. Catherine Bradbury. Room 14," I said, trying not to cry in this cold, empty, windowless place.

"We don't have room numbers here," she said, mysteriously. She swiped at a screen, flipping pages, a single line appearing on her clear brow, and then said with tremendous relief, "Ahhhh. Your mother is on the fourteenth floor, room 11. Right now, you are on the eleventh floor. You must have switched floors and rooms." She deadened the screen and smiled at me, problem solved. "There are no patient rooms in pathology."

I walked back to the elevator much faster than I had left it, *skipskipskipskipping* with my enormous suitcase. Jesus Christ, pathology. Were those saws whirring in the background? Is that what happened on floor 11 at 2 a.m.? They carved up dead bodies? The night had become a horror movie, and when I finally got to Mom's bed on the fourteenth floor, it didn't get any better.

I immediately turned to the nurse who'd brought me to the bedside. "You've made a mistake. That's not my mother."

"Catherine Bradbury? Yes, this is her." The nurse looked firmly into my eyes and held me there, that nurse trick of making you pay attention. I sat down hard on a chair next to the bed and looked again at Mom. I couldn't find her in this face on the thin hospital pillow. Her small chin had been replaced with a large jutting jaw, rigid from the nose down. Death really did take its grip, I saw then. I wanted to pry its fingers off her.

"Hi, Mom."

At the sound of my voice, Mom suddenly lifted her arms in the air like a child wanting to be picked up by her parents. Or like a woman welcoming God, asking him to reach down and take her out of this nightmare with his mighty God arms. I told Mom it was okay for her to go, although I didn't mean it. I said goodbye, I had to, since Death had already stepped up. I'd forgotten who I was dealing with, of course. Mom wasn't asking to be lifted to heaven; her raised arms were a mere visual miscue. She was asking, even on this first night, to be lifted up by me and carried the hell out of this hospital room.

When I arrived back at the room the next day, most of my siblings were already there. And so was Mom. Not fully Mom, not fully there, but enough to make me understand she was still in the game. The death grip was gone from her face, and her eyes were bright as she sipped from a tiny pink sponge that David had dipped in water and held to her lips.

"Mom just said, 'Is that you, Tim?'" David said, grinning.

"Can you believe it?" Tim was sitting beside Mom and laughing, and then we all were.

I kissed her, hoping she would say my name too. "It's me, Cathrin, Mom," but she'd used up her words for the day on Tim. Laura had baked banana bread, and the room, or Mom's quarter of it in her four-bed ward, had the vibe of a house party in that lift-off moment when you're relieved that everyone is going to show up after all. We settled in and got caught up as we sat around Mom's bed, keeping an eye on her and including her in our talk.

And so began the beginning of Mom's end. It would last a little less than three weeks, and it would change all five of her children, though not in the same way. For some of us, it was an experience that would have been better not lived; that she should have died back in her residence room rather than be revived to suffer, to be only her semi-self. The indignity of it. And the monotonous weight on us, keeping her vigil.

And for some of us, it was a life event as important and moving as a birth.

Likely we each wavered between those two states during the next few weeks. Mom's frail body completely turned against her, making it impossible for her to take any nourishment. Being robbed of breath for four minutes stole a good part of her mind as well. But something essentially Mom was present until the end, some energy or life force that was hers alone. James Hillman, an American author and Jungian, wrote fervently about old age and dying in *The Force of Character*, one of his last books before his own death in 2011. His premise was that for centuries, aging was associated not with beating death, as in a contest, but with vitality and character, which age makes stronger. (Although not necessarily better. He pointed out that one's final character could be a miserly liar as easily as a generous and compassionate human. "It pays to live a long life," was the way my brother Tim put it. "Mom wasn't warm with us growing up, far from it, but she got there in the end.") Hillman cited evidence showing that dying, for the old—what he called "incapacitating decrepitude"—lasted only about three months at the very longest. And that it was one of the most social times of life, since people were seldom alone in their dying days. Everyone gathered around more frequently, and most of the dying old had only minor pain, others none. And so it mostly was with Mom.

The scenes at the Toronto General, where we spent about five days, jumbled together. But it was the place where we came to terms with the idea that Mom was not coming home. Well, everyone but Mom did. Okay, everyone but Mom and I did. A young intern came by early on. "There's been some brain damage," he said, his head bent close to Mom's so she could hear too. She'd lost her words, he said, as if they had been mislaid, a handful of forks put away in the knife drawer by mistake. As if Mom's words were mere objects instead of the essential way she connected with us, and always had. Even now, there was a lot she tried to say. Talking was like throwing darts, mostly misses, but as she revived, she managed short sentences.

"Call a taxi."

"To where, Mom?"

She didn't know where, so she tried another tack. "Pack my sweater." And, angrily, to Dad. "Bill. My sweater."

"I don't have your sweater, sweetheart. We don't have your clothes here," Dad said, worried not to fill this small request. He sat beside her at the top of the bed, his spot, near her pillow so he could lean down toward her face and talk to her. Or sing. He sang his own personalized version of a love song. "You're my sweetheart, I'm your fellow. Sweet Cassie Kelly, *something something thing rhymed with 'fellow.'*" None of us could remember the words, surprisingly, because we listened to him sing it six hundred thousand times in the next three weeks.

I opened the drawer of Mom's bedside table and waved my hand, empty, to demonstrate the no-sweater fact. As if evidence was the way to the truth she was after.

"I can bring you one, Mom. The yellow one?" I stroked her arm soothingly.

"Don't touch me." This came out a lot, and it took us back to the silent, pot-slamming mother of our youth. She'd shut you out for days if she decided you'd hurt her; you rarely knew how or when. In the hospital, we eventually figured out that we really *were* hurting her this time. Her skin was so thin my touch must have felt like shoving her arm into a live toaster. The more I watched her struggle in those first few days, the more it seemed to me that her dying was all about not dying. It wasn't mystical; it was a practical, teeth-grinding slog through one minute so she'd be alive for the next. She didn't have the words to explain any of this, so I could have got it wrong.

"It must be hard to talk, Mom," Ann said one knife-grey February morning as we sat by Mom's bed. I'd woken up early that morning to my paned bedroom windows meticulously etched in white frost. "Jack Frost came by last night!" Mom would wake me up when I was a tiny girl, and it still cheered me up. "Frosty!" I posted on Facebook, alongside a picture.

After Ann's question about talking, Mom closed her eyes, concentrating. "Almost impossible," she said, each syllable launched straight at us. It was the most like her of anything she would say in the next few weeks. Her impatience that we were in her way, her anger that we couldn't understand her, her hurt and confusion that we wouldn't take her home. Which did not stop her from trying. Over the next few days, and against the odds, Mom began not only to talk but also to sit up, hoarsely whispering imperatives to anyone who was near. They all came down to the same thing. "Up!" arms outstretched, meant lift me up and get me out of here. "Hurry up!" and "Let's go!," same thing. She pushed sad Dad away—sympathy didn't interest her. She was a bird headed south for the winter with one guiding idea, and that was to get out of this hospital, away from the near-dead all around her.

Mom's four roommates were too sick to need much, though we weren't sure with what. But we got to know them a little, the way you do in a hospital ward, where privacy is a fluid concept. We all cried the day the woman next to Mom said goodbye to her faraway grandson on FaceTime; she was in a lot of pain, so we suspected cancer. The woman with the long undone hair in the bed opposite was surrounded day and night by large conscientious men, sons or brothers, I couldn't tell. I got into the elevator with them one morning, and as soon as the doors closed, they all bent over, crying. In the room, the woman kept her eyes closed, except for the one time the four men briefly left her bedside; then she looked at me, holding my gaze insistently until they returned a few moments later. I wondered if those men needed to leave her alone, if she couldn't break their hearts even more by dying in front of them.

"Every death is different," said the hospital grief counsellor as we sat next to Mom's bed while she slept. I couldn't get enough of this woman. Something in her steady expression and placid hands made me understand that she was wise. "I've seen every kind of death here." This confused me. Was no one trying to make Mom better? "Sometimes the dying want everyone at their side; they wait until the last child arrives from far away, panicked at having missed so much. Sometimes the dying want no one." Like the woman across the room with the long undone hair, I thought. "They die only after everyone goes home to sleep and the last person on watch steps out to the bathroom." The grief counsellor explained that hearing is the last sense to go. "Perhaps think about what you want to say to your mother and find a private moment to say it." I reported this back to the siblings, and over the next three weeks, we each said some final words to Mom. I waited until the last minute, in case she rallied.

About day four at Toronto General Hospital, when Mom was at her liveliest, sitting up and smiling and saying a few words, the doctor and social worker booked a room for us to talk about Next Steps. I admit this much: I wasn't ready for Next Steps. I see now that I was perhaps difficult to handle over this Next Steps stage.

"When Mom made you and Ann her medical powers of attorney," Laura began one day, "I said, 'Mom, seriously? You've chosen the two people who will never let you go.'" Mom and Dad were sitting at their dining room table, Laura remembered, still hale in their early eighties. "No extra measures, no hanging on to the bitter end," Mom said. She talked a good game, but she had no intention of popping off in a hurry. She knew which side her life-and-death bread was buttered on, and her best chance was Ann and me. And what's so wrong with biding your time on the way out, anyway? I intend to. If there's a nuclear holocaust, I'll be scrabbling in the blackened earth for the last radioactive potato. Climate change? You'll find me sucking on my ice cube on the tip of the last sinking iceberg. I've already stocked up on canned peaches for the next pandemic. The point being, I'm not going out gently. And I didn't want Mom to either. "The longer one lasts, the longer one wants to last—for the most part." That was James Hillman again.

I think all my siblings would agree that the room where we gathered to talk about Next Steps was the lowest of the low points. It was one of those badly furnished, windowless conference rooms in office towers everywhere. Dad, Ann, and Tim sat on one side of the large, bland table, and Laura, David, and I sat on the other. The doctor was a lovely man with curly grey hair, and compassionately direct. He leaned forward on his elbows at the head of the table and led us slowly toward the idea that Mom would need to move to another hospital, one that had palliative care. "She can't eat or drink," he said. "We could put a feeding tube in her stomach, and some families do make that choice, but I believe this is medically cruel. Her body doesn't want food now." He persuaded us, gently, that it would be a selfish choice. He got us that far. "Cassie wouldn't want that," Dad said, his voice hoarse.

The next Next Step was which palliative care hospital or hospice Mom would go to. Some, the doctor explained, offered subcutaneous fluids for hydration. This was immediately and unequivocally the hospital I wanted. Others, like the palliative care wing at St. Michael's Hospital, did not offer these fluids, and I imagined Mom begging for a drop of water. How thirsty she would be. Trust the Catholics to try to get you to everlasting eternity faster. Note the everlasting: Why the rush?

"I feel we are hastening Mom's death," I said, glaring at anyone who would look at my fuming face.

"Honestly, Cathrin," Laura said. "Get a grip."

The doctor sided with Laura. "It's the families who want the subcutaneous option, not the patients." He looked at me with his kind clarity. "They don't feel thirst at this stage," he explained. "But the fluids can prolong her life somewhat"—he paused—"if that's what you want to do."

"She is over there sitting up and talking, so I would say yes, that is what we want to do," I said, stating the blindingly obvious, or so I thought.

"I'm not dead!" Tim said in a high squeaky voice.

"You'll be stone dead in a moment," David squeaked back. I'd never heard worse English accents as Tim and David quoted half-remembered lines from *Monty Python and the Holy Grail*.

"I feel fine!"

"Oh, don't be such a baby."

It was briefly funny, and the social worker took her chance to counsel us on an upbeat. "I would advise that you accept whichever hospice has a room first," she said. "There can be long wait lists."

We got fractious after that. There was a lot of talk about do-not-resuscitate. The doctor explained that there was no resuscitation involved in palliative care, fluids or no fluids. There was resentment that Mom had been resuscitated back at Hazelton. "Against her wishes," said David. Panic, rage, and self-pity, that toxic combo most of us carry around in our noisy heads at the best of times, got harder to tamp down. Laura and Ann were at loggerheads, and Laura jumped too soon to funeral arrangements.

"Mom's wishes are the St. Catharines Cathedral," said Ann. "We will abide by her wishes."

She was staring hard at Laura across the table. Whether or not Laura rolled her eyes at this point is a subject of some debate.

"Ann," Laura said, "there is no one left in St. Catharines. The funeral should be here, in Toronto."

And then Ann, giving voice to every youngest-born since time began, replied, "My whole life I've been silenced by you, and I'm not going to take it anymore. I'm sick of your goddamn bullshit." (Since then, whenever Ann has this feeling with anyone, she sits on her hands and tells herself not to speak.)

An outburst of this spectacular magnitude in our family of zealous deniers was new coming from Ann, or any of us. So we did what we do best in a tough situation: we all looked down at our hands and pretended it didn't happen. The doctor wisely left the room, and the social worker shuffled us to a smaller room, where the change of scene did not improve our mood. I latched on to applesauce. I don't know why applesauce; I guess I associated it with being sick and getting better.

"If Mom wants applesauce, I want her to have applesauce. If she says, 'May I please have some applesauce?' I'm giving her the applesauce." Laura and David kept repeating, "Do not resuscitate. Those are her wishes." "What does that have to do with applesauce?" I was furious and crying. Tim, who had been silent, stood up with his head bowed. Then he looked up at us. "If this is going to continue," he said, "I'm going to have to put more money in the parking meter."

He came back a while later, quite a long while, and said, "Here's what I think: I think this is Mom's death, and so it's for Mom to show us how it will go. If she recovers, then she recovers. If she wants applesauce, we'll give her applesauce. And if she doesn't, then we won't. It's for Mom to decide, not us."

We calmed down after that, each finding a place for our own positions to land somewhere on the spectrum of Tim's statement. We agreed that Mom would go to whichever hospital or hospice had a room first. I secretly resolved to feed her applesauce wherever she was, to keep her strength up.

Going home that night was complicated. Ann was supposed to stay with Laura, but after "your goddamn bullshit," she moved to my house. I was trying madly to appease Laura and calm Ann when Ann advised me not to triangulate. "You do that sometimes." We were sitting on the upstairs couch at sooty Number 9, cross-legged and facing each other.

"I do?" I found this statement from my younger sister unpleasing. I liked to think of myself as a deft manager of human emotion, especially as the sister in the middle.

"Yes, you do. There's a difference between triangulation and mediation." Ann had her reasonable union voice on, and I countered with my imperious manager voice. We were well into the wine. "In triangulation, you side with both standpoints without changing them. In mediation, you gradually move people to a new point of view, together," Ann explained. "Like the doctor today."

I snorted. "Yeah, that went well."

We weren't exactly arguing, but it was an easier subject to tackle than our grief. Ann didn't say anything for a while, and then she looked at me, suddenly stricken.

"Did you know Laura has a university fund for my girls?" she said. "She's been such a great aunt to them." Ann went to her room after that, and I could hear her typing in bed on her laptop. It was a long and meaningful letter to Laura, and forgiveness, or the beginning of it, was reached at some exhausted point in the middle of the night, without any help from me.

The next day back at the hospital, we were told that a bed had come up in St. Mike's palliative wing. No subcutaneous fluids. My heart sank. But not Mom's. Mom thought she'd finally got what she wanted. Two tall, nearly identical men in matching navy blue strode into the room to lift her out of her hospital bed and belt her onto a gurney. Ann and I quickly gathered up her few things.

"Ready?" said one of the men to Mom. He'd leaned over her until their faces were inches apart. Mom locked on his blue eyes and nodded. He nodded back and clicked on a stopwatch. "Let's go, then."

Mom smiled goodbye to her roommates, solidarity among the gravely ill. You hold on to the idea of a happy ending. She rattled down the hall on her gurney as the men in navy walked so fast on legs long as stilts that Ann and I had to run to keep up. We were laughing and out of breath by the time we got into the ambulance.

"Do you have a record to beat?" Ann asked one of the men, nodding at his stopwatch.

"Yes," he said. "Buckle up."

Mom was strapped in tight, swaddled like a newborn, and Ann and I put on serious full-body seat belts and held on to leather straps above our heads as we flew through the city, careening around corners, siren blasting. Mom grinned until her face must have ached; she was busting out. But instead, we brought her to a new hospital and a new bed. Her deathbed. I could see in her face that she understood that right way. She took in the hushed hallways and the stained-glass doves over the entranceway and realized that this was where she would die. And so, finally, did I.

I don't know if Mom had tidying up to do as she lay in her palliative bed. She was different at St. Mike's. She'd stopped fighting, I guess that was it. She slept for a long time after we moved her. Something private was going on, that's how it seemed, as she loitered on the doorstep of death. I worried she was still searching for home, but which home would it be? The one where she was raised with her two sisters, where all her stories started? The one on the extravagantly treed boulevard in Grimsby, raising us five kids? Or her last home, those two rooms that their lives had been culled down to at Hazelton Place? "As interiority expands, we move more easily into the small rooms of late-stage quarters, taking up less space in the world," said Hillman. Maybe all Mom's homes were not much more than a chalk outline, but I didn't like to think of her lost in that way. "I can't let go," she said to Laura one day, and Laura worried about her struggle too. But mostly Mom's last room seemed to make her calm.

Kelly said once, "Pay attention to the quality of the light in your memories, Mom. My happy memories are filled with light. The bad ones are dark and grey." "The sun is God" were the last words of J.M.W. Turner, the English painter; perhaps apocryphal, although his light-filled works at the end of his life would suggest otherwise. Mom's sunlit room was filled with flowers and visitors, and was very social, the way James Hillman had said the dying days would be; a lot of people came to say goodbye. Mostly, though, it was us five kids.

"Hi, Mum Mum. Okay night?" Laura was the one who started to call Mom "Mum Mum," and then we all did. I don't know why, since we'd never called her that before. She opened her eyes and smiled sometimes, or sometimes looked worried, the smallest furrow in her brow. "That's pain," said her attentive caregiver, and he'd get something to ease it. Mom had stopped asking to get up, or get out, or get a taxi or a sweater, although her irritation remained.

"Crocheted by the nuns of the pope," said the same caregiver with pride as he tucked a bright orange and yellow blanket around Mom one afternoon. He was a compact, busy Filipino man, and he paused now to smile down on Mom.

"I don't want it," she snapped.

Her lack of interest in God, just as she was getting ready to meet him, was unexpected. We'd prayed often in my family, at her insistence. We said the rosary around the kitchen table for the forty days of Lent, crabbily at first and then lulled by the rhythm of the Hail Marys. We did not miss Sunday Mass. Good Friday was cloudy because it was the day Jesus died, Mom reminded us every year (although only on the cloudy Good

Fridays), and for a long time, I believed her faith was strong enough to make it so. Then, just when I thought she would most want her faith, she cast it off like the crocheted nun blanket. She didn't reject everything, that wasn't it. She welcomed music, waving her arms like a conductor with a baton when a woman came and sang folk songs with her guitar. Mom's arms stayed busy, the way they had most of her life. Sometimes she'd drive a car; sometimes she'd sweep a broom. She'd point and smile to the upper corner of her room now and then; Ann thought it was to her sisters. "Can I come too?" Mom said. Mostly, though, she slept. "This is peace," said the caregiver. "It's not always like this."

During one of her awake moments, alone with Mom, I asked the nurse for applesauce, and without hesitation she brought me a small plastic container and spoon.

"Look, Mom, applesauce." I sat beside her on the narrow bed and put a small amount on the spoon and held it to her mouth. She looked at me for a bit, and if she could I think she would have rocked me in her arms, then closed her eyes, *No.* There was a pink sippy cup of water on her bedside table. She didn't want that either, but she did like her lips to be dabbed with Vaseline, so that was one thing I could do.

At first, I went back and forth to work. My office wasn't far from the hospital. My friend and colleague Jason sat with me one afternoon and talked to me about death. He'd seen a lot of it; his mother died of cancer when he was nine. "Mama will get sicker. And she'll die," young Jason said plainly in a moment caught on film. "I wanted to say what was going on, and I wanted to get it right," he said. "Sometimes you have to wake up to a death; you resist the idea at first." I knew what that felt like.

More recently, when his friend became terminally ill, Jason said he grew closer to him that he might have "if we'd spend our whole long lives together. Death opens up a line, on the positive side." He looked out the window, where the thin February afternoon light was starting to peter out, and then back at me. "'Yeah," he said. "There's only one place you want to be right now."

I raced from work to get back to Mom in her windowed room. Like me, my brothers and sisters figured out pretty quickly that nowhere else felt real, as exhausting and monotonous as it was. I'd break the tedium by texting and emailing from her bedside, my head bent over my phone, anything for a bit of action. After four or five hours in the hospital, I'd collapse in bed at night, too tired even to watch TV. But Jason was right: there was only one place to be. I stopped going to work altogether. Except the day Mom died, March 4.

It feels important to be at someone's bedside when they die. Some of my friends regretted not being with their parents at that moment, even though they, like me and my siblings, had spent many meaningful hours with them in the days and weeks leading up to death. I understood the sting of that the morning Mom died. I decided there was a quick same-day work trip to Ottawa I couldn't miss, and I passed my shift with Mom to David. Tim had stayed overnight in Mom's room, and often talked to her as she slept. She was very still, he said. About 7 a.m., he went home to have a quick shower. The nurse, unusually, called me an hour later to say that she thought someone should come to be with Mom. By then, I was at the airport, about to get on my plane. I called David and asked him to go to the hospital earlier than he'd planned. I was worried, but even then I didn't believe Mom was about to die. I think how those two moments in Mom's dying, the beginning and the end, were bracketed for me by airports, places of transition and confusion. It was only as I was about to board the plane that I decided against getting on my flight. Or rather, my body turned around and started to move in the opposite direction.

It's surprising how difficult it is to exit the part of an airport designed to stream your entry. I felt I deserved this. I pushed past people out of the gate, then tried to read the Enter signs backwards to sort out which entry I needed to go through to get out. I ran to a taxi and then ran again into St. Mike's, into the elevator and off through the hallway, and when I got to Mom's room, the door was closed for the first time. It's one of the worst things I've seen, that closed door. Two nurses were standing outside.

"Your mom died two minutes ago," said one of them. It was 10:02 a.m. The nurse who said this had been crying. She was perhaps forty, or younger, and she had been very kind to Mom.

"No," I said. "I ran all the way."

The nurse opened the large hospital door for me to see for myself. David was looking at his iPad and sitting alone beside Mom, who was unmistakably not alive. If death is an absence, that's what was there on Mom's bed.

"What happened?" I said accusingly, as if it were David's fault. I was aggrieved to have missed Mom's dying, and I wouldn't have been on my iPad two minutes later.

David put his down on the bedside table and looked at me. He was matter-of-fact. "She breathed slowly in and out, and I held her hand. Then she stopped breathing. She took one last breath, a huge breath, and that was it. She died." David didn't cry as he said this, and neither did I as he continued his story. "I walked to the nurses' station. 'I believe Mom is gone,' I said to the nurse, and she broke down and cried." David laughed now beside Mom. "Boy, are you in the wrong business, I felt like telling her."

If people really do choose who they die with, I understood why Mom might have chosen David. He was very like her. Dying needed doing, finally, and he loved Mom enough not to get in her way.

First we called Laura and Tim.

"No, dammit," said Tim, angry like me. "I only just left her." There was a brief, everything-is-all-right-here, let's-keep-going Bradbury forward momentum, when Laura and Tim said they would head straight to the funeral home to make arrangements, but even we couldn't deny death its moment, much as we wanted to. We quickly understood that we all needed to be together to say goodbye.

"Oh, my God." Laura came through the door and hugged me, and then we did cry. Because it was over. There was no more Mom. It was the first day of our lives that we were motherless, and we were still a family.

"So she's gone, then," Dad said when Tim guided him to his place at the head of Mom's bed. He was on a short memory loop, but his wife's death got through, at least on this first day. "I don't have to tell you to go to heaven because I know you're already there," he said, holding her hand.

"Who's hungry?" said Laura. We were all famished. It was eleven o'clock in the morning. Laura and I did a run to Tim Hortons in the lobby with everyone's complicated orders for sandwiches, but at least the coffee was simple. I'm the only one in my family who doesn't take it black. "Your father and I said to each other, 'Let's switch to black coffee so we don't have to be disappointed when we can't get cream or sugar.'" Mom said this about thirty years ago, when they were travelling a lot in their energetic sixties, and cream *was* hard to find in France. I thought about it as Laura and I stood in line at Tim Hortons. About how my parents had agreed on the disappointment of no cream, and how they made a decision together about only black coffee from that point on. How they did this kind of thing for most of their seventy-two-year marriage. We'd hear them talking things over earnestly in bed before they went to sleep. It was hard for me to imagine something similar in my own marriage, this united front around no cream—as if we wouldn't follow our individual preferences—but maybe that's how you get seven decades together. How would Dad keep going without Mom? The answer was he wouldn't, not really. The order at Tim Hortons, or my part of it, came to $17.90. I still have the receipt.

Back in the room, we called Ann, now home in Vancouver, on FaceTime. We showed her Mom's body as we chatted and passed sandwiches. Dad mostly spoke quietly to Mom. She wasn't coming back this time. But she wasn't fully gone either. Her sweetness stayed in the room. "Stay as long as you like," said the kind nurse, popping her head in the door, and we did. It didn't occur to us to leave. We got too loud once, and Dad didn't like that. "Now that's enough. Your mother is dead, you know." And then it was enough. We all seemed to feel at the same moment that it was odd to be there, eating tuna salad sandwiches over Mom's dead body. We put her things in a white plastic bag—glasses, watch, Vaseline, cardigan, some cards and notes, the obstinate, everyday end-of-life stuff—and got into our winter coats and scarves. It didn't feel wrong to leave Mom behind. It was she who'd left us; I got that now.

Outside, we stood around on the pavement for a while, not staying but not going anywhere either. Tim held the white plastic bag, and we huddled from the cold. It was one of those March days that made you feel winter would never let go, the sky and the sidewalk were a seamless grey, and I thought how Mom would have liked that the weather noticed she was gone. None of us knows where the plastic bag ended up.

9.

Prodigal Son, Returned

THAT MY BROTHER DAVID was the only person in the room when Mom died was astonishing and also irritating. He'd been a catastrophe for thirty years. Three packs of cigarettes a day, his first drink when he opened his eyes and his last when he closed them, and it had stopped mattering what kind of drink a long time ago. Sometimes he barely had shoes. "Cathrin, I'm in the snow and my shoes are full of holes. I need shoes right now." Once we got him off the streets, he lived in the worst subsidized housing in the crack-and-booze armpit of Toronto's downtown east end, and even then he was warned by Toronto Community Housing that the condition of his unit "posed a safety risk for himself and his neighbours." The letter was dated February 10, 2014, but by then David was already dying. Or so we thought. He came back from the dead, and also to himself, just in time to see Mom out. He went from raving on the sidewalk to helping manage an organic market; from so wretchedly sick he communicated in guttural grunts no one could understand to a biking, hiking health nut; from a constant worry in my life to a new and steady pleasure.

"Everything is the exact opposite of what it was." This was how David put it as we talked at my round white kitchen table at Number 9 in the weeks after Mom's death. "I used to sleep on my stomach. Now I sleep on my back. I love broccoli. I hated broccoli. My place was filthy. Now I make it shine." It was a complete reversal, an opposite David born out of the ash pit of his ruined self. His transformation was described in a fourteen-page, double-sided, single-spaced hospital report as a medical miracle. But I'll go all the way and say it: it was a heavenly miracle as well, with angels. I get that I'm coming off all Pollyanna here, but if there is a case to be made for straight-up optimism, the story of David is one of the shortest bets. Plus, in my year of hard losses, it was nice to have one hospital stay that didn't end in death.

Was Mom able to comprehend new David before she died that March morning? Likely not. Her groove of anxiety about him had become too deep, that loop you can't get off. Mostly what she saw when she saw David, even the restored David who came back a few months before her death, was her own habitual unease. But for me, my childhood ally was back when I needed him most. When life was at its lowest that luckless winter of 2015—Mom gone, love lost, marriage truly over, and the ugly mess of the house exposed for all to see—there, sitting across from me in the upside-down kitchen of Number 9, was my brother, showing me the features of his new wool cap. As he ran its stiff brim between his thumb and fingers, I saw that his nails were perfectly manicured. For as long as I'd known David, my whole life, they'd been bitten to the quick.

———

My earliest memory is of sitting next to David and eating a boiled egg at the Formica kitchen table in our St. Catharines wartime bungalow. I was at the big table, perhaps only just sprung from the high chair, and maybe that was part of the reason my baby brain latched on to this scene, to remember. It worries me that my first memory involves status, something I've been aware of most of my life—wanting to be at the big table, not being at the big table, finally being at the big table, revelling in the big table. It's not my best side. Then Mom lopping off the egg top to make the little egg cap, that would have been exciting too. But the most important thing about that seminal moment in our bungalow kitchen was that David was sitting beside me.

There are pictures of David and me during this time in St. Catharines, when we would have been six and four. We're freshly scrubbed and pajama-ed for the camera, David with a missing tooth, a blond brush cut, and a sweep of freckles; me ponytailed and with a buttoned-up cardigan knit by Mom over my red-and-pink pajamas. We sit side by side in an easy chair, and the room is empty of decor, we didn't have much, but it's David's face that holds you. He looks like he's about to butt out a cigarette before robbing the corner store. A pipsqueak felon, and the camera loves it. David made trouble like Mom knit sweaters, fast and with natural flair. It was a full-time job for me not to get implicated in his crimes, which he became more blithe about after we left St. Catharines a couple of years later, a move that badly unmoored him.

Our new town was Grimsby, half an hour away in the heart of the thriving Niagara fruit belt. We moved into a wooden one-and-half-storey house on a wide boulevard of blossoming cherry, crabapple, and white lilac trees with smells so intense you would feel dizzy when you woke up in the morning. The boulevard sloped up to the Niagara Escarpment, which gave it a privileged status in the town's hierarchy. To look at it, the escarpment wasn't much more than a backdrop, except for the way the deciduous trees switched colours with the seasons. But everything in Grimsby was oriented by its relationship to the mountain, as it was locally known. The farthest point from the escarpment, past the thick swath of peach and cherry farms and across the railroad tracks, was the Catholic Survey, which was what everyone called the new housing development, and it was where we should have lived. Defiantly, we landed on the other side of the tracks, the first Catholics on our street.

We did not go unnoticed by the sparsely offspringed Protestant families as we all poured out of our station wagon on moving day, Mom pregnant with Ann. All of us but David, that is, because Mom had the idea to send him to camp that summer, so when he left, he lived in one house in one town, and when he came back, he lived in another house in another town. The move knocked me sideways too—there were no talks about change or feelings for any of us—but at least nobody tricked me. David didn't complain about being moved without warning, that wasn't his style, but he didn't get over it either.

He remembered himself as a pacifist when we started at our new school that fall, but I remembered how kids would lean in from a pagan circle in the schoolyard and shout, "Fight, fight, fight!" I pushed to the front of the circle one day and found David standing there, smiling, like he was letting people know he was okay with being hit. If that was the price to be inside the circle, to not be left behind again, then he was ready to ante up. I wanted to take David by the hand to lead him home, but I doubt he wanted me to. He never gave up, David. He had courage. Some fights he won: he'd put his head down and keep swinging. I don't know if he won that schoolyard fight; I slipped away and walked home alone, and it was somewhere in that time that David took up residence in the back of my head. I carried that David around for years, trying to ignore him, until a dull pain would overtake me in a random open moment.

He began to steal and lie with an absence of embarrassment. "Are those my cigarettes?" Mom would ask, pointing to her du Mauriers tucked into David's shirt pocket. "Nope," David lied. He stole Scotch from Dad, got sick, switched to beer—the beginning of a long affair. "I fell in love with it," he said later of his first beer. "The taste, the way it made me feel, everything."

As teenagers, we started to go to the same parties, where this one time there was acid punch. The party was on the other side of town, in a neglected house being rented by older kids I barely knew, but the fame of the acid punch spread all the way to Beamsville, the next town over. "Tread lightly," said an older boy with dark hair down to his waist when I dipped a ladle into the punch. I filled half a Dixie Cup from the giant wooden barrel in the living room, while David gulped down two. The punch was also spiked with booze, for which he now had a steady thirst. I went over to the punch barrel and spoke quietly to him. There were stoned kids lying on the floor all around us, staring at nothing.

"David, you know that has acid in it?" I said as he filled a third cup. He had a hank of blond hair over his eyes and a zip-front bomber jacket.

"I do," he said, swallowing Dixie Cup number three in one gulp.

I had a strict curfew of 10 p.m. and I was peaking, as we said, just as I arrived home.

"What did you do at the party?" Mom said conversationally as I came into the front hall, and I watched as the left side of her head followed the word "do" through the front door and out onto the wide wooden porch.

"Dooooooooooooo?" I asked. The word seemed to go on forever. I had one of those hippie bags made out of old Moroccan rugs, and the zigzag pattern was zigging right off the bag and into my brain. "Oh, right. Do. Not much."

In the den, Dad offered me some bright orange cubes of cheddar cheese and fluorescent Ritz crackers, which had taken on personalities of their own. Between the lively crackers and the lightning-bolt bag, there was a lot going on, but I was holding down the stoner fort. Which was when David yowled through the front door.

"It was in the punch!" he shouted, and ran up to his room, slamming the door behind him.

"What was in the punch?" This was Mom. Her face was super scary.

"I don't know what he's talking about," I said, ignoring whatever the cheddar cheese was trying to tell me as David howled, "My feet, my feet!" from behind his bedroom door. It was a full-on acid freak-out. I could hear Mom crying from David's room as I paced around downstairs, trying to ignore the threatening paisley wallpaper in the dining room, until I was summoned to David's room.

"David says the *acid* was in the punch," Mom said. "Is acid LSD?"

"I'm not sure." This was very thin ice. "Possibly?"

David groaned loudly from under the covers.

"Oh, my God. Bill!" Mom snapped at Dad like it was his fault. Which was way better than it being my fault. "We need to get him to the hospital."

Trips to the Grimsby hospital for tranquilizing or whatever they did for acid comedowns were not uncommon in our town during these early LSD days in the late 1960s, and as Mom guided David onto the front porch, a blanket wrapped around him, my brother stopped on the steps.

"Cathrin, should I let them take me?" He searched my face for the answer as I steered him to the back seat of the car.

"I'm pretty sure it's the right thing to do, David."

He gripped my hand through the rolled-down window until Dad started to back down the driveway and we had to let go. It was a scene that would be repeated—Dad driving David away for help, me standing outside the car holding his hand—almost exactly, thirty years later.

"We'll deal with you when we get home, young lady," Mom snarled as the car drove away. She often said later that those were the worst years of her life, although I was good at hiding my misdemeanours. David was not. When I wondered if he wanted to get caught, he solved that mystery the night he drove Dad's car onto our meticulously mowed, fanatically weedless front lawn. David would have done most of the weeding and mowing, so perhaps he was making a point. He stumbled loudly down to the basement, grabbing an armload of frozen T-bone steaks from our massive freezer. Mom and Dad were on a freezer plan at this stage, and huge amounts of frozen food were delivered by cube van once a month.

"What do you think you're doing with those steaks?" Not a bad question from Dad. This was pre-microwave. What *was* David going to do with frozen-solid steaks at 2 a.m.? There was a shoving match at the door, steaks bonked down the front hall, and David fled, leaving his tracks, literally, across the green lawn, which was covered in wide black tire marks the next morning. For David, getting caught was part of the point, because it's not hard to hide the worst from parents who hope for the best from you. Perhaps Mom and Dad didn't hope for the best from David. Maybe he bore all our sins, the way one kid in a family can. The force of nature, the mystery child, the one who marches to his own drum—there are a lot of names for the kids who end up on the outskirts of a family. The kids who force you to realize you can't control everything, an idea Mom was not comfortable with.

"We are not at all pleased with David's results," Mom wrote on his grade 8 report card, in which he got an F in work habits ("Prompt, attentive, and industrious"). And she was not pleased with the result of David either. She tried to reason it out of him. There were very long talks at the kitchen table. There were visits to the doctor. Punishments for stealing and lying. Mom took David on. She did not give up; she was determined to fix him. And she did, sort of.

David straightened out enough to get a good job as a company manager, like Dad, and his teenage days started to look like a phase. He fell in love with a nice woman who laughed at his jokes; they had a picturesque wedding at a small church across from the escarpment. They raised their dearly loved daughter together in a split-level house in a new part of Grimsby and often had the family over; David was house-proud and liked to show us his latest improvements. He was a steady drinker, but not a disastrous one, not right away, until he started drinking at work. After several warnings, he lost his good job. And then, very quickly after that, his house. And then, the way these things go, his wife and daughter.

He moved to a small cabin on a farm in Vineland, the other side of Beamsville, along with a huge German shepherd and a pickup truck he wasn't allowed to drive because he'd lost his licence, twice. Laura defended him in court on a charge of stealing gas for the truck he was barred from driving. "Within one year, this man has lost his job, his home, and his family," she said in a plea to the Crown attorney and, no small feat, got him off.

At some point, we decided to do an intervention. Mom, Dad, Tim, and me. The setting was pretty: a green orchard in the first push of spring, before the blossoms and before the branches hung low with their fruit, and a small red cabin in the middle. Even David's pickup truck looked charming against that backdrop, until you saw the cab was stacked to the roof with empty beer bottles.

"David, let us in," Mom said in a tone that was hard not to obey. We'd been knocking on the kitchen door for some time, and when David finally opened it a crack, Tim pushed past him and stepped inside, with Mom, Dad, and me bunched behind him. There was nothing picturesque about the inside of the cabin. The kitchen was the first room. Even now, I can't say more about that room than that. We pushed our way through it to a small living room, where we explained why we were there. Tim and I had agreed that he would say this and I would say that, but I was mute. Dad was stricken and also silent, and Mom was crying. Tim did all the talking.

"David, we're here to take you to rehab," he began. "You're an alcoholic and—"

"I don't drink," said David, lounging on the couch. This was good enough for a laugh, and it was the first of many times that he'd hold a Thermos of vodka as he explained that he hadn't had a drink in years.

"Dave, your truck is full of empty beer bottles."

"Somebody else put those there."

Enough time passed like this until I desperately needed to pee. On the way to the bathroom, I passed David's bedroom and noticed a framed photograph lying on top of the unmade sheets. I went closer to see that it was a posed shot of us five siblings, dressed up for a family photo shortly after we moved to Grimsby. Ann was a bouncy baby, Laura had a beehive hairdo, and Tim the beginnings of a rebel haircut. My long hair had been cut short, the coveted pixie. David was in a suit with a pocket square. I couldn't figure out why this was the picture he kept beside him in bed. It was a corny shot, and the little hoodlum from the earlier St. Catharines photos was nowhere evident in David's timid expression.

Back in the living room, Tim repeated that David was being taken to the detox centre in St. Catharines, where he was required to spend three days drying out, and then on to the rehab house we had arranged for him in Toronto. And so it was that I once again stood by Dad's car, holding David's hand through the rolled-down window, as Dad and Tim were about to drive him away to get help.

"Am I doing the right thing, Cathrin?" David looked hard at me. He looked younger than he was. "Should I go with them?"

"Yes, David. I think it is the right thing for you, and I think you should go."

We were both frightened as the car pulled away, but not Mom. Mom had pulled herself together because she had a plan. She loved a plan, and so did I. A plan fixed everything that couldn't be. Mom's plan was for the two of us to clean David's house. And she could have gone back into that cabin; she had that kind of fortitude.

"Mom," I whispered. "The dog shit."

She didn't want the farmers to see David's kitchen, and when I said I'd hire cleaners, she said, "The cleaning people will see it." I shook my head no. Mom looked at me with disappointment, and for a moment I thought she might order me to help her, and I'd have had to obey. But she didn't, and I steered us down the long country driveway, arm in arm; we were shaky on the gravel in our heels. Mom seemed strangely sanguine, the way you sometimes are after the worst has happened, or what you think is the worst. And she did go back into the cabin with Dad after Tim and I left, I learned later, tired as they must have been, and they'd cleaned up after their son, to take away the mess.

Pretty soon, Mom and I saw the roadside restaurant I'd noticed earlier, and we took a window seat and ordered tea and toast. We watched out the window, not saying much until, after a long time, Tim and Dad drove up without my brother. David's huge German shepherd was there, though, his head lolling out of the back-seat window. Dad looked done in as he joined us at our table, but Tim had a lot of energy.

"When they asked him how old he was when he had his first drink, you know what David said?" Tim had ordered a full meal, a hot turkey sandwich with gravy and fries. "He said he was nine." Tim shook his head in awe. "Nine. Jesus."

"Really?" Mom said mildly. "I would have said eleven. That was when my darling boy disappeared from me."

I looked from one to the other, trying to understand what language they were speaking. Eleven was a shock, but nine? The photograph on David's bed suddenly took up the entire frame of my brain. David's new suit, his brothers and sisters next to him, would have been from the time before his first drink, when we mattered more than a bottle of beer.

The rangy, dark-haired man from First Rehab told us he wasn't sure "we got through to Dave," a phrase I would come to understand after David's third or fourth rehab stint meant the twelve steps weren't resonating. For Second Rehab, we got wise and moved David to an isolated country manor, away from the temptations of the city bars, but he checked out the same day we checked him in. "David decided even in Vineland that the easiest way out was to agree with us," Tim said later. "At no point did he take us seriously. Everything had fallen apart for David a long time ago."

It was a swift slide to the streets of Toronto, where he bounced from hostel to hostel. We did get him into that housing unit. We responded to a crisis, like no shoes in the snow. Tim and I took him out for solid meals at a local restaurant, where he'd cough for long minutes while we looked down at our hands. And we all got together with David once a year for Christmas, a holiday event that invaded our minds for weeks before and after. A couple of Christmases back, at Number 9, I went upstairs to get a break. David was in the dining room, coughing on the turkey and pretending his full Tim Hortons cup actually had coffee in it, and everyone else was pretending along with him. I came out of the bathroom and jumped. Mom was right outside the door. She blocked my way, urgently.

"Cathrin, why is David doing this to me?"

"Mom," I said impatiently. Red Christmas earrings bobbed from our ears, the only cheerful thing about us. I was irked by the ego that allowed her to put herself at the centre of my brother's destruction. "It's not David who's doing this; he can't help it. It's an addiction."

"No, it's not," she insisted. "It's David, he's doing it on purpose. Can't you make him stop?"

It was a reasonable question. I've often wondered if we could have done more to help David, even though I know the answer was no, not really. He didn't have much interest in himself. He could get excited about his schemes, and now and then I'd get excited along with him. He decided he needed an e-bike, for eight hundred dollars, and I called the siblings to chip in. Ann and Laura ponied up with enthusiasm, so next I called Tim.

"Absolutely not." I was surprised, and said so. "Cathrin, David desperately needs something ridiculous every other week. Last month, it was a barbell set for his room. My advice is, don't do it." That weekend I met David with the money at the e-bike store, where the bike was already set up in the parking lot.

"Dave, remember what we talked about," said the salesman as he held the bike steady. I don't know what I thought an e-bike would look like, but it wasn't this complicated flimsy thing. "What is the one rule about using this e-bike?"

"Don't drink and drive," David grunted.

"Christ," I said. The bike was the only thing holding him up. David crashed into the curb, then into a parked car, and then he rode past me, waving. "I've got the hang of it now," he said, as he careened onto the heavily trafficked main street. "Thanks, Sis."

"I've just killed David," I said to Tim on the phone.

"Told you," Tim said, and hung up.

After the e-bike, and after he was much worse still, David got a motorized scooter, on which he would visit Tim and Nancy's house at random times, letting himself in with the garden key. Nancy, an even-tempered school principal with a well-developed appreciation of the absurd, would pull up in her car after a long day managing intractable parents and see the deep ruts from David's scooter in her newly planted garden. "Sometimes I couldn't do it," Nancy said. "I'd sit in the car and wait for Tim to come home."

"Here's a story," David grunted to Tim on one of those visits, lighting a fresh cigarette off the butt of another. Tim had to lean in to understand what David was saying. "I thought I had liver cancer." David paused for dramatic effect. "Found out today it was just an infection, thank God. But you know, the whole time, all I could think was, 'Why me?'" Tim still laughs his head off when he tells that story.

We know from the hospital records that in the four weeks before David was wheeled into emergency, on February 27, 2014, too weak to lift his head and his blood pressure so low it hardly registered, he'd lost fifty pounds and was taking four extra-strength Tylenols every four hours. He thought he had the flu, which might tell you how massively he'd dissociated from reality. He had severe COPD and was dizzy and short of breath. The immediate diagnosis was a Tylenol overdose, for which he was admitted. He was given a CT scan, which was the beginning of what would become his real diagnosis:

hemodynamically unstable (blood)
toxic levels of acetaminophen
metabolic acidotic state (kidney)
right-sided loculated effusion with pleural thickening/rind and
   septations strongly suspicious for empyema (lungs)
emphysematous cholecystitis (gallbladder)
right-sided retroperitoneal free air (abdomen)
intraperitoneal free air unknown origin (intestines)
abdominal abscess
delirium
ileus
pleural effusion
renal dysfunction

septic shock
ventilatory failure
wound abscess

We're on page two of the fourteen-page medical report. The only thing David did not have his first night in emergency was any known drug allergies. He was sent to surgery within the hour.

"Mr. David Bradbury is a 61-year old gentleman who was admitted to the Medical Surgical ICU at St Michael's Hospital with a Tylenol overdose." So began the surgeon's eloquent operating-room report. He used words like "a complicated" and "very impressive" patient, which are not good words, medically speaking.

"Given his septic picture and his deteriorating status, we deemed it prudent to take him to the Operating Room," the doctor continued in his report, which read like an explorer's description of a new and surprisingly difficult terrain. There was great respect for the patient, and also a kind of pride and buoyancy as the surgeons solved one problem and moved on to another. "We then assessed the entire situation and realized that there were actually a series of holes." I paused there. My brother's insides were full of holes. It was hard to grasp. "We turned our attention then to slowly elaborating this area so we could determine the anatomy of what had occurred." His duodenum was attached to his gallbladder. That wasn't good. "We said the safest thing to do for this gentleman" was to take out his gallbladder. I wish I had been there to thank them, to tell them what their repair of David that night gave back to us. "We began by carefully dissecting out the greater and lesser curves of the stomach until we could pass a stapler across the antral body junction. We did this using an 80mm GIA blue cartridge of the stapler." There was a lot of detailed description of the necessary tools, like explorers and their life-saving gear: #15 scalpel, #3 monofilament long-term absorbent suture, JP drains, and #1 silk stitches, which sounded nice (the silk part). A chest tube was inserted to drain the blood and fluid from his lungs, and a dozen more drainage tubes were put in his abdomen. And there was this, perhaps the most astounding detail: "The liver is unremarkable."

"Is he going to make it?" Tim asked the doctor after the surgery.

The intensive care unit was a hard-working, hushed place, except for the beeping of the machines attached to each patient, David especially. "He won't make it through the night," the doctor had apparently already told the ICU, but to Tim he was more circumspect.

"It will be tough," he said. The doctor was talking about the original tough guy, though. None of us realized how truly tough that was. For the first two weeks, David needed mechanical ventilation to breathe. His stomach was an open wound, meaning that when the bandages were lifted, you were looking inside him. There was no skin there. To keep him from ripping the bandages, the nurses tied his wrists to the side of the bed. Two nurses, one a respiratory specialist to keep him breathing, were stationed at the foot of his bed, and they kept watch day and night, monitoring their patient.

"Your brother is the sickest of the sick," one of them said to me as I sat at David's bedside. She tapped a thick metal binder that sat at her tidy station. "Everything that could be wrong with a person's insides is wrong with his."

Did we expect him to pull through? Absolutely not. He looked like a man on his way out, not one undergoing a profound transformation. But over the next few weeks in the ICU, his sepsis cleared up. He opened his eyes. He began to communicate, writing notes on a small pad of paper because after he was released from the breathing machine, he needed a tracheotomy, so no voice. Not that we would have been able to understand what he said, anyway; we hadn't for years.

"Will he get his voice back?" Tim asked the doctor.

"That is very unlikely," the doctor said.

On David's fourth week in intensive care, they took the tracheotomy tube out of his throat and moved him across the room, with one nurse stationed at the foot of his bed instead of two. His pain in this time became excruciating. I know this only because he told me many years later. In the three months he was in the hospital, I didn't hear him complain about pain or anything else. None of us did. It was especially bad when he coughed, which was constantly after sixty-five cigarettes a day for fifty years, but David wanted a clear head and refused all pain medication. A nurse told him about splinting, how he could hold a pillow over his abdomen to ease the pain. "In my brain I believed it would take away the pain, and it did," David said. "Because I believed it, it did."

"You know the surgeons call your brother Superman?" said the nurse one wet March night. It had been raining without letup for hours, cold rain on a cold night. I was sitting beside David's new across-the-room bed. He reached over and held my hand.

"I'd better be going," I said after a while. I'd planned dinner that night with friends, and I was late. David held my hand tighter and started to cry. I sat a little longer. David kept crying, though, and after another while, I said, "I have a dinner." I thought when I left that David was saying goodbye to me. He sobbed and held my hand in a way that felt final. "I think that might have been the last time I'll see my brother alive," I said to my friends at dinner, who politely did not ask, "What are you doing here, then?"

But I was wrong about David. After I left the ICU, he couldn't stop crying. Two of the nurses came to his bedside with a plastic basin, soap, and a razor, and washed him from head to toe, then rolled him over and did it again. They shaved him and changed the sheets around him, that nurse trick of replacing bed linens without moving the patient, and tucked him in, the tender white sheets up to his chin. "It was the kindest thing anyone had ever done for me," David said. It hurt my heart to think about how little kindness he'd had for the last thirty years. I don't believe in heaven or angels, but if I needed a testament to the proverbial light that shineth in darkness, it was the anointment with soap and water those two nurses performed on David that night. I think they brought him back to himself.

But that isn't right either. Because the David who was returned was something new, he was the potential David, the person he might have been if he'd been told what was right with him instead of what was wrong. How somewhere along the way, we forgot to notice his strength—the way he was brave and never gave up and didn't ask for or expect anything—and instead spoke to his failure.

"Every time I saw David, I would tell him to straighten up and fly right, that kind of thing," Tim told me recently over the phone, from his cottage up north. He said the birch trees had a brush of snow, and I heard the energy of the first snow in his voice. "A few months before he got sick, I decided to accept David as he was." I could picture Tim looking out his window onto the navy lake with the quiet all around. Nancy would be grading school papers at the table behind him. "I decided to talk not to his crippled self but to a person," Tim said. "I think he noticed. It was important to him. Well, it was important to me, anyway." I wondered if Tim's decision seeded something hopeful in David. Who knows how these things work? Maybe those nurses were able to locate that hope as they bathed him until he finally stopped crying.

When I came to see David the next day, he had his voice back. Well, not his voice of the past thirty years, those grunts and wheezes, and not even his voice from before that. When David got his voice back, it was the voice of a brand-new person.

"Hello, Cathrin," he said. He was sitting up in bed and smiling. He looked freshly scrubbed, the way he had in his pajamas in those early St. Catharines snapshots.

"David?" I looked around to see where the real David had been stashed.

"Yes, it's me."

I dropped my bag and coat on the chair and plopped beside him on the bed. "Jesus, David, you sound great. You sound amazing." I still think about the voice I heard that day. It was touched by something, or untouched by anything, maybe that was it; a voice free of experience and disappointment. It was higher than it had been, and softly melodic. It was simply, pro-foundly, present. I couldn't get over it.

"Call Tim!" I said, and I brought Tim's number up on my cell.

"Hi, Tim," David said into my phone.

"Hi, Paul," said Tim. He thought it was our cousin calling, to ask after David.

"Tim, it's not Paul. It's me. David."

I could hear Tim laughing really hard on the other side of the line.

"Well, hello, David," he said, and laughed more.

On March 31, a little more than a month after he was admit-ted to the ICU, David was sent to a ward. Before they moved him, they'd been walking him around, an orderly on either side. "It was a relief beyond compare, to move again." He was still very ill, but also undeniably on the road to recovery. "It was incredi-bly boring and lonely," he said of his two months in the ward after the ICU. "I would sit and do nothing but concentrate on myself." He laughed. "What else did I have to do?"

His goal was every day to feel a little bit better than he had the day before, and to tell himself so. "One night I might have a calmer sleep; another day I might last a minute without thinking about a cigarette." As he improved, he walked for hours each day, through every part of the hospital. "I had a mantra as I walked, three words: repair, restore, renew. St. Mike's, and I can never thank them enough, put me back together; they repaired me. And now it was my job to make myself well."

The restoration of David wasn't only physical. The harder work was the inside healing. "What choice did I have? Once you stop drinking, you realize the hell you were living. I didn't want to go back to hell." I'm not without willpower. In fact, I'm mostly held together by will, like Mom was. But my will was a twig next to David's. "Let's put it this way," said Tim. "If 99.9 percent of people on the planet went through what David went through, they would not be alive."

After David had been in the ward for a few weeks, Tim and his son Sam went to his apartment to get some kind of paperwork he felt he needed. I asked Tim if it was anything as bad as Vineland. "Vineland doesn't hold a candle to it." The Toronto housing people told Tim that David's unit was the worst they'd seen. "Incinerate it," Tim told them. When Tim decided not to talk about something, he meant it. There were ten years of his early life when he lived on a commune in British Columbia, and he refused to discuss it. Really, he disappeared for ten years and then he came back, and that's the end of that story and good luck to you if you can ever get more out of Tim. About David's room, he said, "Pigeons." I knew enough to leave it at that.

Laura and I sat beside the hospital bed when Tim spoke to David about this housing unit, but we may as well not have been because we were a backdrop to the drama between our brothers.

"David," Tim began. He stood at the foot of the bed and spoke sternly, almost angrily, although his voice was quiet. "You will never go back to that place." Tim was speaking of the room, but it was obvious he meant a lot more besides.

David was sitting up in bed and didn't take his eyes off Tim's face. "I will never go back there, Tim."

"And you will never live like that again."

"I won't, Tim. I won't live like that again."

Tim put his head down and then looked up at David again. "Because I did the math, Dave. And I have only one brother."

"I know, Tim. I know that."

The day David was released, on May 7, he was sent home with seven separate medications and that fourteen-page medical report. I say David went home because he did, to his new home in the one of the best public housing apartments in the city, with a balcony that overlooked the gorgeously treed Mount Pleasant Cemetery, where he went for long strolls with his new walker. He'd abandoned the scooter at the hospital. He'd left a lot at the hospital.

Those first months out in the world, when we thought he was a Budweiser away from being face down in the street, David told us over and over that he wouldn't drink or smoke again. Eventually, slowly, we believed him. He began to fill up his life, or to live a life. He read voraciously, like Mom used to, taking out stacks of library books a week. He helped people in his apartment building and volunteered at an organic market. "I like to make people feel good about themselves. For selfish reasons, it helps me." He didn't make amends, exactly, but he made the rounds, with his daughter and brother and sisters. He cooked us ambitious healthy dinners in his spotless bachelor apartment. He watched over Mom and Dad. He didn't have a lot of money—or any, really—so he discovered free Toronto. He went to weekly jazz shows at a nearby restaurant and readings at his local library.

"I had no idea the dhow ships of India were so fascinating. That keel design, that steep curve right below the prow, has never been replicated." David said this at the round, white kitchen table at Number 9, where we spent a lot of time talking. It was almost summer by then and he'd taken on the job of tending my wild-flower garden, planted by Kelly a few years earlier. David and I surveyed the yellow black-eyed Susans and pink coneflowers, the fragrant pads of lavender and overgrown mint. The garden was an unpretentious paradise, with butterflies and birds, that Kelly had made when he was a young man with ideas. He'd hauled dirt and lugged slate blocks to make a border, then sown the native Ontario wildflower seeds he'd ordered from the University of Guelph, while Mary painted the shed with giant pink and yellow birds. The garden bloomed magnificently, to everyone's surprise.

"Look like weeds to me, Cathrin," David snorted when I pointed out the tall grasses and drooping flowers.

"That's goldenrod," I said, sneezing.

"Like I said. Weeds is what we call them."

I don't want to get carried away with the sainted stuff. David could be irritating. If I lingered over a sorrow, he'd say, "You're alive, aren't you?" He was a genius of the abrupt departure, usually when I was in mid-sentence. "See ya," he'd exit the kitchen door with a backward wave. He trotted out conspiracy theories, like insisting that a pact between big pharma and the government had covered up the cure for cancer for years, and I mostly ignored him. But not the weeds.

"Just don't pull them up, David," I said, irked. "They are native plants." I knew goldenrod was a weed as much as the next person, but what was a weed except a state of mind? A decision that one thing is right and the other wasn't. I felt David more than anyone should understand this.

That Thanksgiving was our first with David in many years, and the last with Mom and Dad. We celebrated at Laura's house.

She'd cooked not one but two turkeys in a burst of domestic enthusiasm, and we made a fuss over David, with lots of gifts. Tim gave a speech and David wanted to respond. He stood up from his chair in the living room, then shook his head and sat back down. On the second try he got out "Nope, can't do it." Finally, on the third try, he said as much as he needed. "This guy. . ." He nodded to Tim before he sat down for the last time. We all looked down at our hands. There was a lot to be thankful for. If you put my two brothers on a graph, Tim would be a steadily rising line and David would be pointed extremes from the top to the bottom of the page, but that Thanksgiving, their two lines joined and stayed steady on together. I had a dream about it, even, where we were on a long road, my brothers walking side by side up ahead and me walking a ways behind. "You don't need to pay that Jungian of yours to figure out that dream," David said when I told him. "You can't catch up with me, and you never will."

Not long ago, David and I met at a boilerplate sports restaurant, where I tested out my miracle theory. The host led us past the humming super-screens to a sticky wooden booth further in and left us with two menus the size of Saskatchewan. David looked more like Dad now that his hair was fully white. He was thin and spry like Dad, too, and as fastidiously neat in a grey Patagonia jacket and one of his lightweight caps, for spring.

"St. Mikes was all over the miracle idea," David said. "They're Catholics, after all." He shook his head. "It's not the word I'd use, although it was beyond description. A totally life-changing event. An old me and a new me. The two are almost not related." This was sounding a lot like a miracle, I thought but didn't say, because what was a miracle other than a wonderfully improbable and extraordinary event with an excellent outcome?

"What would you call it, then?" I was willing to let the idea go, although faced with the alternative of David as a permanent emptiness, I preferred my miracle theory. It felt like the only livable approach.

"I came to my senses, Cathrin. Sometimes I wonder, Was there a reason for it?" Like in a miracle, I thought, where the reason was pretty much always to validate Jesus, who needed a lot of validation. "I don't know the purpose," said David. "I still don't know that." I wondered if he was waiting for one, but if he was, he didn't seem impatient about it.

"Everything all right here?" asked the waiter, a lightly bearded man with a serious haircut, as he cleared our shared plate of barely touched and overly cheesy chicken fajitas. David took his napkin and wiped away the crumbs in front of me. "Here's the thing, Cathrin," he said. "Everyone has a bottom. They say that in AA." David hadn't done AA; he'd gone his own way. "But my bottom was ridiculously low. No one's bottom needs to be as low as my bottom." He shook his head at himself. "And there was only one person whose fault that was, and that was me."

"Funny," I said. "Mom said something similar to me once."

"Well, Mom and I were very close," David said. "She knew me better than anyone. And she was right. It was me."

What Mom would have done to hear that one, I thought. I wasn't sure I agreed with David, addiction is pernicious and life-robbing, but I wasn't going to argue with the person who'd lived it for thirty years.

"You know, Carl Jung had a word for what you're describing," I said. The restaurant was starting to thin out as the lunch crowd went back to work. "The old-you, new-you stuff. 'Enantiodromia.'"

"Enan—what the hell?" David rolled his eyes.

"He said when an extreme one-sidedness dominates everything, an equally powerful counter person or consciousness builds up. The opposite of what was."

David listened. "Not bad," he said. "Like a yin-yang kind of thing."

"Ya, or equilibrium."

We got quiet after that. It was comfortable to wander around in our own heads, apart but connected, the way siblings can. After a while, I asked David something I'd wanted to for some time: Did he blame anyone? Mom and Dad, for not telling him we were moving to Grimsby? Or me, for not taking his hand and leading him out of the fight circle? Could we have done more when he was little, or when he got older?

"I don't dwell on it," David said, sticking to the facts. "I'm grateful for the second chance, and I've made the most of it. With Mom and Dad, especially."

"You were with Mom when she died." I realized as I said this that I no longer resented that he was there instead of me as Mom took her final breaths. He understood death more than any of us. "That meant a lot to both of you."

"I think that's true. And I wanted to help Dad through losing Mom," he said. "I knew how it felt to be that lonely." David nodded at me. "And you helped Dad, too, Cathrin. You had that great idea to give him Mom's urn."

I squirmed slightly on the wooden booth. "Yup, yup. Mom's urn." I'd have changed the subject to what was playing on the big screen if I'd had anything to say about mixed martial arts.

"Remember?" David persisted. "Mom's urn was at your house, and you offered to give it to Dad so he would have her with him."

"Check, please!" I yoo-hooed our waiter, avoiding David's eye.

"Dad calmed right down after that." Would David never let this go? "It changed everything. That was on you."

"Yes," I said. It was on me. David had that much right, and that was enough on the subject. There had been plenty of truth for one lunch, and besides, David didn't need to know everything.

10.

Earn Your Urn

THE CALLS STARTED, one on top of the other, shortly after Mom's funeral.

"Laura, I can't seem to find your mother."

"Tim, remind me again. Where is Mom?"

"Now, Dave, why isn't your mother here?"

"Cathrin, I need to talk to Mom about something."

"Ann, where do you suppose Mom has got to?"

Dad had us on speed dial. Tim set it up for him after Mom died, in our birth order, which made me number four. Our phones rang so relentlessly we'd put them on mute, but then we'd have to hear Dad's cracked, low voice, recorded, which was worse. "I don't know why none of you kids will tell me where your mother is."

What we feared would happen if Mom went first was unreeling before us: Dad couldn't find his way without her. His wife of seventy-two years was not where she was meant to be, sitting next to him in her easy chair or a hand-hold away in the twin bed beside his, and it beat him down, hour by hour. It looked like a betrayal. He was right about that much, and I was his Judas.

When we did pick up, and mostly we did, we'd tell him Mom had died. "Oh no! When did that happen!" You'd have to take him through Mom's death, and his fresh heartbreak, again. Or he'd be hurt that we'd forgotten to let him know. "Now that's not right, Laura," he'd say, summoning the last of his parental authority to let her know she'd disappointed him. "You should have told me. I'm her husband, after all. When did this happen?" The easiest was when Dad said, "Oh, dear. That's right. I forgot." Five minutes later, the phone would ring. "I can't find your mother."

Dad had been on a short memory loop for a few years. It was easy to miss at first because a good memory was never his long suit. He relied on Mom to remember and manage the details and stories of his life. At some point, the repeating started, same as it had with his father and older brother before him, all at about the same age, eighty-eight or thereabouts. Dad's memory went on a long hike, but his upbeat personality stayed behind. Throughout his cheerfully confused dementia, he remembered his five children and ten grandchildren, and he didn't forget the way he felt about any of us, either, or how he felt about long-past events. Emotion, even historic emotion, he remembered. When he started flying again, at eighty-five, he took to the air as if he'd never left the air force. "I'm going to take you all up! Grandkids too!" he said, to our terror. But he couldn't pass the written exam; the massive book he had to memorize was too much for him, and that was our first clue.

It was when he began to lose his long and confident grasp of numbers and his ability to do complicated sums quickly in his head that we realized it was time to bring in help. He called Laura one afternoon when he and Mom were still living in

St. Catharines—it was the first time any of us had heard that panicked voice from our steady dad—to say he had an emergency and needed her to come right away. Laura and Tim raced there to find Dad's taxes spread out on the dining room table in front of him. "I don't understand what any of it means," he said. We stepped up our trips to St. Catharines. On one visit, we arrived to discover that Mom had changed the passcode to their condo building, presumably to make it easier for Dad to remember. Laura, Tim, and I were huddled in the small cold foyer, waiting for Dad to buzz us up.

"Your mother knows the code, but I can't seem to find her." Never mind how Dad could lose Mom in a two-bedroom condo. After long minutes, he came back on the line. "I found your mother. Now let's see what she said, I wrote it down." Dad rummaged. "The new passcode is: 6." We began to realize in the way adult children do about their aging parents, which is to say slowly and with great resistance, that things had gone downhill fast. It wasn't just Dad's once-reliable math that had slipped. Their condo freezer was stacked with frozen Oh Henry! candy bars, the kitchen cupboards with mini pita rounds. Dad could still find his way to the grocery store—he never fully lost his sense of direction—he just couldn't remember what he needed when he got there. "These pita rounds, I'm telling you, they go with everything!" Dad said, waving one in my face before biting into it. "Try one, Cathrin. They're delicious." Food, money, medications were all a jumble to him. Laura called home-care experts to help with the shopping and cooking so that Mom and Dad could remain in their condo for as long as possible; we were still trying to respect their wishes at this point. The case worker sat on the tufted couch in Mom and Dad's ten-thousand-degree living room and asked Dad if he had any preferences about the caregiver assigned to them.

"Some people who have been in the war, like you, Mr. Bradbury, prefer not to have German caregivers, for example." She wrote his responses in her notepad.

"Why on earth not?" said Dad. "The Germans are a great people." There was a pause. "I wouldn't want a Nazi, though. You can write that down."

The case worker said out loud as she made the note, "No Nazis."

On another assessment, this one by a doctor, Dad was asked if he knew what season it was. "Of course," he said, looking from Laura to the doctor as if they were the ones with a screw loose. "It's summer." It was a bleak winter day.

"Okay, Mr. Bradbury, summer. Thank you for that," said the doctor. "And now, what month is it?"

"Well, if it's summer, then obviously it's July." Dad was pretty pleased with that one. He figured he'd passed with flying colours.

Which is all to say, it came as a surprise when Dad began to remember, persistently and accurately, one critical detail about Mom. After a couple of weeks of calls about not being able to find her, Dad's voice took on a new urgency.

"Cathrin, now listen to me. I want Mom." The speed-dial call started like all the others that March morning.

"I know, Dad," I said, still sleepy. It was 7 a.m. "It must be hard, but she's gone and we can't bring her back."

"No, Cathrin, I want your mother here with me. Her urn. You have her, don't you?"

"Oh. The urn." I was fully awake now, sitting up in bed in my T-shirt, my hair stuck to my face. The rubble had been cleaned away and the walls patched. I still hadn't chosen a new bedroom colour, so the holes in the walls were plastered with a white, chalky paste, giving the room a lively, spotted vibe. "You're saying you want Mom's urn?" This was an unwelcome bit of news. How did Dad even remember there *was* an urn, let alone that I was the keeper of it?

"Yes, I do. I miss her and I want her here with me."

"Right, of course, Dad," I said. "I'll bring her over the first chance I get." Which I absolutely, unequivocally, did not. I said I'd put her in my bike carrier and ride her over, but what if I got knocked down and Mom spilled onto the street, dirty car tires driving over her? I said I'd walk her over, but her urn was surprisingly heavy and my arms were weak. Sometimes reaching up to install a new shower curtain made my arms ache all night, in fact, and I didn't want to risk that. Now and then, I really would forget a scheduled plan to bring Mom to Dad. But Dad did not forget. Mom's urn and my promised delivery of it were the two things he finally, unceasingly, remembered.

"Cathrin, bring Mom today, will you?" We were in about the second week of this. I'd say of course, but then a dinner would come up, or a work meeting, or the kids were around, and I'd have to reschedule the urn delivery. He lived four blocks away, after all. I kept thinking he'd forget about it, but alas. After a while, I stopped visiting Dad altogether. It was easier that way.

Mom's urn had been displayed in a gently lit nook in my front hall at Number 9 since her funeral on March 9. A posy of flowers in a low golden vase, Mom's favourite vase, sat next to her on a slender maple table at the bottom of the stairs. The whole set-up was calm and beautiful, not like Hazelton Place, where she'd felt judged by people who were strangers to her. And where Dad could irk the hell out of her with his "You're the most beautiful girl in the world" this and his "I love you, sweetheart" that. Forgetting he'd just said it. "Be quiet, Bill," she'd snap. Mom was unpestered in my hallway nook.

As for me, I loved coming through the front door at Number 9 and chatting with her. An over-housed homeowner, I sometimes rattled around in my Miss Havisham manor at 3 a.m. Every sound woke me up, and I'd have to creep downstairs, tiptoeing around corners looking for intruders, peeking out windows into the backyard, my finger on the emergency number of my iPhone. I lay awake thinking how sad it would be to be murdered. With Mom there, I began to sleep better, skulk less. I didn't have cats or shelves of ballerina figurines. But this urn thing occupied my mind. It felt like Mom was around in spirit, as they say.

"Hell-oo-oo, Mum Mum, it's me!" I'd plunk down my coat and boots and bag in the front hall, toss my keys somewhere it would later take me an hour to find them, and pat Mom's urn as I headed into the kitchen to pour myself a glass of Sauvignon Blanc. "What a day, Mom. Not a minute to myself." I'd sauté a couple of chicken thighs and trim green beans and throw Mom the odd comment—"So I said to Angela, 'If Jonathan and Kevin don't get along, let's just move their desks apart,' and you know, it made me think that it was something you might say." It wasn't the first time I'd realized my workplace-management skills came mostly from watching Mom multitask as she raised five kids, coming up with practical solutions to conflict, setting boundaries and priorities, getting the best out of us. I liked talking to Mom about this at the end of the day. I kept these talks to myself, though. I wasn't as far gone as Laura, who would report back on her conversations with her fluffy white dog, Buddy.

"I was saying to Buddy the other day"—Laura would phone to tell me this—"I'm thinking of making Mom's lemon squares, or maybe the butter tarts. What do you think, Buddy?"

"And what did Buddy say?" I'd ask this calmly. I didn't want to let on that Laura had possibly lost her once-firm grip on reality.

"Cathrin, Buddy is a dog. He doesn't answer me, for God's sake."

"Okay. That wasn't entirely obvious to me, Laura."

Mom didn't answer me, either, although I felt she listened. Now that I lived alone, I talked to myself quite a lot, but having an externalized person to talk to, even one made of dust, seemed more explainable than talking to your own brain. There wasn't anyone else to chat with at home anymore, except sometimes for Kelly, who'd returned from Banff for Mom's funeral and stayed on. His first night back, he'd opened the front door with the same key I gave him when he was twelve years old, and I hugged him right as he stepped into the foyer. I broke down and cried. "Mom!" he said, alarmed by too much emotion from his mother, but he became tender as he absorbed my sorrow. I was really sobbing. "Oh, Mom, I'm sorry."

That tenderness was not on display tonight. I was full flight into a chat with Mom's urn when Kelly came strolling into the kitchen, startling me. "Ooo!" I jumped, to his infinite annoyance.

I couldn't get used to him popping up, this full-grown, broad-shouldered man with a beard, towering over me.

"Hey, Mom," Kelly said. "Who are you talking to?" He said this in a deceptively light tone, but I could tell he'd come downstairs to catch me out.

"You know, just to myself." I knew better than to say I was chatting with his dead grandmother.

"You were having an entire conversation." Kelly grabbed a bag of chips and trudged slowly back up the stairs, glancing back at me to say, "Possibly you are losing your mind?" I could see the burden of my long-term care furrowing his brow. Isn't it wonderful how quickly our children judge us senile? Although I was perhaps going a bit far in my conversations with Mom's urn. They were perhaps getting a tiny bit odd.

Mom's wake had been at Number 9, which is how she got there in the first place. The siblings had gone together to the funeral home to choose this urn, blue and silver and sleekly shaped. It had serenity. We'd had Mom's name engraved on it, and the dates of her birth and death. We took a lot of time and care over these decisions. It mattered that Mom's urn suited her. I remembered another time I had sat in a funeral home much like that one, with John, and his brother and sisters, picking their mother's urn. Those siblings talked for a long time about the right urn for their much-loved mother. One too elaborate for her sumptuous, unerring taste was quickly passed over. Plain pine suited her; she was a brilliant outdoorswoman who could build a fire, make campfire coffee, and whip up a delicious breakfast in her matching khaki pants and top, plus jaunty neckerchief, without getting a smudge on her. I'd be covered in soot from head to toe just watching her work. When John's father, a problematic man and difficult to love, died, most of John's siblings phoned in to the meeting at the funeral home and agreed in under five minutes to go with the cheapest urn.

My siblings and I discussed but did not argue this time over where to have the funeral. We explained Mom's wish to be seen out at the St. Catharines Cathedral, with a High Mass, to Father Victor at St. Basil's Church in midtown Toronto. Laura had steered us to this gorgeously light-filled church tucked into a small side street and run by the Basilian order, and the rest of us loved it on sight. "Let me ask you this," Father Victor said when we worried about fulfilling Mom's request. He wore cowboy boots and was super chill. A lot seemed to have changed in the priesthood since I'd mumbled Hail Marys in the hard wooden pews of St. Joseph's Church in Grimsby. "Do any of you go to church?" Cool Father Victor asked, his boots stretched out in front of him. "Because a funeral is for the living, not the dead." And so it was that a High Mass became a simple prayer service for all of us.

We arrived at the small church on one of those indecisive Canadian March mornings that was neither winter nor spring, but the sun shone bright and cold. We processed up the centre aisle, kids and spouses and grandkids, Dad leading the way with his walker. Tim gave a beautiful eulogy, and some of the grandchildren stood at the front of the church and gave the parting blessing together.

Go forth into the world in peace.
Be of good courage.
Hold fast that which is good.
Support the weak, help the afflicted, honour everyone.

I'd wanted the funeral reception at Number 9 because, finally, as if it was planned that way, the rewiring of the house was finished. The holes had been plastered, the walls mostly repainted, and the furniture put back in place. There were a lot of empty spaces where John's half of the furniture had been, but the flowers for Mom, arriving in a steady flow, filled up the house. The night before the funeral, I stayed home alone and dusted. I blasted Leonard Cohen from when I was young and Mom was a force to be contended with. "So Long, Marianne," "Sisters of Mercy," "Suzanne." Mom threw *Beautiful Losers* in the garbage when she found the book in my room when I was thirteen; I have a vague memory of Father Murphy denouncing Cohen's novel, which blasphemously featured saints and sex, from the pulpit. But *Songs of Leonard Cohen*—I used to crank it up for hours at a time and, more quietly, into the night on the family's massive oak console in the living room—that album, Mom liked. I channelled Leonard and Mom as I dusted. I didn't sing Cohen's words, I let them fill me up. He knew how to welcome grief. I dampened a soft flannel cloth with vinegar the way Mom taught me and slowly wiped away the domestic dirt, communing with her around the household art of putting things in order. "Look up *and* look down when you dust; most people don't do both." She taught me how to clean a house and iron and fold clothes, hem a skirt and sew a button, and that was the Mom I remembered as

I dusted. Not the random destroyer of books but the woman who took care of the way our home looked and felt and operated, and who showed me how to do the same. I wrapped a vinegar-dampened tea towel around my straw broom and swept the crown moulding in the living room. Leonard sang about saving ribbons for thee. I didn't cry, I concentrated on the work. I rubbed the mahogany side table in the dining room until it gleamed, and it took vigour, no feather dusters or Swiffers. "Put some elbow grease into that," Mom would say, and I did. "No one can make the bathtub shine like Cathrin," she said when I was a little kid, and I loved pleasing her with the ring-free tub. It didn't occur to me until much later that being the best at scrubbing made me her willing charwoman for years, and when I did get wise, I used the same strategy on my own children. "Look at the way Mary organizes the closet. No one does it better." "I sure wish I could untangle knots like Kelly." They figured me out much sooner than I did my own mother. I'm glad it took me a long time, though, because even as I began to balk against the constant tasks, it was a straightforward, homely way to show my love for Mom.

After the funeral, it was Mary who found the perfect spot in the hallway for the urn, and she took a picture of it in soft candlelight with flowers. "Peaceful and pretty," said my cousin Mary-Pat. We cried a lot back at Number 9 after the service at St. Basil's. Tim's son Sam made a speech about his weekly dinners with Mom and Dad—"free meal!"—when he was attending Brock University in St. Catharines, and how they waited at their door for him to come off the elevator. The grandkids sat crowded together on the couch as Sam spoke, jammed in so they were almost on each other's laps. "Every time I came to visit, Grandma would say, 'Here he is. Here's our Sam.'" The kids all wept then, and I understood that Mom had reached into them in a way that was less complicated than it had been for her own children, and that each of her grandchildren felt loved by Mom in his or her own private way, no small trick of love. Although we all knew what it was to be welcomed home by Mom and Dad. As long as they had a home, it was our home too. It was the least I could do for Mom, to give her a good spot in my own house. Her urn was part of the newly rewired, put-together-again Number 9. Sometimes it felt like the most important part.

As March turned to April, I patted Mom's urn as I left Number 9 and took the Ottawa trip I was meant to go on the day she died. With the smallest promise of spring budding on the maple trees, people were out running and biking along the Rideau Canal, and the city felt young and fit. I walked along the canal and then over to the Alex Colville exhibition at the National Gallery. I loved the energy of his work and the emotion, sometimes the menace, so contained it felt like a tightness in your chest to look at it.

"Start at the end and work your way back," said a friend who had been to the show. "You'll understand why when you see it." I walked briskly along the polished wooden floor to the final room, trying not to be distracted by the paintings of charging horses and bending dogs, and found myself in front of a late portrait of Colville and his most intimate and enduring subject, Rhoda, his wife of seventy years. It was called *Living Room*, and in it, Rhoda and Alex sit next to each other, him on a chair, her behind the piano. They are very old. Her legs under the piano are scrawny; he's lost his shape and his stomach sags. It's a quiet, private domestic scene, and as I stood and looked at it, I felt I'd tumbled into something important about my own parents' marriage. In the next room, one of Colville's daughters described on video how her aged parents sat side by side in their easy chairs. "I love you," Alex would say to Rhoda. "It's the one big fact of my life." That blew my mind. Not just the seventy years and the paired easy chairs, right out of my own parents' marriage playbook, but that the two husbands described their wives in almost the exact same way. "Dad," I'd said on a visit to their condo when Mom was still alive. He'd told her he loved her for the fifteenth time, and fed up, she'd left to take a nap. I was exasperated too. "Why do you love Mom so much?" He looked at me as if I had missed the plot line of an action-adventure movie. "She is the most important thing in my life. She is the making of me."

Rhoda was initially dubious of her future husband. "I wasn't terribly impressed when I met him," she said of Colville in the video at the exhibit. Mom's knees hadn't buckled at the sight of Dad, either, and I'd long assumed she married him to be adored, something that had been missing from her childhood with a father who reached around her to get at a cold beer. But at the Colville show, I began to understand that's not how Mom saw it. She wasn't in it to be cherished, or even to be conventional. She was in it to become someone new. Mom and Rhoda both decided at a young age that choosing a partner is a way of choosing your future self, the self you will become together. It's an old-fashioned idea, but perhaps not a wrong one. I think Mom saw in Dad a kind of confidence and bravery to push ahead, and she bought into the bargain that Dad's best self would be realized through her too. Did they transform together, the way the bishop of London said when he married William and Catherine, becoming their best selves through their union of matrimony? Hard to say. I didn't know them when they were twenty and twenty-two, but I think they did lift themselves out of one thing and into another.

As I walked backwards through the Colville show, I followed the love story of Alex and Rhoda in reverse. The way he painted the slope of her shoulders, the intimacy of his knowledge of them, when she was an old woman in the bathtub and, at the beginning of the show, a young woman standing naked in front of an open fridge. (Rhoda said she wouldn't have been caught dead standing naked at the fridge door, any more than Mom would have.) Around the middle of the show, there was a quote from Alice Munro below a painting of Rhoda on the beach: "He wanted never to be away from her. She had the spark of life."

Going home from Ottawa on the plane, I was seated next to a large man who snored loudly. His head kept bobbing until it rested on my shoulder. This tends to happen to me on planes and once even on a subway car—people fall asleep on me, as if I'm a homing beacon for the weary. "Sir!" I said, shaking him off. "I beg your pardon," he said, and moments later he was right back there, snuggled into my shoulder. I shook him off again, more roughly this time. I had my own weariness to deal with. With myself, mostly. It wasn't just that Mom understood more about love than I gave her credit for. She was better at it than I was. I'd failed to emulate Mom's practical approach to love with Promising New Man because I had it wrong. She might not have told and retold the story of the night she met Dad, but she created the narrative of her life that began that night at the YMCA dance and sustained them both for seventy-two years. They had the very stuff of a happy marriage, the kind you'd expect to find if you checked in on a pair of Jane Austen newlyweds fifty years on.

"Okay, Mom. We're heading out." Back at Number 9, I'd wrapped the urn in a soft wool blanket and put it in a carrying bag, which I held in my arms next to my chest as I walked the few city blocks over to Hazelton Place. It was more than a month after Mom's funeral, and the crocuses and snowdrops were out, hits of purple and white in the drab ground. Forsythia bushes popped yellow. The spring glut had begun. All that life teeming around could make me anxious, but today it perked me up. I was doing the right thing, and I felt like the blossoms had come out to cheer me on. I thought better of jaywalking across the four lanes of Avenue Road to get to Dad, because of the Mom ashes/tire treads worry, so instead I walked up a block to cross at the light. When I got off the elevator on the second floor, he was waiting at the door.

"Here she is, Dad. Here's Mom."

He took the urn wordlessly and put it on a small table across from his easy chair. "So I can look at her," he said.

"Nice," I said. And it was. We sat there together, looking at Mom and not saying much.

After a while, Dad glanced over at me. "Thank you for bringing her." He was like David; he didn't hold things against you. I put my coat on and patted Mom goodbye and gave him a kiss.

"See you soon, bye-bye."

"Bye now, honey." He often sang around the house when we were kids, and the song he sang at breakfast came into my head as I left him with the urn. "Honey in the morning, honey in the evening, honey at suppertime. Be my little honey, and love me all the time." He'd kiss Mom at the end of it, and she'd smile, not at him but at us kids at the table, eating our Cocoa Puffs. The sudden memory made me happy.

"Now, Cathrin." It was Dad on the phone, a couple of days after the urn drop-off. I bowed my head; here we go again. "I need to get some VO5 hair balm," he said. "Can you go with me?"

I went over and helped him with his winter gear. I had to move at a clip to keep up with him and his walker as we sped down Avenue Road. The Rexall drugstore was in the basement of Hazelton Lanes, a high-end shopping centre a couple of blocks south of his residence.

"Hello, Mr. Bradbury!" said the woman at the till. She seemed happy to see Dad, and he her. "I haven't seen you for a while." She had dark curly hair and an open, unthreatened stance.

"We're looking for—"

"Aisle six, bottom shelf," the woman interrupted me. "I know what Mr. Bradbury likes."

Dad put three of the red, white, and black VO5 boxes in the basket.

"One should do, Dad." He had at least six more back at the condo.

"I don't like to run out, Cathrin." It was more of a plea than an order, and we headed to the cash with the three boxes.

"How's Mrs. Bradbury?" said the kind woman at the till.

"Oh. Well, she's dead, I'm sorry to say," said Dad.

"Oh no!" the woman held her hands to her heart and then started to cry. "She was such a lovely woman," she managed to get out.

"She was," said Dad, and then he was crying, and then so was I, the three of us bawling our heads off in the Rexall drugstore in the basement of Hazelton Lanes.

"But it's okay, you know," Dad said as we pulled ourselves together. "I have her there with me."

"Of course you do," said the woman. "The people we love stay right here with us." She put her hands over her heart again.

"Why, yes," Dad said with his unfailing courtesy. "But what I mean is, Cassie is back in our room. Waiting for me."

The kind woman looked from me to Dad, but she didn't ask any more questions, and I didn't say anymore either. It was private, this urn-love thing, and not for talking about.

11.

Meryl and Me

IF YOU DECIDE TO GET back in touch with that first friend, the friend from when you were maybe six or seven, the one you haven't talked to in years and years, the one who knew you best before the world got hold of you, that Rosetta Stone friend who has the clue to the true you, and if you do this in a year when who you are is open to interpretation, hoping that this first best friend will provide some answers, you'll likely begin with a text, not a phone call. We might be sixty, but we're not living in caves; we keep up. You start with a long-time-no-see text to your friend, which leads eventually to the Phone Call, stage two of the unification of Germany. This Phone Call tears down the wall that's stood between you and your friend for twenty years, twenty-five, if you add in that stretch after you threw a book at her head when you were sixteen, and pretty soon you decide to meet in person, because that's what friends do. And it's great, that meeting. There's the nostalgia part, the old-boyfriend-reveal part, the trip-back-to-your-hometown everything-is-so-much-smaller! part, and that leads to the difficult-conversation part, about the dark night you've never discussed that's all tied up with your mothers. It's big, this conversation, and it takes place precisely six weeks after your mother's death and six weeks before her mother's death, so wow, that's the universe working in strange ways. You get to the bottom of that night and your role in it, and you're pretty pleased with yourself until, much later, your hairdresser suggests that you seem not to understand anything at all about your best friend of fifty-four years. This is an unwelcome bit of news because it means you have to talk, again, to your once-lost friend about things not said, like that book-throwing, when you missed her head and wished you hadn't, and somewhere in there you begin to ask yourself what you're holding on to in this can't-let-you-go friendship that in fact does let you go quite often, and maybe will again.

So if you're given the chance to do something similar and track down that original friend who feels like youth, hoping that he or she can bring back something steady and simple and clear in your life, I'll just say this: think twice before you hit Send.

Hello Meryl. this is my best 60th birthday present. long time no see. xx Cathrin.

I tapped my pithy note to Meryl the same night Tim showed me her birthday text. The temperature in Toronto had nosedived to –18°C—"Nobody alive today has ever experienced a colder month of February," reported the *Toronto Star*—and snow was coming down in a white curtain outside my bedroom window. It was the kind of night when Meryl and I, at twelve or thirteen, might have gone out for an epic winter adventure, leaping over the ice hills that rimmed the shore of Lake Ontario. Newly sixty, that sounded like at least one broken hip. Meryl wrote back within minutes, and we were off, launched into stage one of unification, which lasted that winter through the dying, death, and funeral of Mom. "You look alike," said Laura when I showed her Facebook pictures of Meryl, and we did, except Meryl looked younger. "No, just the same," Laura said, and I thought about the first time I saw Meryl across a paved school-yard, dark and compact and watchful like me, and how it was like recognizing something important in myself. But let's not get sentimental right out of the gate. Meryl, in her first text back, said maybe we should meet in the real world, but that felt a bit hasty. Sometimes I never thought about Meryl, sometimes I thought a lot about Meryl, but the one constant was that she was safely situated in the past. This one-text-away Meryl was very present and I proceeded with caution. Meryl was the first to relax into randomness, describing whatever was going on outside her window, a lively bird or a tree that came down in a storm, and then digging back to remember some old boyfriend. We lingered on the soft pillow of nostalgia but didn't smother ourselves with it. We were moving toward something—that was mostly the feeling in the early texts—whether we meant to or not.

The memory-syncing part was cool and mysterious, once ours were linked. When Meryl mentioned the Tea Room on top of the Grimsby Escarpment, a rickety stick building teetering at the very top of the mountain suddenly appeared in my mind. *It was made of logs,* wrote Meryl, and the Tea Room stopped wobbling. It had shut down long before our time because it's not the wisest business model to put a tea room in the middle of the woods, but giving it shape together made our memories if not free of falsehood—we both tilted toward the positive—then at least real. The magnificent magnolia tree at Livingston and

Main needed no prompting. *Big! Bold! Pink!* But more satisfying than putting Grimsby back together again was that Meryl's memories made my version of things less dubious. It had been a long time, possibly never, since I'd felt that I was a reliable keeper of the past.

We caught up on our adult lives, too, as we texted back and forth. I'd gone to Meryl's wedding when she was twenty-one. By then, it was six years after the book-throwing incident and we were talking again, and even as we went different ways—Meryl had kids and jobs, I had school and jobs—we made time at night in our twenties and thirties for hours-long phone calls. Now she sent me pictures of her three grandchildren, each one another large-eyed version of herself. She still worked as a florist, as she had when we last spoke. And she'd stayed in the same Ontario town since her marriage and raised her three daughters there. *Still in the same house, it is now yellow.*

The moms were a steady topic. They were both ninety-one and both living. Or to put it another way, they were both ninety-one and both dying. Mom had just lost the part of her mind that would have remembered our childhood, and Vivian was in her right mind but couldn't talk properly after a recent stroke affected her speech. Our mothers' connection to each other, separate from Meryl and me, was mostly invisible to us growing up, but it was a subterranean current in our lives. Mom and Vivian weren't friends, but they were deeper allies than we understood. They were both liberals and both prodigious and mostly indiscriminate readers, Vivian of newspapers, Mom books. They were terrified of lightning. Vivian would hide in her front hall closet, and Mom would shove us down to the basement after pulling out all the plugs. "Don't touch the metal doorknob," she'd snap as she pushed the door open with a broomstick. (Electrocution by metal doorknob during lightning is a thing; I've done the research.) Mom had a penchant for housedresses, a very small step up from pajamas, but Vivian dressed with flair because she was different from the other moms—she worked full time, and at good jobs too, or as good as a woman without a degree could get. This was exotic in Grimsby, Ontario, in the 1960s. "You have to put a price on your head, to know your worth," Vivian would say, miles ahead of her time; she was the first working mother I met. "You have to know what you will do and not do." She marched out the door every day, her red hair swept into an updo. It gave her mystery, and her own agency.

When Mom collapsed, Meryl was the first person I wrote from my Vancouver hotel room. I didn't mention I was lolling on my bed, eating a clubhouse sandwich as I texted her. As Mom lay dying, I remembered that I hadn't asked about Meryl's father, Clayton, a handsome, broad-shouldered man with a head of thick black hair. Clay was a former hockey player from a family of hockey players in Northern Ontario. He played defence for a feeder league and would have followed his brothers into the NHL if the Second World War hadn't interrupted. After a stint with the navy, Clay returned to hockey in San Francisco, where he and his team members were given medals of honour for pulling passengers from a flaming train that had collided with an oil truck in Fresno. "I never in my life saw boys with so much guts," the coach told the *Oakland Tribune* newspaper, but Clay was out for the season with severe injuries. When he couldn't make a living at hockey, he returned north to work in the gold mines, marry Vivian, and eventually move south to Grimsby with her. Vivian's mother offered her a sizable sum to move south without Clay, because by then he was a drinker. Vivian declined, hoping the change would be the cure. *Clay died 12 years ago*, wrote Meryl.

On March 15 at 7 p.m., eleven days after Mom's funeral, Meryl and I had the Phone Call. Our first phone call, I'll mention again, in twenty years. I was nervous enough to think of texting that I was sick, or tired, or sad, at least two of which were true. I called Meryl from under my covers, and she answered from under her covers. She's been cold since she was twelve years old. "Just an extra sweater, coat over that, blanket over that," she said, and we picked up where we'd left off. Neither of us finished our sentences, letting our thoughts dangle dementedly. "I just think . . . Here's what I'd say about that . . . My strong feeling there is . . ." We digressed so often, and at such length, that we rarely got back to where we started. Our conversation would have been incomprehensibly, mind-numbingly inane to anyone else, but we understood each other. We'd lived our life in the same place, we saw things the same way, we didn't need to explain ourselves. It was blessedly, nourishingly familiar. A high point of the unification, and there will be glorious high points if you do something similar.

"What do you remember about our last call?" I asked Meryl before we hung up. An unsatisfactory phone call, I remembered that much.

"You had to go," she said. "I remember where I was: in my rec room. And it wasn't a good call. You sounded a little exasperated with me. I think I could be exhausting. We were not on the same wavelength for a talk at all. You said, 'I'll call you right back,' and it took you twenty years."

That Meryl and I were moving irrevocably toward the Meeting filled me with unease. In a year when arrivals and departures stacked up like Pearson Airport during spring break, with me trying to figure out what to let go of and what to hold on to, Meryl felt like another challenge. We chose the weekend of April 25, more than a month away. Ambitiously—reconnecting with Meryl, I began to see that grand thinking was typical of me in a way I hadn't noticed before—I suggested Paris. *To recover from my awful winter.* I'd found an inexpensive hotel, well located, but Meryl wasn't going to get carried away. She arrived at Union Station early on a Friday evening. There were at least fifteen texts about the time of this arrival—*Meryl, I woke up thinking you should get the train that gets you in at 5 on Friday . . . What time does the train arrive exactly? . . . Is it a GO train or a real train?*—and on and on, which was when I realized how old we'd become. When did "See you in the park" turn into sixteen thousand emails about what time a bloody train arrived? About six months ago, was my guess. Of course, I lost her at Union Station. *Where are you?!? . . . I am here!! . . . Where is here?? . . .* Cue fifteen more emails until I saw Meryl across the chaos of the station's endless renovation. Her head leaned left like the first time I saw her, and she had the same unconvinced look on her face, as if I was the one who had to prove something. She was an overpacker like me, I saw from her suitcase, and she'd slung a leather handbag over the shoulder of her slim black-hooded jacket. "I love a hood," Meryl said, and I remembered that she did. We laughed as we hugged and mostly stared at each other on the subway (why did I choose the subway? would she hate that, or would it be fun? how should I know?) until we got to Number 9, where Tim and David were coming to meet us.

Meryl had practically lived at our house growing up, and David said right away that he wanted to come over the night she arrived, and then Tim said he would come, too, because he'd brought us together, after all. "Why did you?" I asked Tim later, and he said it was serendipitous, mostly. He'd bumped into Meryl's brother, Ken, at a window store, secured Meryl's email, and corresponded with her for a while before he broached the idea of connecting us. It was such a kind thing Tim had done, to give this friendship back to me. I was not kind in return. "We have only two nights, so you can't stay long," I said, but Meryl and I were delighted to see them. It wasn't just getting lost at Union Station. What had we got ourselves into, planning three days together so soon into the unification? I could see the panic on her face as clearly as I felt it on my own. Tim and David calmed us down, briefly.

"Two peas in a pod," said David. "Always have been, always will be." "News of your arrival has occupied my family for a month," I said to Meryl. The four of us found quick familiarity and talked easily until David said, "The thing I remember about you two was that you were the town tarts." (Hussies? Floozies? I can't remember the word, but it wasn't complimentary.)

"We most certainly were not," Meryl and I said in unison.

"Sometimes you went out with the same boy at once." He was getting on a roll, as David could. ("The good news is, David is back," Tim said not long ago. "The bad news is, David is back.")

He took a swig of his water and looked at Tim for collaboration. Tim said nothing, wisely.

"We most certainly did not," I said.

"We both went out with the Candle Maker, but that was sequential," said Meryl, nodding at me to help along the memory. The son of a prosperous fruit farmer, the Candle Maker would dip massive candles, each one bigger than the one before, and leave them at our front doors. Dad would go out for his morning coffee on the porch and walk into a five-foot-tall, multicoloured phallus of dripping wax. This did not please him.

"But neither of us had sex with the Candle Maker," I said.

David guffawed. I stood up and cleared plates and glasses noisily. The brothers had worn out their welcome.

"Can you believe David?" I said after they left in mild disgrace. "We were virgins the whole time we were in Grimsby." I was still irked.

"We were practically virgins the whole time," said Meryl. That the timing of our virginity mattered forty-five years later said a lot about the free love sixties. If a girl had energy around her sexual desire—went all the way, put out, balled—the word shaming was brutal. Fifteen years old when you lost your virginity? You were a slut, the worst word of all. By eighteen, the shaming went the other way, and you were frigid, with graduated stages (fast, tease) in between. Going all the way, in other words, was a meticulously planned strategy. A boy was there, a boy wasn't there, they left us, we left them—we couldn't figure out exactly when and why, none of it was continuous or logical. The only thing that tied it all together was the escarpment, where the boys were and the grown-ups weren't. It let us loose.

Which is perhaps why a trip back to the escarpment was to be the centrepiece of our reunion weekend. The next morning at Number 9, the second day of Meryl's visit to Toronto, we took the bus to Grimsby, about two hours away. The sun was high and bright but gave no heat. April was like that. We walked past the giant pink magnolia tree, now severely pruned, and bought flowers to put on Meryl's father's grave, which was on top of the mountain. We found the foot of the escarpment path behind the big brick house we used to say was haunted because we never saw anyone come or go from it. Now the lawn was covered with bright red and yellow plastic toys, and little kids ran around yelling.

"Let's find the cave," I said. I wanted something to be the way it used to be. The nostalgia part of the unification wasn't fully co-operating. Even the narrow dirt path was wide and well groomed. To the right of the path was the Point, so called because it jutted out for a view of the town, the abandoned cars below the Point, now cleared away, along with the guy who'd lived in those cars—"Jigger," said Meryl, her memory for detail was astonishing—and the deciduous forest, the trees of my youth. Red oak, sugar maple, trembling aspen, and preciously, black walnut. I'd collect their leaves for school, ironing them between waxed paper and then pressing them onto white Bristol board, simple-mindedly printing labels beside each: *The Compound-Leaved Poison Sumac, The Alternate-Leafed White Birch*. Labelling leaves gave life a manageable order I never lost the taste for. To the left of the path was the cave, the creek bed, and the other side of the mountain. A third of the way up, we stopped at the dank cave where some teenagers, not us, had sex.

"Remember when Dave moved into the cave for the summer?" I said. "It was Alan," said Meryl. She didn't flaunt her reliable grip on the facts and names of our childhood and youth; it was just there, useful to both of us. "I think I necked with Dave right over there," I said, pointing to a bright clump of birch trees on the sloping hill. Dave and I would wander off the path to kiss in piles of fall leaves. That was the thing to love about those trees, the way they changed with the season, and the way we changed with them. He'd pick the stiff birch leaves out of my hair as we walked back down the path in the dark, his arm loose on my shoulder.

"I never could stand that Dave," said Meryl. "I couldn't figure out what you were doing with him."

"Pardon? What?" Dave was my first love, and I still loved the memory of him. "What was wrong with him?"

"He was arrogant and full of himself. And not very nice either. He wasn't very nice to you." Meryl didn't say this unkindly, just matter-of-fact, as if I would obviously agree with her. This gave me considerable pause. What else had I been wildly romanticizing, for one thing? And had I been choosing the same type of men since I was seventeen years old, for another? As we climbed to the top, the first of the spring flowers were poking through the forest floor, protected by the trees, and Meryl knew their names. Hepatica, yellow lady's slipper, marsh marigolds, jack-in-the-pulpit.

"Trilliums!" I said, and pointed to a shady mound blanketed by the only plant I could name outside of grass and dandelions.

Meryl bent down to look at a petalled white bloom close to the ground. "Bloodroot. It looks nothing like its name."

She smiled happily at the flower and was six years old again, and so was I, smiling at her smiling at the flower, and I was briefly pulled back to when a flower was enough. I ran my hands like a little kid along the birch trees that rimmed the path as we climbed the rest of the mountain.

"They're so white," I said. The birch trees in Toronto were a sad grey colour.

"It's the red soil," said Meryl. "It's why the fruit trees did well, Clay told me. He loved that red dirt."

At the top, we walked the flat plateau to the Point, and just as we called out our old houses—"there, there"—like we did when we were kids, two red-tailed hawks circled overhead, their tails turning golden in the sunshine. They cocked their heads to look at us, as if we were the unexpected ones. "Look, two hawks," Meryl said. She took them as a sign, I wasn't sure of what.

We made our way to Clay's grave, where we put our flowers on the stone Vivian had designed; it would soon be hers as well. Meryl lingered under the struggling sun, and I stayed a little ways back until she was ready to leave. Down in the town we walked to the library, where the wide lawn had been turned into a parking lot. Much of Grimsby's downtown had been turned into a parking lot; the town council seemed to have an aversion to magnificent trees, cutting them down with abandon. I took it personally and railed at Meryl. "Talk about paving paradise. What the hell, Meryl."

"Didn't these library steps used to be higher? Everything is so much smaller," she said. If the escarpment was where we'd lost ourselves, the library was where we'd discovered who we were. It was on one of the town's back streets, hidden from strangers, but if they happened onto it, they would have found a pleasant red-brick two-storey building with a broad, welcoming front door and wide, high windows. It had the same open stance as Number 9, I realized as I stood in front of it. I was a book-shelver at this library for several years, pushing my trolley up and down the alphabetically ordered stacks and chastising customers who absently put Steinbeck in front of Salinger. "If you don't know where the book goes," I'd say in my spooky girl's voice, squeaking up to a patron with my trolley, "then it's better not to put it back at all." Today on our Grimsby tour, the library, now a community centre (the library proper had moved next door to a lively modern building), had mounted a typography show and we each bought a blue lithograph of the town's grid as viewed from the Point and a poster that said, "Everything speaks in its own way."

Back in Toronto, we had dinner at a midtown bistro, and finally got to the hard conversation. Not the book-throwing incident when she was fifteen, but the dark night more than a year before that, when Meryl tried to kill herself. "I can't believe Vivian is ninety-one," I said. I'd asked for seats at the bar because I thought it would be more intimate to be side by side, but I saw my mistake right away. To Meryl, with people on either side and a bartender hustling in front, the bar felt like a decision against intimacy. I'd been trying to make her feel safe and comfortable since she'd arrived, and I seemed to keep getting it wrong. "I think of Vivian as more my own age," I said. "Of course that's not right, but you know what I mean."

"I can't wait to tell her you said that. She liked being one of us."

To a point. One afternoon in her bedroom, Meryl and I got high, a steady preoccupation once we turned thirteen. "We rolled down the stairs, laughing hysterically," said Meryl. "She told us to stop laughing. 'Stop that right now!' We wouldn't and she slapped me. It was the only time she ever hit me."

"I would have slapped me," I said. "We were idiots a lot of the time." I poked at my arugula salad. "I'm sorry I didn't know Clay died, Meryl."

"Those hawks today." She'd finished eating and turned to look at me as she spoke. Her brown eyes held the pencil flames of the candlelight. "When our middle daughter left home, John and I sat in the parking lot, watching her plane take off. We did that with all the girls, watched until their planes were out of sight." Meryl grinned and shook her head. "We don't do that anymore. The girls come and go a lot."

"All finished here?" The bartender didn't wait for our answer as he cleared our plates, revealing the Thousand Islands of crumbs that had formed around mine. I wiped the smudge of lipstick off my wine glass with my napkin and wondered not for the first time how people didn't leave crumbs or smudges, a talent I couldn't master. Meryl's place and glass were both pristine, like her memory. I'd been drawn to her memory from the start, as I had to my husband's; it left room in my brain for idle thought. There was a downside. John's having all the facts in our marriage meant he rarely lost an argument. Even when I thought I knew something, like the right direction in traffic (so, so rare) or the turn of a story from the past, I mostly kept it to myself. There were other ways to get at the truth. Also, I didn't care about being right the way some people did, that was the simple fact.

"As our daughter's plane disappeared, a hawk came and sat on the fence," Meryl said, taking a sip of her wine. "An Indigenous man I'd been chatting with said the hawk was a protector and my daughter would be fine on her flight." Meryl paused and smiled. "So today when I saw the two hawks, I kind of thought it was your mom and my dad, protecting us."

"I love that story," I said, but really I was having a hard time concentrating. It hadn't been a plan, exactly, to talk about the night Meryl tried to kill herself, but after twenty-four hours of conversation, it had begun to seem pathologically evasive not to, even for me, the queen of let-it-lie. Forty-five years had passed since that night, enough time perhaps to finally broach the subject. I glanced over at the tables, where people did look more comfortable than the two of us on our bar stools, and then asked my question.

"So I guess there are a couple of things we haven't talked about this weekend. Like that night?"

Meryl didn't change the subject so much as make her way toward it, ahead of us in the distance. "Remember the time we climbed the mountain by the creek bed? We would have been twelve or so. I remember that."

"I think so." I saw the faintest sparkle of a creek as I dabbed my finger at a lingering crumb. "Why do you remember?"

"I dunno," Meryl said. "We were barefoot."

"We don't have to talk about that night," I said. Talking about difficult things was not who we were, Meryl and me. Not talking was what bound us, even. How could I have forgotten that? I racked my brain for a new subject that would sweep this one away like the crumbs.

Meryl looked at me calmly. I was beginning to suspect that I was the panicker, not her. "No, I want to," she said after a while. "I mean, I never have, but I want to now."

We both paused then, and I thought about the part of the story I knew. It would have been a couple of years after the creek-bed climb. Meryl was fourteen, and she took enough pills to die. She was rushed to the hospital by Vivian, barely in time to save her life.

"Things weren't great at home in that time, you'll recall," Meryl said finally. She looked me straight in the face and waited.

"Yeah," I said, although I didn't, or only faintly. We'd finally acknowledged the thing we'd never discussed. We'd said out loud that it had happened, and that was enough. That was plenty. "You weren't depressed or anything," I said.

Meryl kept looking at me, until she seemed to make a decision to leave it there. "I often think if my mom hadn't come to my room and asked me if I wanted pizza, I'd be dead now. I often wonder about that." She looked down at her lap, then up again at me. "And your mother was very kind in that time. She tried to help me, after. She took me to see a priest and told me I could talk to her anytime."

"I remember being mortified that she took you to a priest, of all things." I rolled my eyes, which made me wobble slightly on my bar stool.

"I think maybe I'm more religious than you are now." Meryl let me absorb this new idea of her before she continued her story. "Your mom's taking me to a priest was an act of concern. That meant a lot—the act, not that priest." She raised her eyebrows. There was something more there, but we'd have to come back to it. "There wasn't therapy or anything remotely like that. It was a private, shameful event. Even now, it's a shameful event. No one, not even you and me, Cathrin—we never talked about it." It wasn't exactly an accusation.

"Meryl." I skated over the fact that it had taken me almost five decades to mention that night and instead went back to what I knew: that Meryl had called me and told me she'd taken pills from the medicine cabinet. I thought she was trying to get high, our ongoing commitment, and asked her if it felt good. She said it did, but also that she felt kind of funny. "Cool," I'd said, and went back to watching *Star Trek* or whatever was on TV. But as we talked on our shaky bar stools, what happened after that call took on more shape.

"I'm pretty sure my mom told your mom, and that's why Vivian went into your room." My words seemed to ring out, although I was speaking quietly.

"No, that's not how it happened," Meryl said, and I might have left it there because she'd been right about everything else. "It was dinnertime. My mom thought I was hungry." Meryl smoothed her napkin on her lap and spoke again without looking up. "How would your mom even have known?"

My heart was pounding. I was getting in the way of how Meryl remembered that night, but my words were too fast for me. "She knew because when I hung up the phone, I told her," I said, and I knew that it was true. Even though at fifteen, I'd made hiding things from Mom a defining purpose of my teenage life, I must have understood that Meryl's life, and in a way mine too, depended on my telling Mom, because what might life have been if my best friend had died that night, on my watch? Not great, was my guess. Now, sitting side by side with Meryl, our shoulders almost touching, I wasn't only sure that my memory of that night was accurate, I cared that it was.

"If that's true, then it was your mother who saved my life," Meryl said. She looked directly at me with what could have been anger, but I think she was concentrating on getting the facts straight, like I was. "If that's true, then it was you who saved my life."

"Well, you called me, so I guess you saved your own life."

We both took time to settle after that. I became so lost in my thoughts that when I looked at Meryl again, I was surprised to see her still sitting beside me. She looked like she'd wandered a long way too.

"It wasn't a condition, you know," she said. "It was an episode. That's how I think of it."

"Yes, I get that."

"I don't talk about it because I don't want to be defined by it. I'm not defined by it."

"I think that's true," I said. "It was an incident, not a lifelong affliction." Incident, episode, that night, that time, before, after. We were careful with our words. The other words felt too violent, and further from the truth.

"I'm proud of myself, how I rallied," Meryl said. It was a statement, for both of us. "It took longer than people realized." All weekend I'd been carrying around the idea that I needed to take care of Meryl, and in that moment, I let it go. She didn't need looking after by anyone.

Back at Number 9, we put on our mothers' pajamas, as we'd agreed we would. We were both wearing our mothers' clothes a lot at this point. I wore Mom's dramatically flowered red-and-black silk muumuu with its massive flapping arms. There was enough material for this garment to take flight. Mom's usual bedtime style was modest and belted, but this muumuu had been her sister Mary's, and Mom never washed it because it smelled of Mary and now I didn't wash it because it smelled of Mom. That's thirty years of smell on one muumuu. Meryl came out of my spare bedroom in her mother's leopard-print silk pajamas.

"Very Vivian," I said.

"Very Vivian," she said. Meryl liked to repeat my words; it was her empathy.

The next day, she left Toronto with a simple factual question she could take to her mother about the sequence of events that night. They hadn't talked about it either, so it wasn't a small thing when Meryl sat with Vivian and asked her, "Mom, did you come to my room that night because Mrs. Bradbury called you?" *And my mom locked eyes with me, her eyes wide and so much pain in them, and she didn't have the words, but she nodded yes.* Meryl wrote this to me right away. *To have this talk finally when she could no longer talk. It was strange, Cathrin. It was sad. It was huge.*

I read the note from Meryl in the kitchen at Number 9 and started to cry, my tears plopping on the round white table. It sounds dramatic to say that, because getting the details right on that long-past night was simple enough. Mom, Vivian, and I would have done anything to save Meryl, so it didn't matter who told whom. But knowing that it was all four of us, and that Vivian and Meryl had been able finally to nod that truth to each other. And knowing for sure that I didn't go back to my *Star Trek* show. Beside the ordinariness was a hugeness, like Meryl said.

Six weeks after Meryl's visit, Vivian died, and it was remarkable how that midtown bistro conversation happened when it did, exactly between the deaths of our mothers. It changed things for Meryl and me after that—if only we could have told our moms. Meryl would have asked Vivian to forgive her and told her how glad she was to have lived that night. And I'd have told Mom that I finally understood she had been my ally in important and even life-saving ways. It wasn't just ancient Mom who saw me as I was, beaming at me back in her room at Hazelton Place. Mom had been paying attention all along. My idea of her changed, but not only that, a new idea of myself began to take hold, a more reliable, less rickety one, like the Tea Room on the mountain. I wondered if my version of more things was right, or at least not wrong. I noticed something begin to grow in myself. A voice, maybe.

They buried Vivian next to Clay on top of the escarpment. Meryl's brother, Ken, read a poem, and Meryl laid flowers on her mom's grave, as she had with her dad on our day on the mountain. Meryl liked to think of them up there together, Vivian and Clay. I did too.

Several years after the great success of my dinner with Meryl, a work colleague took his own life. I was badly troubled by what I'd missed. We were trying to make changes at work, and he said he'd get on side, but he wasn't capable. I plowed ahead with my agenda, as usual. His death knocked me sideways for some time, although I'd known him only briefly.

"The look on his face the last time I saw him. I don't know how to describe it." I was talking to my hairdresser, or rather to her reflection in the mirror as she clipped my bangs. I'd been going to Kaila for several years, since before Meryl and I reunited in 2015. Like the best hairdressers, she knew a lot about my life.

"Agony," Kaila said.

"Yes, agony." I looked at her in the mirror, waiting, because she was often wise.

"Suicide gives you access to a part of you you didn't know was there." She held a hank of my hair between her fingers before she took her scissors to it. "I've had four people in my life commit suicide."

"My God, four people." I'd never heard anything like this.

"Yeah, way too many." She told me her connection to each of them, and some of their stories.

"I've never been touched by suicide," I said when she was done. "But this sure is reaching into someplace I didn't know was there, you're right about that."

There was a pause. Kaila looked at my reflection in the mirror, as if she was trying to decide whether to say something. "Except didn't you tell me once that your best friend almost died that way when you were young girls?"

My reflection stared back at me, agog. That I hadn't made the connection until this moment, sitting in my hairdresser's chair, between my outsized grief over the death of a brief work acquaintance and my best friend's attempt to kill herself at the apex of our relationship was a surprise to me, to put it mildly.

"I guess I put it out of my mind because my friend and I got to the bottom of that night when we had dinner. It was remarkable, really," I said, "that between the deaths of our two mothers, we were given the opportunity to figure it out."

"Oh, that's good," Kaila said. "It's important to do that." She was gently blowing the hair off my face and neck with her silver Dyson hairdryer. "So why did your friend take the pills?"

"Pardon?" I was suddenly at sea again.

"Oh, I thought that's what you meant when you said you figured it out, about why and everything."

"Well, things weren't great at her house in that time," I said.

"Oh, I see," Kaila said, and I could see that she did not.

She ripped open the Velcro on my black salon cape and shook off the hair, then hugged me goodbye, as was her habit, and I went through the motions of paying up as her question about Meryl rat-a-tat-tatted inside my head. Back at Number 9, I kept replaying that dinner conversation as I wandered room to room with my freshly cut hair, now and then looking at myself in a mirror. "Things weren't great at home in that time." That's what Meryl had said, and I hadn't asked her any more, out of deference or avoidance or lack of interest. I thought again about how Meryl and I talked and talked, and about how we didn't talk and didn't talk. We had two modes. Why did Meryl take pills that night? I had no clue. What had I missed in my best friend, and in myself, when we were two girls trying to break free? Again, I came up blank. And there were only two people left who could fill in those whacking great gaps now that our mothers were both dead: Meryl and me.

Also, that book I threw at her head did matter. I just needed to find out how.

12.

Two Girls Talking

I'VE SOLVED MOST PROBLEMS in my life by never discussing them. I managed to get divorced without talking about why. If I had a rift with a friend or family member, I'd let the dust settle and call again in a month or so. I was a genius at avoiding work conflict, hiding in the bathroom when I saw someone I should have been managing out of some hole or other. "Avoid at all costs and it'll sort itself out" was my motto. Meryl was something similar. We didn't worry every little thing into the ground. "Not talking is talking," Meryl often said. Exactly.

After my hairdresser conversation, Meryl and I tried something new. We talked on the phone about things we never had, for twelve hours, in three-hour increments over four days. We got to the book-throwing incident and other less expected places, like friendship and betrayal. This time I'm going to start at the beginning, to listen to two girls talking.

Most of the kids stood in noisy packs of three or four as I waited for the bell to ring, so I could at least join a line and not be so obviously friendless on my first day at a new school. I scanned the paved yard of St. Joseph's nervously and stopped on Meryl.

She stood at the entrance to the laneway that ran along the side of the school, an off-limits place because it was out of sight of the teachers on patrol. She had a daringly fashionable pixie cut, enviable next to my tight braids. She wore a caramel-coloured dress, as did I, only mine had a large tulip and Meryl's shiny white buttons up the front; again, cooler. But more than her hair and dress, important as they were, it was the look on her face that caught me. Bored, pissed off, an I-dare-you face. She looked ready to burst into inappropriate laughter, although it would turn out that she was more likely to burst into tears when the teacher called her up, and I was a nervous vomiter. Inside, I was called to the front of our grade 2 class and presented as the new girl. It was a big crowd, 35-plus, and a big event, the arrival of a new kid. The sheen wore off fast if you didn't live up to it. ("Little girls are cute and small only to adults. To one another they are not cute. They are life sized," wrote Margaret Atwood in *Cat's Eye*.) My eyes again settled on Meryl, who studied me from her seat toward the back of the room, and I looked at her with the same open interest. A few days later, I arrived at school with a pixie cut, just like Meryl's. We became fast friends.

Meryl started to come into my house after school, to wait for her mom to be finished her day's work as secretary to Mr. Odd, the principal at Grimsby Secondary School, which was just past where I lived, on the other side of town from St. Joseph's. We'd sit at the kitchen table eating the milk and cookies Mom laid out while she hovered in the background. Mom was always there, making me wish she wasn't, but for Meryl she was the mom she wanted, the mom who waits for you with cookies. She couldn't get enough of Mom, and Mom treated her the same as me; she expected Meryl to be there. Pretty soon, Mom let me walk the three or four extra blocks with Meryl to the high school, dodging the older Protestant boys going in the opposite direction. "Let's go in this door," I said, pulling Meryl through a forbidden red door on the side of the school. We looked for evidence of bravery in each other rather than in ourselves, and for Meryl, my grabbing her hand and screaming up and down the stairs made me the brave one. She was calculating the whole time: "Okay, if we go through the red door, then how do I find my mom?" At her desk outside the principal's office, Vivian gave Meryl paper and sat her at a typewriter. The first word Meryl typed was "Ken," the name of her older brother. Ken, Ken, Ken, Ken, Ken, Ken . . . to the bottom of the page. It was an easy word to type. But also, it was Ken who was Meryl's ally when Clay came home drunk. Ken was only eight or so himself when he said being home was like living with a bomb ready to explode.

The next daring idea, after the red door, was to climb the escarpment because by now we were twelve and old enough to be out of sight of the moms. "Let's go up by the creek bed," one of us said. "Let's do it barefoot," the other said. It wasn't Meryl or me who was brave, it was the way the two of us combusted together. The rocks were almost submerged by the spring rush, and we jumped fastest when the next rock looked farthest so we didn't get stuck by our fear. Halfway up, we got drenched in a thunderstorm, the thick rain hitting us twice, once on the way down and once on the way up, after it bounced on the rocks. As we surveyed our domain at the top, the sun came out again, and it was suddenly hot, as if spring had come not gradually but in that very instant. We came into ourselves, too, in that moment, Meryl and me. Our most free selves, and it lasted for another year or two.

"I love you, sun!" I shouted over the noisy creek, my arms reaching to the yellow ball overhead.

"I love you, boulders!" said Meryl.

"I love you, creek!" And the way the sun glinted in the creek as it flowed down the mountain did feel like love.

"The best day ever," said Meryl. It was a big pronouncement. "Water nature beauty free."

In grade 7, Meryl and I became bad. That was how it was put to us. Our downturn began with mocking God. Throughout my Catholic education, which I swallowed whole, I loved the spectacularly murdered martyrs and longed to join them on their high-speed escalator to heaven. Meryl put an abrupt end to my saintly aspirations the day she sneeringly recited the Our Father in the schoolyard and made me repeat it after her. Lightning did not strike. Which was when it occurred to me: without God, we could do anything. I can't overstate the power of this sudden insight. Without God, we could do as we liked, and so we did. We'd sneak down the forbidden side lane at recess for a cigarette with the Protestant boys, and for our Catholic teachers, we may as well have joined a Satanic cult and roasted babies on a spit. The day I came back to class with burrs on my clothes—the hill we escaped by was overgrown, and those burrs were the evidence of our truancy—Meryl was blamed. She was the bad influence, everyone said it. She worried about being the one who got blamed. It wasn't that she did anything bad; it was that she wondered if she was bad. She decided it was important to hide the way she was different. When they accused Meryl, the day of the burrs, I chastised the teacher, standing on principle like those martyrs, but Meryl was too worried about what was going on at home, and worried that it was her fault, to argue with a teacher.

We became teenagers with a ferocity that exhausted our mothers. We didn't so much argue with them as flaunt our disdain for them. We began to go barefoot everywhere, not just up the escarpment. We walked in the rain without umbrellas, and it was this last detail that Mom would not take in. Barefoot *and* wet in the rain—it was a step too far. We scoffed at anything with polish or shine or 1960s zinginess to it, a look Vivian loved. She bought Meryl snappy psychedelic tops, and Meryl would glare at her. "What part of you thinks I will wear this?" Her brown hair was still short but longer than a pixie, with her bangs covering one eye completely. She had a steady handle on what was cool and what wasn't, and I tried to keep up. We snuck out in our mothers' fur coats, their hems sweeping the snow as we prowled the town. We prowled the hockey arena and we prowled the bowling alley, looking for boys. We walked up and down and up and down Main Street, waiting for something to happen, or for nothing to happen.

When we skipped school, we'd sneak into Meryl's reliably empty house through the basement trap door. Meryl lived in a big white house toward the peach and cherry orchards that led out of town. It was a grand manor that had seen better days, not like my relentlessly ordered house, where every room had a person and a purpose. Even when it was quiet my house had a hum, as if someone had just been cooking and cleaning, which Mom had. At Meryl's, we spent most of our time in her bedroom on the second floor or the TV room off the kitchen, which was where we were when I worked up the nerve to ask my question. This TV room had a lot going on. The pet bird lived there, and the fish. Vivian often sat on the couch with Poncho the chihuahua, under the shelf of Ken's hockey trophies. We had dinner there most nights. On the floor was a large brass heating vent where Meryl leaned her head to dry her hair as I asked my question.

"My dad and I are going on a canoe trip," I finally began. Mom had offered me a summer gift that year: I could go on a weekend shopping spree in Toronto with her or on a northern canoe trip to Algonquin Park with Dad and a friend of my choice. To everyone's astonishment, my own most of all, I chose the canoe trip, and thereby cemented the obvious but important lesson that an authentic experience, preferably outdoors, will in most circumstances trump shopping.

"It's kind of a family tradition." That was a lie, but I felt it gave my request an impressive formality. "I can take one friend, and I wondered if you would like it to be you. It will be the wild outdoors, and possibly dangerous," I added, sweetening the pot. We hadn't openly talked about our friendship since we were little kids. It was easier to tell the trees we loved them.

"Why me?" said Meryl, not sufficiently interested, or so it seemed to me.

"Because you're my best friend." And there it was, and then we knew that we were.

We had two jobs on the canoe trip with Dad: to put up our own tent, which collapsed on us in the night, to our screaming hilarity, and to do the dishes. Meryl dropped the cooking pot off a cliff (why were we doing dishes off a cliff?) and we'd have left it at the bottom of the lake, but Dad sent us back.

Meryl dove off the high rock, her body making a brief arc against the blue sky, before she straightened out to land soundlessly in the flat black lake. "Come in! It's so warm!" It was so cold I thought my head had been severed from my body as Meryl swam serenely past me to the shore.

"Go to sleep," Dad moaned from his tent that night as we replayed the day from under our flannel sleeping bags. "He's so relaxed, your dad," said Meryl when we got sleepier. "My dad would never, ever, I mean *ever*. He would not have taken us on this trip or ever had an interest in . . . a canoe." I wasn't surprised by this. I thought I'd die of boredom with a father like mine; I couldn't figure out what I'd done to deserve this fastidious man who soaked his sweaters in Woolite and spread them out to dry on a towel beside the heating vent. Who parked his Pontiac in the driveway and came through the side door for dinner at precisely five thirty each night. Of course it wouldn't occur to Clayton to spend a weekend slogging around with a pair of twelve-year-old girls. He was the cool dad.

Clay took Meryl to church on Sundays, and they both loved to dress up for the occasion. He put his strong arms around her and Vivian during lightning storms and explained how they worked so they wouldn't be afraid, and Meryl adored that father. But drunk Clay took her by the scruff of her neck when she came home late one night and held her face to the kitchen clock. "What time is it?" he said. "I hate you!" Meryl screamed at him. When Clay was violent, Ken would stand between his father and mother, to protect Vivian, but he didn't always succeed. Meryl mostly stayed in her room with her ears plugged. Dinner was the worst. "You never know when he's going to blow in,"

Vivian would say at the set table, ready for a fight. "Just don't say anything," Meryl would tell her mother when they heard Clay's car in the driveway, but Vivian was not prepared to stay silent.

Soaping the school windows wasn't exactly a silent act either. As a parting gift to St. Joseph's School in our final year before we graduated to high school, Meryl and I soaped the windows of the grade 7 and 8 classrooms one night, writing spectacularly vile things about our teachers. The next morning in class, Mrs. Newbury called all the grade 7s and 8s together. "My husband is not a violent man," she began quietly, her updo trembling on top of her head. "But when he catches whoever wrote these things—and he will—he will take their heads and smash them against the brick wall." Meryl and I couldn't decide which would look less guilty, staring out the window or looking straight ahead, so we tried both, and no one guessed it was us.

This was the Meryl I knew: God mocker, cliff diver, window soaper. After some sin or other, Mom had had enough and sent me to a Catholic high school in St. Catharines, in the hope that the nuns would set me straight. "How's it going?" Laura asked. "I'm not doing so well in math," I said. Laura was an unfailingly good student, always at the top of her class. She asked what grade I'd got. "Zero," I said. This was December of the school year. Out came the Kleenex box as Mom wept at the kitchen table. I stared at her, stone-faced. She shouldn't have sent me to that Catholic high school. Nothing good came of it. Going to school in another town put a space between Meryl and me, for one thing. It meant I wasn't with her that lonely Saturday night.

Meryl walked alone to the bowling alley. She'd turned fourteen a couple of weeks earlier, and some boy or other broke up with her as the balls thunked down the alley and the pins tumbled around them. So no boyfriend, and I wasn't there, and Meryl couldn't figure out why. She didn't take the pills because of me, but we weren't together, either, and as she walked home, she thought, Well, this is what I'll do. It wasn't a plan exactly, more an idea that she followed through to the end. She was tired of feeling frightened all the time. She was just generally very, very tired. No one else was home, and she went quickly to the medicine cabinet in the upstairs bathroom and opened the pain pills from when Ken had broken his leg months earlier. She swallowed them by the handful. It took some effort.

"Pizza!" her parents called up from the front door. They'd been to Ken's hockey game with the Grimsby Peach Kings, where he was the star player, and it was one of their good nights; they were laughing and happy. Meryl went downstairs and had a slice with Vivian and Clay, and then got under the covers of her parents' bed. She rarely went in there, it was huge and often cold, but it was the only upstairs room with a phone. After Meryl's call to me, things happened quickly. I told Mom, Mom called Vivian. Vivian tried to sound casual as she went into the bedroom and asked Meryl if she wanted another slice of pizza, but she saw how bad things were right away. At the hospital, Vivian had to stay in the waiting room while they treated Meryl, not knowing what the outcome would be. A stranger, a kind woman a little older than her, held her hand until the doctors came out to say that Meryl would live.

The Grimsby hospital was a small and pleasant white building, just past Meryl's house. I didn't visit her there. It was too embarrassing to see her lying in a hospital bed, and besides, Meryl wasn't the kind of person to do something like that. She'd acted impulsively; she had a dramatic side. It was stupid, she knew that as soon as she'd lain down on her parents' bed, and it was better not to rub it in her face by talking about it. After a suitable silence to let the dust settle, I called on Meryl at home one afternoon, but she'd been taken up north to be under the care of her devoted aunts and to take the cure of the northern December air. She came back to school that January wearing a glamorous camel-hair coat with a detachable fox fur collar, a gift from her parents. She felt like everyone was staring at her. She said what she had to say, and nothing more. It was a struggle to get herself back on track, and she kept that hidden too. She closed her circle. She became another person, introverted and quiet.

One Saturday after Meryl got home from up north, Mom drove us to the St. Catharines Cathedral, where she'd made an appointment for Meryl to talk with a priest. We didn't discuss why. I slouched in the back seat, embarrassed that Mom was doing this. Meryl sat in the front, looking straight ahead. When she walked into the priest's office, she recognized him right away. She'd met him at a wedding when she was eleven years old, barely at puberty, and he'd given her a dime, eyeing her up and down, and said, "Call me in ten years." When Meryl saw him sitting there, she said, "I guess I'm using that dime, eh?" It was an awkward conversation after that. She waited until Mom dropped her back home to throw out the pamphlets he'd given her.

You might have thought the trouble in her house would make her want to get away, but it had the opposite effect: it made Meryl want to stay closer to home. My stupefyingly ordinary home made me want to get out into the world, and fast. I began to formulate a plan that would make us free and unafraid, the way we had been

on our climb up the creek bed. We went to the Pedlar in midtown
Toronto, then a tiny bike store you took steps down into, to buy
ten-speed bicycles. Red for Meryl, blue for me. My plan was to
ride these bikes across Canada, and we applied for government
grants to subsidize the trip. They were giving grants away like
flyers in 1969; it was the era of grants and free money, before the
era of loans and no free money. An optimistic time, right after
the spectacularly successful Expo 67 in Montreal, where we
and the world saw Canada at its most hopeful. My plan called for
us to bike from Grimsby to the East Coast, and to tell the story
of small-town Canada in photos and words. "We'll interview
people and take their pictures and publish their stories as we go,"
I said to Meryl. "How are we going to do any of that?" she kept
wondering. The *Grimsby Independent* ran a photo of us on the
front page, shaking hands with the local member of the provin-
cial parliament, our government grant application in his hand,
but he turned his back on us the moment the photo op was over.

When we didn't get the grant money, we got jobs at Spanky's
Submarine on Main Street. "Would you like Spanky's secret
sauce with that?" we'd ask customers in our yellow button-downs
with the Spanky's logo on the chest. We began to train for the
bike trip, riding to the next town over and back as fast as we
could, catching each other's slipstream. We were our own pelo-
ton, the Tour de Grimsby. Meryl took a corner so close to the
ground her shoulder caught the curb and she got badly cut up,
but nothing stopped us. We got more ambitious and biked to
Toronto, although outside of this training regimen, our plan was
a bit loose and Meryl was not getting great feedback at home.
Our trip was not flying with Vivian at all.

"Where will you sleep?" said Vivian. "What will you eat? What if your money runs out?" There was not enough information for her to be satisfied. Meryl was having her own qualms. Some part of her, a big part, never fully believed the trip would happen. It was not a win-win situation for Meryl between me and her mother.

On the night before we were meant to leave, our saddlebags packed and mounted on our bikes, Clay stood close to Meryl and said, "You are not going. Period."

Meryl called and asked if I could come over. By this time, they'd sold the big white house—"the bad luck house," Vivian called it—and were moving around a fair bit. We stood in Meryl's bedroom in their latest apartment, near the library.

"Cathrin," she began. She was standing next to her bedside table, holding a book. "I have to tell you something. I can't go on the bike trip." Meryl handed me the book. "This will explain everything," she said.

"I don't want your fucking book," I shouted, and I threw it at her head, missing (I have terrible aim), before I stormed out the front door I had just come in through. I got as far as the library, lit up after closing like a 7-Eleven, where I cried in the shrubbery for some time. It was late, so no one was going to catch me bellowing in the bushes; I must have calculated that much. I made my way home to my parents, but not back to my friendship with Meryl, and so our first silence began. I've often wished since that I'd taken that book. It really would have explained a lot.

———

And here I must interject.

Up until now, Meryl's story and mine, the one we put together over our hours-long phone calls, merged neatly enough. True, when I said I'd seen Clay as a hail-fellow-well-met kind of dad, Meryl was astonished. "Seriously, Cathrin? That's all you saw? I mean, he was that too. He could be. It's what he would have wanted you to see." But mostly, Meryl would remember one thing, I would remember another, and we would build the story together. Not this time, though, with the scene in her bedroom the night before our bike trip.

"What book?" Meryl said blandly.

"What are you talking about, *what book*, Meryl?" My fury was instantaneous.

"I have no memory of a book," Meryl said again.

"I've regretted not taking that book from you my whole life," I said. "*My whole life.*" I was not without drama myself.

"It was likely just something at hand. I needed something to calm you down," Meryl said. She muffled the receiver and spoke to her husband. She put me on hold, for Christ's sake. "John is baffled that any two people could talk for so long," she said. "I do remember it was an explosive exchange," Meryl said. "There was nothing I could say to make you forgive me. But as much as I loved planning that trip, I never got it in my head that it would happen." She paused. "My parents cancelled things all the time. I guess I thought it was okay to do that."

I wasn't saying a lot on my end of the line.

"I'm sorry, Cathrin," Meryl said after a while. "I'm sorry I didn't go on the bike trip."

We ended the call soon after that. I wandered around Number 9, tidying and thinking about how Meryl had stood up to the full force that must have been me at sixteen, bulldozing through her fear with my plan to break free. The tugboat, the bulldozer. I saw a pattern emerge, and not a welcome one. I thought about the strength it took for Meryl to recognize that she didn't have that trip in her. Not a lot of people would know that about themselves at fifteen. Most of us go along, whether it's good for us or bad. "She really was the brave one," I said out loud. "I was right about that." It wasn't much to be proud of.

"I'm sorry too, Meryl," I said to her the next morning. It was the last of our series of phone calls. "I'm sorry I didn't know what was going on with you." I could feel Meryl nodding at the other end of the line.

"I remember it was a big shift in our friendship," she said.

I didn't ask whether Meryl meant my missing her struggle with her father or her missing the bike trip, because it was both. The cancelled trip was the disappointment of my youth, and I'd held on to it for a long time. I was less familiar with the idea that I'd let her down to the point where she'd opened that medicine cabinet.

"I've been trying to remember that book. I think it was red," said Meryl. "Do you remember red?"

"Maybe," I said. A small redness began to take form in my head. "I think I wondered if what was in the book was that Clay hit you, or worse." It wasn't exactly a question.

"I think it was a library book, maybe about friendship," Meryl said, before she answered my real question. "No. It was Ken who bore the brunt with my dad. And my mom."

There was a lot of activity after the cancelled bike trip. Meryl almost immediately moved up north again, this time for two and a half years. Vivian finally left Clay. Everyone was on the move but me, and I was the only one who wanted to be. On my third day of crying, Mom took me to Mass, where she hoped I'd pull myself together, but I bawled all through the Apostles' Creed.

"It was really bad," said Laura recently, recalling that period. "Something had to be done." She came back to Grimsby from her home in Toronto and offered to bike to Montreal with me. "Yes!" I shouted, without pausing to think that Laura didn't own a bike, that she didn't like riding a bike, and that she would have to leave her husband and job behind to do this extraordinary thing for me.

"If I hadn't done that, I don't think you would have survived, really," Laura said of her unexpected trip with me forty-five years ago. We were talking in her living room in Toronto, sitting on her sleek sectional sofa. Buddy, her fluffy white dog, sat beside me, ears up.

"Why was it so important?" I asked her. Laura and I hadn't talked much about this bike trip either, and I wanted her help to piece it together.

"There was no stopping you," Laura said. "You were ready to go, and I understood that because I'd left home too, and I knew how much it mattered." She took a sip of her Prosecco, chosen to go with the mild cheeses she'd laid out. Buddy yawned extravagantly. "But you know, the bike trip fixed all that; it did the trick. We did meet great Canadians, and it did make me realize there are great stories out there, like you said in your grant application.

"You and Meryl, you both knew what you needed," Laura said. "They just weren't the same thing."

Meryl and her family did their own intervention with Clay, and unlike ours with David, it took. At fifty-two, Clay joined AA. He got a job at the detox centre of Hotel Dieu Hospital in St. Catharines and worked there until he retired. He tried to help my brother David, too, visiting him in his kitchen to convince him to come over to the sober side. David was a fail, but Clay found his way back to himself and his family, if not to Vivian's forgiveness.

"Suddenly he's the hero?" Vivian said to me once, sitting at her dining room table in their new apartment in Beamsville, her anger on full boil. She never lost her fury toward her husband, even after he'd been sober for twenty-seven years. But she couldn't deny him either.

"Vivian was for the underdog," Meryl said. "She had the ability to see the good in a person. She saw he was worth fighting for. And he was, in the end."

Meryl made her peace, not just with her sober father but with her drunk one too. "It wasn't like he wasn't a good person when he drank. He was another person." I was still making my own peace with Clay for the way he'd terrified my friend when she was a vulnerable girl. I liked the clarity my anger gave me, but Meryl was more familiar with forgiveness.

"You meant a lot to Clay, you know," she said. "Our friendship meant a lot to him. In the years we didn't talk, he never stopped asking me about you." Meryl laughed. "'How's Cathrin?' he'd say, over and over. 'Have you called her yet?' It drove me crazy."

I thought about my brother David, and how a person could transform. And about the string that tied not only me, Meryl, Mom, and Vivian, but also David and Clay, when we were young and again now. I'd read another quote from Alice Munro at that Alex Colville show in Ottawa: "Something happened here. In your life there are a few places, or maybe only one place, where something happened. And then there are the other places, which are just other places." I thought about how Grimsby had been like this for us, a place where something happened. And about how understanding what went on there might help us understand what went on everywhere.

Meryl and I revisited Grimsby recently. It was nothing like trip one of the unification. We'd parsed the mystery of our youth, so that was behind us, thank God. It's great to have a mystery late in life, and even better when it's solved. We'd got to know each other again, how we were the same and also different. Meryl had the perfect degree of bossiness, not unlike me. We made a detailed list of our weekend plans and crossed things off one by one, to our mutual and vast satisfaction. We changed several times a day, without embarrassment, discussing and comparing outfits. We both sneezed terrifyingly loudly. I thought she'd fallen down the stairs when she bellowed "A-CHOOOO!" and have since modified my own sneeze. She talked to everyone, at exasperating length. I know the life story of most of the sales clerks in Grimsby thanks to Meryl. She reminded me of what E.M. Forster said about the kind of aristocracy he believed in, not of power but of "the considerate and the plucky. Its members are . . . sensitive for others as well as themselves, they are considerate without being fussy." And we gave each other energy, still. I was beginning to ask myself if that energy needed to be directed solely toward the future, as Aunt Helen had believed, or if going back has its own value. Maybe figuring out the me I'd been with Meryl really could help me sort out my current self. It was a work in progress.

"I didn't want my mom to die," said Meryl.

We'd rented a small wooden house that backed onto the escarpment, and the bare grey trees outside the window felt like our ghosts, staying near, watching over us. We lounged on the roomy living room couch, which faced a groovy gas fireplace with a remote control that we constantly adjusted. I liked the flames big.

"I didn't want my mom to die either," I said.

"I held on to a scrap of paper she'd written on." Meryl shook her head and the gaslight ran along the tips of her brown hair, like tiny fireworks. "My girls were going to do an intervention, it got so bad."

"I kept a bit of chain from Mom's bedside drawer." (Never mind that urn thing.) I sat up on the couch to dangle an imaginary chain at Meryl, who looked at it with interest. "I thought maybe it was one of those hopscotch chains, from when she was young."

"Don't you think sometimes that my life was your mother's life, and your life was my mother's life? I think about that sometimes," Meryl said. "My house even looks like your mom's house. You had the wonderful care in your home. The wonderful ease."

Meryl described how her husband had been a gift, coming into her life when she was barely twenty, like Dad had with Mom. "We collided with each other. There was never a question that this was it. He devoted himself to me and the girls. Not through words but through devotion." I could see that Meryl's children had been raised with calm and ease by their parents, never moving from the house they were born to. And that my kids had not, or at least not toward the end of my marriage, when we were a long way from a happy home. "Dinner was the worst," said Kelly recently of the tension between John and me, reminding me of what Meryl had said about her house growing up. Work saved me, as it had Vivian, but maybe not my children, or not as much. Would any of us have been better without the lives we had? I wasn't sure, and neither was Meryl.

"Sometimes I think if we had gone on our bike trip, and come back and got lives in Grimsby, never left, I think, Would we still have the same friendship we have now?" Meryl said. "I'm not so sure."

I thought about Meryl's question, and the long and sometimes furious silences between the two of us, as I rooted in the kitchen for something to eat. It was 2 a.m. and we'd worked up an appetite talking on the couch.

"I think being apart was what kept us together," I said as I laid out salted peanuts, pistachios, olives, gouda cheese, and crackers. We ate, not saying much, until Meryl told me about a morning with Vivian, before she'd had her stroke.

"She was reading the obituaries at the kitchen table when she started to cry, hard," said Meryl.

Vivian didn't cry, not even when life was lowest. Meryl was alarmed.

"'What's wrong, Mom?' I asked her.

"'That woman died,' my mom said.

"'What woman?'"

It turned out Vivian did talk, once, about the night Meryl took the pills, to the stranger who had sat beside her in the hospital waiting room, holding her hand.

"'The woman who was so kind to me at the hospital, that awful night.'" Meryl laughed, telling me this in front of the gas fire. "'That awful night,' that's what she called it."

The woman had stayed beside Vivian in the waiting room the whole time, and Vivian had told her what happened to her daughter. "Your daughter will be all right," the kind woman said. "The apple doesn't fall far from the tree."

"Nice," I said. My eyes started to close, and it was hard to keep them open as I rested my head against the arm of the sofa.

"Do you think we'll stop talking again?" Meryl asked after a while. I was surprised awake by the question, because if history was our guide, well.

"No," I said firmly.

"No." Meryl said. "I don't think so, anyway."

13

Keds

IN THE YEAR WHEN Promising New Man decamped, when half the furniture was hauled out of Number 9 and my bank account was cut in two, when Mom died and absence heaped on absence left me with too much time to think about my stupidity in my best friend's near death, I won't say the lowest point was not being able to buy a new pair of white Keds. But it was. Not having new Keds to replace the pair with the loonie-sized splotch on top of the right shoe, a bit of the previous summer's spilled coffee, took me down to the futility of everything.

Every year in June, I'd head out to buy a few new pairs to get me through the summer. I liked my Keds spanking white, whiter than the sunlit clouds in the cramped urban sky outside my kitchen window. It was fully, extravagantly spring. The trees heaved with blossoms, and my backyard feeder was at maximum bird capacity. The sparrows and chickadees were rapacious as hell with those seeds; it was like watching *Macbeth* play out on the ledge of my backyard feeder. Or like me at a sample sale. My unseemly avarice was one of the reasons I was in this bind with my stained Keds. Because in this year of many confusing changes, I'd also given up shopping, a decision that felt mildly mysterious to me, six months into 2015. It might have had to do with how much had given me up, and how little say I seemed to have. Quitting shopping was a way for me to leave something instead of it leaving me. Also, I was saving money with the one hand so I could give it to my giant mortgage with the other. I'd stuck with it too. Resolve, I was good at. Half the year was over, and I hadn't bought a single item. Until these Keds.

As I watched the chickadees struggle for their place at the feeder, a hum started in my chest, a tiny bird need that took hold and would not let go. It was like wanting a cigarette long after you'd quit the habit. Surely my moral rectitude did not depend on one pair of forty-dollar shoes. No one would be the wiser either. I could get away with it, easy-peasy. If I wanted to buy a new pair of Keds, I could buy a new pair of Keds. If I wanted to buy a new pair of Keds, I *would* buy a new pair of Keds, dammit. The sudden decision gave me fresh energy and purpose. I put on my helmet, got on my bike, and headed east, for the siren call of the Bloor Street stores.

There's a lot to be said for, and there is a lot that has been said about, not shopping. There's the unseemly greed, as mentioned. The social approval to be gained by reducing the toppling piles of landfill made up of my five black coats of varying lengths. The utter lack of need to buy anything new, ever again, when so much already exists, and when so much else matters, so much more. A full-on material life keeps a lot at bay, too, so quitting opens a space for valuable self-reflection. If only I had a knack for that.

I'm not sure when shopping began to feel dodgy. At a certain point, I'd get lost and panicky wandering the racks, and if I spent too long undecided about this or that top, I could become uncertain about much more than the clothes. Something would start to tug at me, like the shark in the opening scene of *Jaws*, when he takes his first nibble of the swimmer. A four-foot-square dressing room was not where you wanted to be yanked to the dark depths. Was I shopping to escape dread and death and pointlessness? Obviously. Who wasn't. But the ping-ponging back and forth between satisfaction and guilt was getting more exhausting. It was distracting me from one of the things I loved best about shopping, in fact, which was not to think about why I was shopping.

Even my ample walk-in closet had become more of an affront than a pleasure. I'd spent many happy hours in that closet, putting everything in its place, first by category (pants, skirts, jackets) and then by the more visually satisfying subcategory of colour. A work colleague asked me if I had a lime-green section in my closet. "I do," I said. Also, "closet," singular, is not quite right. If I was honest with myself, as Kelly forced me to be one day by sternly counting them aloud, my closets had been propagating like spider plants from cuttings. I was up to four if I added my seasonal storage closet (otherwise known as Kelly's closet) and my coat and sports closets, which I preferred not to do. On the continuum of "It's so pretty!" versus planet-destroying greed, I was on the wrong end.

My decision to quit shopping was not met with widespread approval. This surprised me. Some people got hostile. "Just buy a pair of underwear, for Christ's sake." (I may have been complaining.) My sisters were unimpressed. Far from lauding me, Ann told me I was out of step. When I'd admired a woman's expensive and understated ensemble in shades of slate blue and tan, she said, "Nothing about that appeals to me. Why would you want to identify as the one percent, Cathrin?" Ann had stopped "participating in fast fashion, except in a second-hand sense," and had recently bought a dress for a party at Value Village for eleven dollars. "I wore it with velvet-lined leggings and my Doc Martens, and it felt perfect for the occasion."

Laura, on the other hand, objected to my Lenten habit of self-denial. "Why go to these extremes, Cathrin?" It was true I liked to test my resolve around just about anything. A couple of years earlier, I'd vowed to eat food made only with love. More recently, I went vegan. I am no longer vegan. About shopping, Laura said, "Buy what you need and don't buy what you don't need." She was not alone in her inability to grasp that shopping for clothes had nothing to do with need. That it wasn't going to the podiatrist to be measured for a set of orthotics.

"Wait a minute. Are you saying you shop and you don't have any idea what you're going to buy?" This was my friend David, a couple of months into my shopping fast. I was at the fishing cabin, that weekend of my sixtieth birthday, putting away groceries in the big country kitchen, and the news of this fast was going down like a lead balloon.

"Correct," I said, puzzled by the question. "Do you mean you don't like to shop and shop for hours and hours and talk and talk about tops and pants and sweaters?"

"No."

"So are you saying you shop only for something you need—some striped French scarf—and it has nothing to do with an unspecified longing to fill the gaping maw of existence?"

"Yes," said David.

"What about underwear?" asked his wife, holding aloft a package of spaghetti as she eyed me up and down.

"No."

"Earrings?"

"Ixnay."

"Hats?" Janice was thorough.

"No hats of any sort."

To understand how hard it was for me to give up shopping, let me explain how much I love it: so, so much. I often remembered an event best by what I had on. This past New Year's Eve, for example, at the annual dress-up party—the same party I went to alone after PNM cancelled, and also the same party where I decided to give up shopping for clothes for the year (the two were perhaps connected)—I was wearing a reimagining of the classic kilt. It was in a silk Douglas plaid with a side swath of small polka dots, plus front pleats stiffened with narrow plackets of shiny black backing material. The fine details of the skirt, perhaps a secret only to me, gave me confidence. And the kilt itself—well made and understated, a man-skirt with a Celtic kick—suited me. True, it had cost more than Ann's eleven-dollar dress, but it also felt just right for the occasion.

My love of shopping was written in the stars, even. When Georgia Nichols, the horoscope woman, told me that my Venus in Capricorn was not great news in the love department, she added that it was excellent news in the clothing department.

"You'll always feel confident in great shoes and a good suit." This was true, and the fact that she said it over the phone, without physical evidence, added mightily to my faith in her clairvoyant powers. I liked my open-ended shopping sprees. I'd roam the racks, alive to possibility. Crimson pants were not something I needed, but trying them on created a world there in the dressing room. I imagined the unexpected relationship the crimson pants might have with the high-backed Alexander Wang shoes at home in my closet. I imagined walking into a Christmas party wearing the lively combination of the elegant cream shoes with black piping and the daring crimson pants. I'd be holding a Manhattan as I tried to look unsurprised by the electrifying effect these pants had on the assembled guests. "Sensational!" "Bold yet chic!" And then—voila—I was bold and chic, even if I sometimes felt otherwise.

When I shopped with Mary, she found the thing she wanted, bought it, and hugged me goodbye. It was about a small necessity, and it was all wrapped up in an hour, but for me this robbed shopping for clothes of its complexity. It wasn't a mindless pleasure, or didn't have to be. New clothes were rarely as simple as choosing them. You had to wear them too. Then they posed questions that demanded answering, not only about who you were but also about who you wanted to be. If you weren't comfortable with the answers to those questions—and who is?—you'd better brace yourself for the wobbly uncertainty that comes next. Kennedy Fraser's *The Fashionable Mind*, a sharp, intellectual collection of essays from forty years ago that still holds up today, had this to say about the mind and fashion: "The dimension in which fashion operates is an amalgam of the mental and the material—a miasmic half-world where ideas have functions and prices, while objects are hung about with thoughts and dreams." It's the thoughts and dreams you try to see when you shop, not the image in the mirror, although you do stare at yourself at least half of the time. It's a supremely egotistical pastime.

My most reliable shopping companions were not shy around a mirror. Once the kids were grown, I'd call Ellen up the street on a Sunday morning, sun shining merrily, and say, "Let's go shopping," and she'd be at my door in five minutes. Ellen is a glamorous five foot eight and smooth from top to bottom, like a model. I'm five foot two and my figure has been described as parabolic, but we shared a taste for well-made tailored clothes, a hangover from our days of Catholic school uniforms. Those nuns, who taught us never to covet that which we did not have, were with us as we spent money with quite a lot of ease and a complete lack of judgment. I'm not saying we felt morally justified, but we weren't doing heroin. We embraced the unselfconscious vs. ego-enhancing yin-yang of shopping. It gave us something existential to think about while we tried on white jeans in the Bahama-beach-at-sunset store lighting. "Oddly slimming!" And they were, until we stepped outside into the pitiless Canadian light.

When the kids were younger, my friend and work colleague Johanna and I took a trip to New York for Mother's Day, with shopping an important feature of the weekend. We understood that we deserved this as hard-working mothers holding down two jobs, running a magazine on the one hand and our homes and kids on the other. We were well matched in energy and agreed on the essential rules of shopping: Dress sensibly. Be systematic. And no breaks. (Mom used to bribe us with sweets to squeeze another hour of shopping out of us when we were little. Ann threw up in the aisles of a department store after scarfing an entire bag of snowballs—chocolate rolled in coconut with a soft minty filling. "It was spectacular," said Ann.)

Johanna and I didn't get lost in each other's taste either: the dreaded style drift. You'd do the rounds with someone you admired, who looked dazzling in flowing, unstructured dresses, and the next thing you knew, you'd be wafting through a party in an orange pup tent. In New York, we made a beeline for Loehmann's, the sprawling discount department store on 7th Avenue, for the deeply marked-down designer labels in the Back Room. As good as the deals was the communal, multi-mirrored dressing room, where everybody changed in the open, and all the conversations happened between your reflected selves, which made them more open too. When a nest of nuns in navy looking for dresses to wear to a wedding slipped off their modest habits to reveal *a lot* of undergarments, one of them spoke to Johanna's reflection as she spun around to check out her ass in a black-and-tan mesh gown, a dress that was the antipodal opposite of nun garb. "It's pretty on you," said the nun to the mirror. "I like the straps." Next to the nuns, an Upper West Side woman in a thong with a lot of opinions looked mirror-me up and down in my snug and satisfyingly discounted Calvin Klein Couture knit navy evening dress. "You'd be crazy not to buy it, honey." Johanna and I bought both those dresses that day. They embodied the life we wanted, if not the one we had. A life we could at least imagine we were living when we wore them.

As a seasoned shopper, Johanna knew that need was not only secondary but anxious-making. "Say I need black pants. Suddenly, the world is either empty of black pants or astoundingly full of black pants. How do I know these are the right black pants?" Instead, she searched for a deeply discounted item that made her feel like she was getting away with something. "But mainly the magic purchase is finding a thing that makes me look the way I want to look."

I was a steady gifter of my purchases, although not that evening dress I'd bought twenty years earlier, because you never know when you might need a skin-tight evening gown in your sixties. Like me, Ellen could give something away the same week she bought it. She had a fantasy to take all the items of clothing she had ever purchased and lay them out end to end.

"To think about what you should never have bought," I said, with my well-established self-denial sensibilities.

"To think about what I should have kept," Ellen said.

I locked my bike in front of Holt Renfrew, a fancy Canadian chain, and took the escalator to the less expensive third floor to look for my Keds. I knew they wouldn't have them there, but I wanted to check out the spring trends to better arrange my own closet. In the Theory section, with its muted and gently tailored clothes perfect for work, I was immediately greeted by Olia, a superb saleswoman with big curls and a confidence that made you trust her frank assessment of anything you tried on. Olia put her hands on her hips and looked me up and down.

"Where have you been? You missed the sales."

"Shopping fast," I said.

"What's that about?" she said, and I struggled to answer about greed and panic and introspection and sharks in dressing rooms, until my words dwindled away in the air.

"Wisdom," she said, as if she were pronouncing a jacket just the right fit. "It's about the wisdom of letting go." She looked at me, mildly suspicious. "What are you doing here if you can't shop?"

"I'm just looking," I said, fondling a pale blue summer cardigan with small tufts of silk sprouting from its sleeves like prairie grasses. A summer garden party came to mind. I'd be holding a gimlet. "So pretty!" someone would say. "Smart *and* subtle!" And as the cocktail murmur grew, I saw the ways I might be smart and subtle, both at once.

I went to Talbots next, because it was next door, and also to calm myself down. Talbots was the blandest of stores, the domestic cruise line of shopping. Everything was semi-affordable and everything was a variation on the same theme, racks of elastic-waist pants in every colour. Although the optimistic Easter-egg-yellow pants were fetching for summer. Not something I had done before, yellow; there wasn't a yellow section in my walk-in closet. But I was open to the experiment, or I would have been if I were actually shopping. I let myself lament the loss of that for a moment before I made my last stop of the afternoon. I walked into a well-appointed shoe store and was stopped in my tracks by a pair of gently flowered Keds on a pedestal, offering themselves to me, their tiny red, blue, and white flowers quietly beckoning. A perfect posy of a shoe.

"Would you like to try those on?" asked the saleswoman, coming over and smiling at me. I stared at her, startled. She'd called me over from far away. I was deep in those shoes and the possibilities they offered. I silently asked myself the same question the saleswoman had just posed. Would I like to try on those pretty Keds? Yes, more than anything, at that particular moment. I looked down at the stained and ugly pair on my feet and felt hopeless— and worse, shabby. I hit bottom for a moment, until, slowly as a Prius going uphill, a new thought made its way into my head. Maybe my experiment with not shopping had its own unexpected possibilities. Something more than shopping would change. An opening-up that was coming. It felt like a turning point, six months into the year, although I wasn't sure toward what.

The old Keds were good enough for now, I decided. They'd do while I considered other things. I looked at the saleswoman and shook my head no, and then walked out into the warm afternoon and rode my bike home, slowly and thoughtfully.

14.

Built to Work

THE ONE THING THAT DIDN'T let me down in the year when many other things did was work. Work was my vocation. It gave me purpose, it made sense to me, it bent to my will. In 2015, I had the best job I'd ever had, in fact. Men and wiring systems come and go, but work never disappointed. And I would say this even if I hadn't been fired five times. Wait, six.

On a windless September morning, I glided on my bike to the foot of the city, where the *Metro* news office looked out onto a strangely smooth Lake Ontario. Work was strangely smooth too, given what was going on everywhere else in the newspaper industry. I was editor-in-chief of a national chain of local dailies in a business where 50 percent of journalists had lost their jobs in the past ten years. "We all have PTSD," said one colleague, and it was true that as a tribe, we were jumpy as hell. But so far, at *Metro*, we were holding our heads above water. More than that, we were participating in a new idea of the news. It was the beginning of a massive shift in journalism, when its impartiality was being called into question and new and inspiring voices were coming forward. The *Metro* reporters weren't shy around a point of view; it was another necessary version of the story, and also, whose point of view had the news been reporting from for the past hundred years? Not theirs. A few months earlier, I might have been balkier about having the purpose of my life's calling challenged, but I was getting better at standing beside someone else's story, or getting out of the way of it altogether. The year was teaching me that. I wasn't handing over the keys to journalism. I didn't have the keys, and never had.

That fall morning, I locked my bike and bounded into the newsroom of sixty or so mostly millennial journalists, taking my seat in the news hub, a round circle in the middle of the room. It was here where we would decide what mattered most that day for our 1.5 million readers. I say "we" loosely, as every day began with valuable and necessary tutoring—of me, not my staff. "From my perspective," I began the morning meeting, recognizing my misstep as soon the words left my mouth. "You mean your white, gender-normative, privileged perspective, Cathrin?" interrupted one colleague, who also happened to be sitting in my boss seat with the view of the calm lake. Working with those journalists as they remade news for a new generation with the same commitment and energy they gave to the vast quantities of healthy food they consumed every day—a coffee area that used to have actual coffee instead housed personal blenders, glass canning jars, and nut milk bags—was the most thrilling job I've had. They gave *Metro* an optimistic, purposeful soul, reporting on the best versions of our cities. "Metro Ain't Having It" was one of their recurring story banners. It was their future to remake the news as they saw it—until, four years later, the *Metro* papers were shut down and almost everyone lost their jobs, me included. I was hoping it would be the last time I got fired. It certainly wasn't the first.

If you made a shoestring documentary of my life of work, it would look something like this: A kid is on a two-wheeled bike for the first time. She grips the handlebars like life itself, pedal, pedal, *CRASH!* Get up, pedal, pedal, ride, ride, *CRASH.* Get up, *CRASH.* Get up, knees bleeding, ride ride ride ride—she's going the distance! Look, no hands!—*CRASH.* Add in a couple of steep hills, three crazy descents, biting dogs, and a head wound, and it's the story of my forty-five-year career. I've seen thrilling heights and poke-pins-in-my-eyes daily drudgery. Most of what I understand about loyalty and some necessary self-regulation, I learned by going into an office and being around people every day. Work let me figure out what was important to me, about how I thought about things, what moved me, and what was worth fighting for, if not always what wasn't worth fighting for. I'm still getting the hang of when to stay silent (my current boss calls it CLC, or career-limiting candour, which she also suffers from). But for all the years I've worked in my life, I've never learned more about work than when I haven't had any, usually after being fired. *CRASH.* It's the pitiful sloughs, crying into my Cheerios in my pajamas in the middle of the day, that offered the moments of enlightenment I'm about to share. I call them Six Lessons of a Six-Times-Fired Working Woman. We'll begin with my most recent firing. It means jumping ahead in time a bit, to 2018 and the day I got fired from that *Metro* job I've just described.

I was called into my boss's bland pale brown office. It was 11 a.m. on a Thursday on November 15. Each of those details was important. I knew from my own history of doing the firing that any date closer to Christmas than mid-November was regarded as unseemly, that morning was preferred, and that Fridays and Mondays were verboten because they were too close to the weekend. I don't know why not Wednesday, but it was never on a Wednesday. There's a rule book somewhere. My brilliant capacity for denial made me miss the sledgehammer clues of month, day of week, and time of day as I sat between the head of human resources (clue!) and my boss, looking woeful (clue!).

"Hey, guys, how are you doing?" I liked these men; they seemed to have held on to a ribbon of their humanity as their main job became to kill papers and fire people. Although my guys, we'll call them Thompson and Thomson, didn't use words like "fire." R.W. Holder's *Dictionary of Euphemisms* (later renamed *How Not to Say What You Mean*) holds up thirty years later as a funny and astute guide to the language of "evasion, hypocrisy, prudery and deceit." Let go, laid off, made redundant, discontinued, relieved of duties, released, downsized, lateralized, streamlined, managed out, dismissed, negotiated departure. This firing of mine was part of a "restructuring measure to improve overall efficiencies and help fund our transformation." There was a large envelope on the table. There always was. "It's nothing personal." This was Thomson, who reminded me of Hilary Mantel's Cromwell: someone who was interesting to know even as he chopped your head off. It felt pretty personal to me as my head bounced off the round table. "So you're firing me?"

A brief period of buoyancy generally followed a firing. The worst had happened, the slog of work—there was a mountain of it right before you were axed—had finally ended. The possibility for something new, or blessedly, for nothing new, opened up just ahead. Also, I had the satisfaction of being right. "I told you I was going to get fired," I said to the various people I called to share the news with. My friends had thought I was paranoid. *Well, yeah.* It takes only one firing for you to understand that there is no such a thing as terra firma in the world of work.

That night, Mary had invited Ellen and me to see how she'd decked out her new midtown apartment. As I walked to the subway, my firing envelope in the small olive-green knapsack on my back, a guy on a guitar sang Cat Stevens's "Wild World." His voice echoed achingly down the long tunnel, singing about the damage the world can do, breaking your heart in two. The world was mean, and my heart was broken. I bent down and dropped a toonie into the singer's black guitar case, and we nodded meaningfully to each other as he continued in his ringing alto about all the bad people out there. *Be-wa-are.*

I should mention here that being fired also makes you sad. Hopeless, even. In the lobby of Mary's building, I said to Ellen, "Don't tell her. I don't want to ruin her evening." "I've been fired, Mary," I blurted moments after we walked through her door. Two bottles of wine and a single toke from a joint that had the strength of fifty horses later, Ellen and I stood on Mary's eleventh-floor balcony, crooning Cat Stevens's lyrics into our salt-and-pepper-shaker microphones while Mary took pictures of herself wearing a wreath of twigs, which she had made on a recent visit to the country. *I love you mom*, she wrote under the picture of herself on Instagram.

"Mom," said Mary firmly when we collapsed on her couch after several rousing rounds.

"Cat Stevens is one of the *truly greats*." I slowly looked at my daughter and tried to sound formal before I spoke again. "Is there something you would like to say to me, Mary?"

"Yes, there is." She sat on her sole chair. It was a bachelor apartment, so there was a couch, a chair, a bed, and a small kitchen table all within close proximity, but so deftly laid out it felt like the one room contained at least the idea of a bedroom, a kitchen, and a living room. Mary looked at me with something between worry and disappointment. "Why do you get fired all the time?"

"I do *not* get fired all the time." Mary's couch was so comfortable, I thought of stretching out and falling asleep, possibly forever. "This is a shameful fallacy perpetrated by my enemies. Just this one time, and the one time before that." I stared at her, ready.

"Didn't the time before fire you twice, though?"

"Well, yes, that is correct. There was a downscaling. I was rightsized." Ellen and I cackled.

"And there was that job at the magazine. Your first job?"

"Uh, yeah. I forgot about that." I had too. Why did I tell my daughter these things from my distant past? To shore her up, maybe. There was no time more terrifying than your twenties, when everyone seemed to be speeding ahead of you and life felt full of failure. I wanted her to know from the vantage of my later success at work that my own twenties had been a rout. I'd spent half of them living on peanut butter and lying in bed staring at the ceiling.

"And then you got fired from the next job after that," Mary continued. "With those cult people."

"Sufis," I said. "Not a cult. Mystic Muslims. Muslim mystics." It was hard to say. "True, true." I'd forgotten about that one too, and over the next few days, I began to see that being fired was a deeper pattern in my life than I had realized.

I called Meryl because she was my very first workmate, back in Grimsby. "I can't believe I've been fired five times," I said, recounting them.

"Six," said Meryl. "Don't forget the egg-grading factory."

My first job, the one that had propelled me to move up to egg grading, was picking cherries at one of the lush fruit farms that stretched between the escarpment and Lake Ontario in Grimsby. Meryl was twelve and I was thirteen, and we stood on our wooden ladders, six-quart baskets hooked to thick leather belts around our waists, and picked the trees clean of their fat clusters of red cherries, twisting them from the end of the stem as we'd been taught. We were paid seventy-five cents a basket, which at our pace meant we'd made three bucks at the end of the day.

"You needed more cherries in that one," said the farmer, who wanted the baskets overflowing.

"Full is to the top, so it's full," I protested, and was docked ten cents. After a few days of this, I said to Meryl, "What we need is a factory job."

The local boys had jobs at E.D. Smith, where the fruit was turned into jams and jellies, and they were paid by the hour. E.D. Smith wouldn't hire us at our age—or more likely because we were girls, a theme to be continued—but we got taken on by the Grimsby egg-grading factory instead. Why Dad happily left us at that factory when we were so young, smiling proudly from his brown Chevy as he waved and drove away, I do not know.

Inside the massive shed, our new boss explained the huge, noisy roller coaster of an assembly line that was right out of a Dr. Seuss village. There was the egg-washing station; the egg-grading station, where you studied the eggs under ultraviolet light and discarded those that had blood or tiny chick fetuses; egg size sorting; and egg cartoning, in that order. The most important part of this three-minute safety lesson was the large RED BUTTON, which was to be pressed only in case of emergency. I took my place at the egg-washing station, where it was important to place the cartons on the correct groove so the eggs wouldn't be smashed by the washing brushes. "Cathrin!" Meryl pointed up the line after I'd loaded my cartons for a bit; my eggs lay there in a crushed, slimy heap. I ran and pushed the large RED BUTTON, and the assembly line came to a creaking halt. It was a satisfying amount of power. Day two, Meryl's yellow work smock got caught in the assembly line as she stared at the eggs under the ultraviolet light, lost in thought. She liked that post on the line because it was warm, but I hated seeing those dead chicks. "Help, Cathrin! Help!!" I looked over from my station to see Meryl running along the line, her smock jammed in the spinning wheels of the conveyor belt. "Take your lab coat off," I shouted. "Help me! Save me!" shouted Meryl, in a real panic. So I pushed the large RED BUTTON, and the line stopped again. It was terrific. The third day we decided to ask for a raise, and also when we got our paid holidays. I was hoping it would be very soon. It was hard work on the line. "We would like two weeks," I said. "You're fired!" the boss shouted. "And don't come back!" he added to our rapidly retreating backs as we walked out into the bright sunshine of the day. We did get a very tiny paycheque at some later date for our three days' work. Meryl and I had steady chores at home, for which we were not paid, and the egg-grading factory was where I learned the first essential lesson of a working life, the defining purpose of labour, even: it is better to be paid for work than to do it for free.

The second job I got fired from was where I learned the second most important lesson of a working life: you need to show up. I was hired right out of university as an editorial assistant for *Gifts & Tablewares* magazine. One problem was that the concept of *Gifts & Tablewares* was elusive. Another was that this job was a very long way to get to by subway and bus, so I was often late, and this lateness became so embarrassing that I soon concocted stories about why I couldn't show up at all. Laura called me at work one day to be told I was not there because my grandmother had just died. "Oh no!" she said, before she remembered both our grandmothers had died years earlier. A month or so later, my boss, a tall man with a long hank of black hair that he kept pushing out of his eyes, called me into his office from the sickroom, where I'd been lolling on the slender cot, reading. "You're fired," he said sadly. I felt bad for him. He was a kind man. And note the use of the word "fired." Those were clearer times.

I'll just mention the third firing, and the not one but two lessons it taught me, before we move on to better times. It was the next job I got, as a copywriter for a public relations firm located in a vertiginous office tower, and it had the benefit of being near where I lived. The men at this firm had large windowed offices overlooking the city; the women sat either outside those offices or, like me, in small windowless rooms at the end of a long corridor. I've never worked with a man who abused me physically or sexually. The abuse was of money and power. Men in the bigger office. Men calling the shots, running the show, pulling the strings, getting the top job *every single time*, until at last, after forty years of work, I was put in charge of the *Metro* newspapers—another reason why that job was glorious. Of course, the male editor of the bigger, more important parent paper, on a higher floor in the same building, was paid twice as much. The white guy sitting next to me, doing the same job, made about $400,000 more than me over the long span of our careers, if you added it up, which plenty of pay equity studies had done. It wasn't only gender; discrimination based on race or disability was worse. It hasn't changed, or not nearly as much as it should.

The problem with that copywriting job, aside from the in-my-face sexism, was that I couldn't sort out what public relations was. People thought one way about a pen, say, and I was meant to make them think a new and exciting way about the pen, to tell its story so winningly that journalists would run it on the front page of their newspapers. Actually, as I write this, it sounds like the way we live now, when everyone is a brand worth publicizing, not just a pen. I couldn't think of anything to say about the pen except that it wrote and was slender to hold, which was when one of the men in the big offices said, "You're fired." I was indignant. "I have more talent in my baby finger than you will have in your whole life," I said, one of the least evidence-based statements I've ever made. Still, the public relations job did teach me my third valuable lesson as a lifelong woman of work.

To review the first three of Six Lessons of a Six-Times-Fired Working Woman:

1. Make money.
2. Show up.
3. Have a nominal level of competence in the job you choose or the career you think you want.

Another refrain that ran through my early work life like a second theme in a concerto was me getting in the face of the men I worked for, starting with that farmer I argued with over how full my cherry basket was (who, by the way, paid the boys five cents more for their baskets). I'm not going to add "Don't argue with your boss" to my list of things I've learned about work. Or maybe I will.

4. Argue more.

I wish I'd fought harder, and for more important things, like fairness and respect in pay and position and title for everyone at work, in every job I've had, instead of worrying over whether I was good at writing about a pen.

I have no secret but hard work . . . Labour is the genius that changes the world from ugliness to beauty, and the great curse to a great blessing.

—J.M.W. TURNER, circa 1800

One of the fallacies I've heard throughout my working life is that no one ever wished on their deathbed that they'd worked more. No one ever said, "I wish I'd worked harder." But at two of the deathbeds I attended, both men spoke proudly of their work. It was among the last things they said. "Work hard, try hard, do your best," said my uncle Jack to Kelly. "Find work you love, and someone you love to work for, and work your heart out for them," said Dad, also to Kelly, three days before he died. I forgave those men for not telling my daughter to work hard. It didn't occur to them. They were the last of the unquestioning patriarchy; they'd done their duty by their families and society as tax-paying workers for fifty years without pause. And they were on their way out.

"'I wish I'd chilled more.' Who's going to say that on their deathbed?" This was my work colleague Jason, who'd just been fired himself. Jason and I were having a drink at the plushly cushioned bar of the King Edward Hotel in downtown Toronto. He'd ordered a rare beer because being fired is no picnic. A few months earlier, Jason had been pulled out of his role as the talented creative director of *Metro* and put into a job that involved idea sprints and imagination boards, supposedly to find a solution for dying media. "We began each day standing in a circle to say what we had accomplished the day before, what we would accomplish that day, and what we would accomplish the next day," Jason said, leaning back in his chair and grinning at me across the wooden bar table. He is what you would describe as ridiculously handsome. "The problem was, I could never remember what I had done the day before."

"Oh, my God, I love it." Dianne, another work friend, arrived and was already laughing as she shook off her coat. We'd taken to rallying for a drink whenever one of us got fired. It happened more often than we might have liked, and when we got together, we gave each other fast entry to a whole world, our world of work.

"'What are your blockers?' people would ask me, as if I knew," Jason continued.

Dianne clapped her hands with glee. "Blockers! It doesn't get any better than that." Dianne had small, pretty features, a chic bob, and a laugh that could only be described as joyous. She was still an employed journalist, in between her own firings.

Jason, Dianne, and I had been work friends for many years, over many criss-crossing jobs that brought us together and then sent us apart, sometimes to flourish, sometimes to be fired, often both. We didn't have dinner parties or travel together or call each other every day. We didn't kiss or hug when we met. We rarely talked about personal things like kids or marriage or private sufferings. It was our particular talents and obsessions that gave us commonality.

"I was speaking English, and everyone else was speaking Agile Methodology Language." Jason's long hands were covered in ink. "Optimize the iterative feedback of beta-testing velocity spike board domain timebox!" Jason said each word perkily, as if together they formed a winning sentence, then leaned back and sighed loudly. "I was the fish out of water, that's for sure."

I told Dianne about my deathbed theory, how people spoke of work in their final hours the way you might remember a dear and meaningful lifelong lover. She became serious.

"If it hadn't been for working, I don't know how I could have lived," she said, putting down her wine. "Work changed every-thing. Finding the right job and the right people, it was bigger than marriage." Dianne's voice and colour rose slightly as she spoke. "They knew me in a way that my husband and my parents and my kids did not." She looked from me to Jason. "You get into the work you do by accident and find it was there waiting for you. It was pure happiness."

"Work friends unlock a part of yourself that's realized only when you're with them," said Jason. "We share a collective work-brain palace, like a disco ball shedding light in every direction." He held his hands in the air, and we all looked up at his imaginary disco ball. "The way we agreed and understood what was important."

"The look across the table in a meeting." Dianne wrinkled her nose to demonstrate meeting-face. "The raised eyebrow. We knew exactly who we were together."

We all thought about this for a few moments. "It's not the way it's supposed to be, is it?" I was thinking about my own divorce, and how my most painful firing (coming up) was as deep a blow as the loss of my marriage. And why wouldn't it be? Humans spend about a third of their lives working, around twenty-five years, if you strung one working life from end to end like a clothesline. "I think labour creates its own meaning," I said, waxing. We'd all ordered another drink, even Jason, which was unprecedented. "The sacred power of work that Karl Marx described." I thought about my egg grading and pen pushing. "Not what you did. More the simple fact that you worked."

"We're built to work," Jason said simply.

I began a story about a picture book that my aunt Mary, a lifelong working woman, gave me when I was a small child. This was a random tangent I was introducing; I had a gift for the non sequitur when drinking. "It was called *Katie and the Sad Noise*."

Jason and Dianne listened politely, waiting to see where this was going. "Katie heard a sad noise no one else could hear, and so she packed a lunch, a detail I found fascinating, and set out one night with a flashlight to find the source of the noise. Her father went with her, but it was her agency to find this sad noise. I read that story over and over and over." I stopped there. I had no idea where I was going with this, but my work pals would not let me dangle.

"This Katie had a lot going for her," said Jason.

"It's the story of female corporate success," said Dianne, and we all nodded sagely.

I didn't only get fired. I had female corporate success too. After the rocky start in my early twenties, I began to take my career seriously and prepared for weeks to land a good job at a new fashion magazine. That job began a twenty-year stretch that took my career to the top of the hill.

Domino was one of a raft of new magazines the *Globe and Mail* started in the can't-spend-enough late 1980s, when one advertising executive said he'd drive around town with his car window open and let people throw money at him. *Domino* was run by a woman named Ray, my first female boss. She wore bright red lipstick, oversized black sunglasses, and a very tight bun, which loosened strand by strand throughout her sexually liberating divorce, until her hair was a wild mane of bouncing curls down her back. Her diet remained strict, however: cigarettes, black coffee, and rare steak. She also had a strict no-colour rule. Her Fiat Spider convertible was beige. Her two Doberman pinschers, who were as frightened of her as the rest of us, were black and beige. Her impressive closet of large-shouldered Armani suits, beige, beige, beige. The new red dress I wore the day she hired me would have immediately disqualified me if I hadn't spent two weeks preparing for the interview. A week later, I started my first day as managing editor of the brand-new fashion magazine. It was a terrific stint. Ray would send four of us at a time to Milan or New York or Paris, not to cover the fashion shows but to soak up their world, wobbling through the streets on our high heels, talking about how wobbly our high heels were. "I hate it," Ray would say of just about anything we showed her—any story or photo shoot we'd laboured over— and then we'd go back and make it better. Her standards were high but not unattainable.

The publisher who built the magazine division and then watched it flame out five years later was a tightly wound Irishman with a volcanic tick on his right cheek and a serious motorcycle in the parking lot. When ads began to decline, I protested some ugly shape for the way it disrupted the flow of words. "Bradbury," Ed the publisher began quietly, his twitch a warning, "if some-one wants to run an ad in the shape of a snake on every goddamn page, that's what we're going to do." It was the beginning of the end of big-spend media advertising. Not long after, *Domino* folded and I jumped to the division's travel magazine, where I sent a reporter to golf the coastal courses of California in what was to be a lure for the lucrative golf advertisers. When I ran his stream-of-consciousness story on the front cover—"Me golf. Wind bad, golf bad, golf stupid idiot smackdown asshole game"—and let it like continue like that, verbatim, for five thousand words, Ed prowled the halls. "Ed's on the hunt," an editor alerted me as I ran to the bathroom for cover. We had the best of it, but we didn't know it at the time. Ed quit his own job the day he finally had to shut down the magazine division and fire the rest of us, me included. He was in the prime of his work life and announced his decision to a small huddle of staff without fanfare and refusing accolades or send-offs. It was an act of bravery I've not seen replicated at work by anyone, myself included, and it taught me the fifth of my Six Lessons of a Six-Times-Fired Working Woman:

> 5. It's the moments of integrity and decency in the rumble
> of work that you don't forget and want to emulate. I try
> to remember that when work pushes me to compromise
> on the important things, like truth and basic humanity.

I was in my thirties when the magazines shut down, and I thought work was over for me. It was six weeks before Christmas, naturally, so I put my energy into making my own wrapping paper. "You need a job," said John, looking down as I knelt on the kitchen floor painting tiny green leaves on my homemade fruit stencils, and a month later, I got hired back by the company that had just fired me, this time to be the national editor of the *Globe and Mail*. The problem with this job was that I didn't know anything whatsoever about the news. Reporters would loom over my desk six-deep and ask how many inches I wanted them to file on parole hearings and school board mandates; the editor beside me would discreetly nod yes or no, and I'd follow her lead.

Worse than the incomprehensible story pitches was the blurred pace. I was in over my head. Ed called with advice. "Walk in every day with your head up and say to yourself, 'I love the smell of napalm in the morning.' Never let them see you blink, Bradbury," he said, thereby cementing a work principle I have stood firm by ever since, which is not to be afraid of what you don't know; it'll come to you as you do the job.

Not long after Ed's call, I muscled a story onto the front page about the newly diagnosed hantavirus. This deadly virus, transmitted by mouse droppings, hit just before the May long weekend, when many of our readers would be sweeping out mice nests as they opened their cabins and cottages. The next day, the newsroom revolted over my plebeian values. "It's the beginning of the end," the political editor said as he slapped the paper on my desk. Still, people read it and talked about it. A lot of people, right across the country. That story gave me the beginning of a confidence that carried me over the next fifteen years, overseeing big news like 9/11, when the massive machine of the newsroom would come to life, when you'd call into the wide room of typing reporters, "Who's got fifteen inches on the American flag?" and someone would call back, "On it!" I didn't actually stop the presses—there were no RED BUTTONS anymore—but I held them up more than once.

My boss and the editor-in-chief at the time, my second male editor, let's underline that, was Richard, a raffish product of London's finest public school system. His body was loose and his tongue sharp, and he used the combination as a form of torture.

"Cathrin," he said as I held up the press to get in a feature's complicated-to-format footnotes. He spoke in a singsong voice, smiling so sweetly I thought he was going to say, "Your editorial judgment is unequalled." "You are a complete disaster, aren't you? You don't have a clue what you're doing, do you?" He promoted me all the same because we worked well together, and I flourished under my next editor-in-chief too, another man, and gained "renown as one of the country's best feature editors." That last part is from my firing letter, written by my fourth and final male boss, a cracker-thin, three-month-in editor who was that keen to fire me he all but swung an axe at my head whenever he saw me. New editors liked to fire people right out of the gate, to make their presence felt. I'd survived three of them, watching as they came and went. I wasn't going to survive a fourth. The new editor emailed me on a Tuesday to ask if I had a minute to join him in his glass office. I went outside and called Laura, pacing up and down on the grey-stained sidewalk. "Whatever you do, don't cry," Laura said. "You'll regret it later."

"Let me put this into the bigger perspective," the editor said as I sat across from him, dry-eyed. "I'm going to be doing every-thing differently." It was a little short on perspective. "I hope you believe me when I say you are a brilliant editor." He spoke in a low, considered voice, and I could see why people said he had integrity. The bright green envelope in his disconcertingly pretty hand shook slightly as he put it between us.

"The pension is the most important thing, not the money. Focus on that," said Dad, who was deeply disappointed in the paper's publisher, who he believed had an interest in my career matched only by his own. Laura got me an excellent lawyer who loped into his first meeting with me in a fitted dark brown suit, tightly cropped hair, and the focus of a coyote about to rip into dinner. With a good package to tide me over, I watched the empty days multiply like a marauding virus. The lowest point in this, my worst firing, was the afternoon I failed to change a complicated light bulb. "You can't even change a light bulb," I said out loud, standing in my pajamas on my dining room table, and I went back to bed for the rest of the day. It was a long recovery. But it was a reckoning too. I found out that I wasn't as funny as I had been when I was the boss and everyone laughed at my jokes. And I was called up short at a party at the Toronto Film Festival, where I was introduced to Irish actor Colin Farrell.

"And who are you?" he asked politely; he was meeting a lot of people to promote his latest film.

For the first time in thirty years, I didn't have a job title to put beside my name, and I stared at him blankly for a moment. "I'm nobody," I finally said.

His face opened into a huge smile, and he grabbed my hand and shook it vigorously. "So am I. I'm nobody too."

My final lesson of Six Lessons of a Six-Times-Fired Working Woman is this:

6. It's painful to get fired from a good job, and it hurts your whole life. You'll go off, too, when you least expect it. Someone at a dinner party might say, "I was reading in the *Globe* the other day," and you'll leap to your feet and shout, "You know what, fuck you and your fucking bullshit," and then storm out into the night. Just go with it; there's nothing you can do about it.

A couple of weeks after I got fired from Metro News, the sixth firing, I sat at the round white table in the kitchen of Number 9 with Kelly, thinking about what to do next. Between the *Globe* and *Metro* firings, ten years had passed, and I'd worked hard all through them. I wondered if it was time to stop.

"I think I'll get a new dog." Pierre the poodle had been gone for a while. "A wiener dog," I said to Kelly. I was looking at puppy pictures on my computer. The puppies were bouncing around on a wide blue trampoline.

"I wouldn't," he said, not looking up from his magazine. He'd taken to reading *The Economist* cover to cover.

"I'll call him Billy."

"You're not done with work, Mom. Get a cat, if you must."

"Billy and I are going to head out one day and walk west. I've always wanted to do that, walk and walk, heading west."

"Mom," Kelly said, looking at me now, "that is the most just-fired thing I've ever heard."

"I wonder how far we'd get, me and Billy?"

"About four blocks."

"Remember how Mila used to pour boiling water on the ants?" I asked Kelly after a bit. Mila had been one of our most beloved nannies. "She didn't like those ant hills, the way they poofed out of the dirt between our patio tiles."

"It was super fun," said Kelly. "She drowned mice too; she was really into that kind of thing."

"Those ants. They seemed to be running all over the place in pointless ant frenzy, but they built snappy little hills all the same, tiny pyramids of ant mastery. A life of toil. You live, you work, you die. The end."

"Dark," said Kelly, and went back to his magazine.

15.

Vincible

"WE'RE NOT GETTING ANY YOUNGER."

This was Tecca, who had a plan to face that particular problem head-on. "We'll go on walking trips. It'll keep us young."

It was one of those ideas that sounds terrific over a lively dinner and is sure to be shot down at breakfast. Except this one wasn't. We woke up the next morning and it was still a good idea.

"I propose Ireland," I said over my coffee with cream, thinking of the land of Mom's ancestors and the vague tug I felt to be among them.

Tecca, Johanna, and I were staying at a seaside house owned by Johanna's brother-in-law in Rockport, Massachusetts, and we each looked straight ahead from our lawn chairs at the Atlantic Ocean as we drank our tea and coffee. Waves crashed over the high rocks, so we had to raise our voices slightly to be heard. Tecca's initial idea was that only women would go on these walks. She and I were both divorced and it could be unmooring being the odd woman out in a group of couples, but we quickly agreed that the trip should have both sexes. My partner-less future was looking shinier than it had at the beginning of the year—there was a lot to be said for the steady availability of solitude—but the company of men was still something to be desired. The bulk of men, the way they embraced solitude without guilt. Their comfortable lack of interest in small talk, or even, sometimes, in talking, period. How their combination of impatience and confidence could lead to unexpected adventure.

Our search for men hikers started with Tim and Frank, the generous owners of our Rockport digs, but two weeks shambling around with aging straight people was not high on their list of holiday priorities. I called plain-speaking Matt in New York. "I'd rather pour acid on my hands," he said at the thought of daily forced marches with eight people, which was the number we'd settled on. It was Ron who saved the day. Tecca was visiting Gillian, who is married to Ron, when he walked through the front door with an armload of maps.

"What are those?" asked Tecca, sniffing out fresh prey.

"I'm thinking of going on a walking trip," he said. "Maybe the Cotswolds."

"I've got the trip for you," said Tecca. "There's just one thing you have to do first."

She listed out the kind of men we wanted, like the children in *Mary Poppins* describing their ideal nanny: if you want this choice position, have a cheery disposition; be kind and never cross, don't dominate or boss. Ron enthusiastically took on the job of finding such men, and on a cool October day, eight hikers, four women and four men—two of them couples, two divorced, two married without their spouses; a good mix—descended on a B & B in the tiny village of Aughrim, in Wicklow County,

Ireland, like the gnarly dwarfs pouring into Bilbo Baggins's cottage at the launch of their great adventure.

Tecca, Johanna and Ian, and I were the first to arrive, banging on the B & B door in the pitch-black at 5 a.m. until Margaret finally opened up. "Early birds," she yawned. She wore a fluffy pink dressing gown, two sizes too small, and her blonde hair stood straight up, adding six inches to her already impressive stature. "It's the Canadians!" she shouted to her husband, waking Michael, a thin, genial man who came up to Margaret's assertive bosom. "I have only one room ready." Margaret cinched her tiny dressing gown. "We'll take it." Half an hour later, the four of us were in a deep sleep on one bed and a cot, and our Irish walking trip had begun.

Ireland would be the first of many hiking trips with a group of people who, despite our advanced ages and long-established personality quirks, would prove that your butt doesn't have to be the only thing that gets wider as you get older; your circle of acquaintances can too. Most of us were sixty or still in our slap-happy fifties, and we thought we were invincible, so our plan to hike together every *other* year seemed reasonable, until we realized that after sixty, at the bottom of the sudden-onset decrepitude ramp, time was our most precious commodity. We would hike every year, united in our optimism that getting older could be less an unfortunate decline and more a critical growth spurt.

That was the shining public part of our hike. The private part was darker. This first hike took place between the deaths of my parents, which had a way of cinching my own sense of mortality. But even without that, the trip scared me. The whole year had been a mountain to climb. I wasn't sure I had the strength, physically or emotionally, to climb the actual Wicklow Mountains, so high and bare and steep. I was even less sure that I had the nerve to face the steady reminder from the coupled pairs on the hike that I was on my own. It was a struggle I was still coming to terms with. I was getting older, too, and feeling more fragile, although I also hated to admit that. There was a lot I was trying not to think about, in other words. I needed shoring up if I was going to get through the peaks and valleys, not only of the hike but also of my aging body and worn-out heart. I decided the easiest place to start was at the ankles. I broke my shopping fast and bought new boots.

I found them at Mountain Equipment Co-op. They were expensive, but I reasoned that they would be the last hiking boots I'd buy, a calculation I'd taken to doing since turning sixty. (My simple French press coffee system doesn't need that fancy update. Or, This will be my last blender, so why not the Breville Sous Chef food processor with multitasking S-Blade System?) My new Italian leather boots were called Asolos (imagine every play you can on ass-hole-oh, and you get the tenor of many of our hiking conversations) and were so big it was like wearing small children strapped to my feet. But I felt they would ground me as I trudged through the home of the Kellys and the Keoghs, Mom's people. Mom's motto, and that of her mother before her—"Never go back; always go forward"—was embroidered on a small sampler that had moved after her funeral in March to my front foyer. But it fit less with me as I prepared for this October hike. It took energy to live by a slogan like that, a determined hurtling that didn't leave room for much else. As I clomped around Number 9 in my new Asolos to break them in before the trip, I began to feel not just steady but hopeful. Maybe being more uncertain—about everything?—didn't also mean I'd float away like a puff of dandelion seed, not if I was heavily shod. With my feet firmly on the ground, I could search not just for the route, which would have its own challenges, but for the pace of a new, more thoughtful momentum.

As the first day of our trip rolled on, we met up and caught up at our Aughrim B & B. Most of us had some connection to Ireland. (The country's diaspora is galactic: I once stood on a beach in Liberia, and a Black woman from the nearby village said she had Irish roots. "Ireland and Africa, we're the same," she added.) It broke the ice. That night we had dinner at a local pub, where we were surprised to learn that we were considered noisy. The Irish were low talkers. You needed to work on them a bit to get them to warm up. "Be quiet," someone near us said, beginning a theme that would find us segregated into our own rooms at dinner so as not to disturb the local guests.

"How about a wee dram of whiskey?" Shane asked after our highly excited inaugural dinner. Shane, brother of Gillian, was a Berkeley psychiatrist, musician, and on this trip especially, Irish whiskey connoisseur. He'd researched a local whiskey bar, and after a murmured conversation with the bartender, Shane and Tom (retired banker, tall and cheerful strider) ordered the first of many flats of eighteen-year-old Bushmills for the table, at fifteen euros a shot. I'm not a whiskey drinker, but my first sip tasted like warm gold. Which it may as well have been. For the next three towns, our reputation preceded us. "Are you the Canadians who spent €375 on whiskey?" the owner would say as he unfurled his primo list.

The other thing we had in common besides our Celtic roots was that most of us were going through some kind of transition, divorcing, retiring, moving, thinking about a new kind of future. We were at that age. But we rarely talked about those things as we walked the Irish countryside. It was our forward pace that bound us. We'd debated whether to hike out from a single rented house or move from place to place to place. We chose the direct line of walking, starting near the foot of the Wicklow Way and heading north back to Dublin. We liked the accomplishment of going somewhere, partly. Going forward cast our thoughts forward too. "Perhaps / The truth depends on a walk around a lake," wrote Wallace Stevens, who composed many of his poems on slips of paper while walking to work as an insurance executive. Walking was about the pace of your feet, and also your thoughts, wrote Stevens, agreeing with many other artists and writers. Rebecca Solnit, in *Wanderlust*, an expansive study of walking, put it this way: "The mind, the body and the world are aligned, as though they were three characters finally in a conversation together, three notes finally making a chord." My own mind darted from *want cheese sandwich now* to *must find good pee spot* to *ouchy-wah-wah neck hurts*, but the more we walked, the more I think we all let our minds become their own terrain. We accordioned over the moss green hills, stretched out end to end, catching snippets of conversations that travelled up and down the line. "And every time we hit a bump, my Icelandic seatmate's inflatable arms would float up into my face," Tecca's words wafted past me as I lagged behind. Most days began with a long upward climb out of the low glen towns and onto the bare hillsides. Any climb slowed me down, and Ian joined me at the tail of the group for a while one wet afternoon. A newspaper reporter, he roamed the line from back to front, listening, culling. The cold and wet energized him, and me too. I loved to travel in the miserable off-seasons. The scrubby landscape, the wind, the grey time of year suited my Irishness to the bottom of my new Asolo boots.

"The coastal people, Saxons. It's where my people are from," Ian said happily as he bent down to fiddle with ancient hiking boots held together by increasingly elaborate applications of duct tape. He had a sentimental side.

"My people too," I said. "I wonder which I am?"

"You're a Pict," he said without pause. His precise pronunciation suggested Pict was the last thing anyone wanted to be.

"What's a Pict?"

"Short, pugnacious. Oat eaters."

"And what are you?"

"I'm a Viking. You can tell from my blond colouring." He grabbed hold of his hair, which was standing straight up in the wind, to pat it back down on his head, a classic Viking gesture. "The Vikings killed Pict kings. They'd cut off their nipples first, because they were a sign of succour, and then fling the kings into the bogs."

I scanned the landscape for murderous bogs and landed on what I hoped was our next inn, a long, low lodge winningly called the Glenmalure. "Look," I said, pointing down to the wide green glen dotted with angry Irish cows, and suddenly the sun shone and the white lodge glowed up ahead.

The lodge's rooms were organized around the bar. This bar had a lot going on. There was a live fawn that wandered among the tables, being fed snacks. Many sayings were painted on wood nailed around the bar: "If you want breakfast in bed, sleep in the kitchen." And there was a portrait of Nazi field marshal Erwin Rommel in a back room, binoculars around his neck, hands in the pockets of his leather bomber, and on his face a fed-up expression that suggested we should all get off his back. We couldn't figure out how Rommel had ended up on the wall of an Irish pub on the Wicklow Way. "Why Rommel?" Ron wanted to know. He didn't get an answer, but we got Ron's nickname for the rest of time: Ron-mel. What next, Ron-mel? Hail-o, Ron-mel. Except Ron was the least Rommel-like of any of us. "This trip needs more sheep," he said on the Wicklow Way the next afternoon. Ron was another journalist and also a lifelong walker and polymath, who sometimes talked and walked and sometimes talked and stopped walking as he described prehistoric mosses or Pierre Trudeau's thought process. Now he, Gillian (Buddhist scholar, empath, dawdler extraordinaire), and I held back while the rest debated which way to go next, each pointing in a different direction. There was a lot of that. The Wicklow Way was marked in the Irish sense, which meant sometimes it was and sometimes it wasn't. ("Be careful to watch for the markers at each junction because if you miss one, it could make for a very long day," said our guidebook. We had more than one very long day.)

There were two map systems: the Word, which the women preferred, and the topographical map, favoured by the men. Neither group trusted the other's system. "The map places you in space; it's a metaphor for where you are. Words are like nagging. Do this, go there," said Ian. "Words are not little dots of colour on the page," Johanna said. "The Word has history, local land-marks, eccentricities."

Ron, Gillian, and I ignored all systems. "Baaaa," said Gillian, and I joined her, bleating onto the heath. "I'm 100 percent sheep." I'd spent too much of my work life herding people; I loved following the map-holders as I drifted from one thought to the next and one town to the next. Ballymaghroe, Shillelagh, Tinahely, Glenmalure with the Derry River flowing through, Enniskerry. In Glendalough, the Valley of the Saints, we lingered at the abbey, where we found ourselves staring up at one of the few still-standing tenth-century stone walls. The wall featured a ten-foot-long oval hole with jagged edges. "*Vagina dentata*," said Shane solemnly, referring to the ancient fear of a toothed vagina designed to castrate any man who ventured near. ("The toothed vagina is not a sexist hallucination," wrote Camille Paglia. "Every penis is made less in every vagina.") "Oh my, you're right," said Gillian, as we gleefully snapped pictures. That night, Shane dug out a catchy ditty he'd written for his band some years before and emailed the song around to our rooms. We all dozed off to the sound of Shane crooning,

> *It's a tricky approach,*
> *going in slow,*
> *is there something else*
> *I should know?*

Va-gin-a den-ta-ta. Strings swelled, an organ throbbed. Was there a French horn? The next morning, we couldn't get the tune out of our heads as we walked to the Glendalough grocery, where a lovely woman made robust sandwiches for each of us, and it's true there's not much better than a generous sandwich on a long hike.

"Ach, Mary Rose, sweet Mary Rose," began front-of-the-line-always Tom as we set out on our day's hike. His brown fedora made him even taller than he was.

"The way she asked, 'Cheese?'" said Ian.

"Did you see how much time she spent on *my* sandwich?" said Ron.

"My full name is Mary Cathrin Rose," I said to them as we paused at the bottom of our day's ascent.

They all stopped talking and looked in my direction as if they'd heard words in the air but didn't know where they came from. Shane picked up where they'd left off. "The light on her cheek, sweet Mary Rose." We women lagged behind, we'd had enough, and they strode far ahead with their Mary Rose delusions. Her name was Brenda, by the way.

Three Irishmen in shorts heading in the opposite direction stopped when they got to us. They were well into their seventies and had covered our full day's hike in three hours, they told us.

"You'd better hurry up if you want to catch those men of yours," they said.

"We don't," said Tecca.

"You won't want to get lost out here, though, and that's the truth." They told us a story of a night when helicopters had to be sent out to find a missing woman. "And where do you suppose they found her but in the bar at Tinahely!" It took less than a minute for their silhouettes to disappear on the heath, and I thought it really would be easy to disappear. I could feel Mom everywhere on the lonely hill. I don't mean in an abstract sense. It felt like she was just over there, as lost and forlorn as the landscape, which I suppose was more how I felt without her. I started to cry. "I miss my mom," I said. "Of course you do," said Johanna, hugging me before she poured me tea with sugar from her bottomless Thermos, which did cheer me up.

I felt all my ancestors who went before Mom, too, as we continued our walk. Ann Keogh, my great-great-grandmother, rode horseback over the Wicklow Mountains to deliver an endless tally of pink and rashy Irish-Catholic babies, so the story goes. The spelling of her last name turned out to be important. Back at our Aughrim B & B, I'd told innkeeper Michael that my relatives lived in Carnew, further south on Wicklow Way. "Would they be Keoghs or Ke-hoes?" he asked and was greatly relieved when I said Keogh. "Better not to be a Ke-hoe," he said as he piled more sausages onto my plate. (I eventually met my Keogh cousins on a trip back to the same part of Ireland with my siblings. "Isn't it amazing that we live halfway around the world and look exactly alike," said my cousin Jim as we crowded into a bar in Carnew, and there was a kinship. These dozen cousins lived in the same town where they were born. "We look after each other," said Terry, who took us to the original stone hut, now an outline of rocks in a pretty green valley, where Ann Keogh had lived 150 years ago.)

I blew my nose after my tea and kept walking, wondering if any Keoghs were preserved in the bogs, where the Irish had begun to dredge up the Bog People, murdered Picts, as Ian had said. Often their hands were still tied, and some still had parts of their faces or long tufts of red hair. Or maybe my relatives had fallen in unawares; the bogs were a steady warning not to stray off path.

The day we ascended Scarr Mountain was a textbook bog-sucking kind of day, and I imagined the sour look on my face when they yanked me out a century or two later. "I told you we should have taken the low road." If the weather is not good, "stay on the Wicklow Way." The weather was not good. Ignoring the reliable Word, we took the high detour north, for the view. Which I did not see. I saw nothing but my Asolos as I tried not to blow off the lip of the mountain. "Whee, whee," called Shane as he tripped past in his Irish tweed cap and John Lennon sunglasses, and we found him a little ways on, in the lee of the mountain, flopped in the windless heather. Shane and Tom scouted our lunch site each day, finding a warm spot like this, out of the treacherous wind. We'd spread across the brown landscape with our apples and water and sandwiches like characters in a Jeff Wall tableau. First we'd eat, quiet and hungry. Then we'd stretch out, and maybe nap. Ron practised Burmese meditation, and I told him I'd felt a crazy tingling in my left calf whenever I tried it, which he did not find insane. "It's fine, it's just vibration." Ian was trying to meditate while walking. It wasn't going so well. "Walking distracts me from meditating, and meditating distracts me from walking."

"Many a Viking before you has said the same," I said.

Tecca turned out to be another self-identified Viking. "The Vikings are tall," she said, putting her hand on her own head. "The Celts," she reached down in my direction, smiling sadly, "are short."

Near the end of our hiking trip, we walked along another stone wall that stretched for miles in both directions, marvelling at the effort it must have taken. Gillian wandered off path to gather the blackberries that grew from vines poking out of the crevices. "Look at her," said Shane. "She'll stand there eating those now for half an hour," but it was never disappointing to lag back with Gillian. She was doing a master's degree on Burmese Buddhas. "Worshippers applied gold leaf to Buddha statues as a form of devotion," she told me, "and they become so altered over time with the gold overlay that they're almost blob-like." That image has stayed with me. That was the best of the walk, when our spirits were high and we munched blackberries and talked about golden Buddhas together. Before we became a house divided. Before I set out on my own.

As the afternoon wore on, we walked down and down with no sign of a marked path, and the map readers became fractious. "There's a gate right there," said Tecca, pointing to a white wooden gate. "The Word says, 'Go through a gate,' so let's go through a gate." The men with the map found a better route, a shortcut, maybe. "Like that deer trail through the woods that saved us ten seconds?" Johanna flapped the Word, but the men turned away from the gate to follow their map. Hours later, after a long and ugly detour through an endless landscape of chopped-down trees, Tecca and Johanna were proven right. I pictured how sad those dead trees would have been to pass through, and how silent my hiking companions would have been on the dreary stretch, but I don't know for sure because as they argued over which way was next, I looked up at the high ridge to our right and then my legs started to go in that direction. My idea was that just beyond this high ridge would be our village, and I would be there in no time. As a plan, it sounded better than it was. "Cathrin, stop!" called Tecca, but I didn't.

I kept going. I don't know why I did this, because I was immediately terrified. I thought my fellow hikers would see the wisdom of my decision and follow me. They did not. I'd made a stupid misstep but was too proud to turn back.

"Wait up, Cathrin!" I turned to see Ron, who'd decided to join me because I shouldn't go alone, or because I'd chosen the high road, which also appealed to him. I've rarely been so relieved to see someone. We weren't the wisest pair to go off-map together. It wasn't so much that Ron had a bad sense of direction as that once he made a choice, he stubbornly stuck to it ("têtu," said Gillian). I, on the other hand, should never take the lead. I once hiked on the Yorkshire Dales and stopped at a stepped stile to ask a handsome local man walking toward me if I was headed in the right direction. "You are going in *precisely* the *opposite* direction you need to go," he said with the unreserved joy the English take in giving directions to the wrong-headed. "You need to *completely* retrace your steps." I wished he was here now on the high ridge, directing me with the same zeal. Or maybe it was my emotional traffic that needed directing. Maybe I was trying to get lost on that ridge, like Tim the Jungian had said. Maybe I'd be found that way. This was a supremely wishful thought.

At first, the idea of the village over the ridge seemed plausible, even wise. "Just over this rise, we'll see our inn," I said. "I agree," said Ron, and we went forward at a happy clip. There was a grand view in every direction as we walked under the vast clouded sky. The problem was that just over this ridge was another ridge, and then another, and another. "The ridges seem to go on and on," said Ron as we paused on top of the mountain, looking into the distance at the bare brown crests ahead of us. The view was less motivating as it became more monotonous. We looked back down the mountain then, and our companions were lost to us; their dots had become smaller and smaller until they vanished into the landscape like bits of scrub. After an hour or two of this ridge walking, we decided to revisit our plan. The sky was a darker grey now, not from inclement weather but from the encroaching evening. I was really worried, not only that I'd put myself at risk but that I'd put Ron at risk too.

"I say we head down the side of the mountain," he said gamely, as if this had been stage two of our plan all along. It was steep and we started to slide, too fast. "Hold on to the gorse," said Ron. "It's prickly!" I protested. It was heavy going and complex to calculate your next step within reach of the next patch of gorse. About a third of the way, we sat down to catch our breath, two sheep on a hill. Mountain goats passed by. "I'm sixty-seven years old," said Ron, shaking his head. I clutched my bit of gorse, worried how it would be when my body was no longer as willing as my spirit. Worried that maybe that moment was right now, tired out and lost on the side of this mountain.

After a while, sitting under the blunt sky, we stood up and, bent low at the knees, slowly made our way down the rest of the mountain. At the bottom we came to a walled and rocky stream, which we scrabbled over, exhausted, and some way after that, we arrived at an unexpectedly pleasant grass road. Thirty seconds later, our group appeared behind us in a staggered, spread-out line.

"Where have you been, for heaven's sake," I called out, trying to look miffed. It was terrific to see them. "Ron and I have been waiting here for hours."

Everyone laughed, and it was a huge relief to be back together. If we'd gone through the white wooden gate, we really would have been here hours ago, but we were too happy for recrimination.

"Just don't do that again," said Tecca as we walked beside each other toward the town and our inn. "We don't separate; that's not what we do."

I had, though. I'd climbed the mountain and come down again, and it meant quite a lot, although I didn't know it at the time. At the time I'd thought I was foolish, and said so. But leaving the group for the mountain was a way to leave myself too. I wasn't running out on them, I was running out of myself. Running, and returning. Because you can't stay up there, with the broad view. I had to go back down to my friends and my life, or a life, one with a lot less certainty. It was time to think less about what I was going toward. It was time, even, to think less about what I was moving away from. John, Mom, my childhood with David and Meryl. Instead, it felt like I should ask myself, finally, what I was coming back to that was right in front of me, which was a new and more complex thought. One of the last things Rousseau wrote about walking, before he died of a stroke at sixty-eight, was about what was left for him to do. "I am now alone on earth . . . But I, detached from them and from everything, what am I? That is what remains for me to seek," he wrote, and I thought I was ready for something similar. To find a slower, less relentless version of myself, as I began to see that being vincible was a way forward. And that pretty soon, it wouldn't be just another way forward but the only way.

My iPhone suddenly rang out in the cold. This was unusual.

Only one call had got through on this trip, from a shop in Toronto that was repairing a light fixture for my front hallway. "I'm in Ireland!" I said to the light man. "Well, hang up right now, then!" he laughed. Now I pulled my phone out of the pocket of my red windbreaker and answered it for the second time on our hike. It was almost dark and the grass road looked black under our footsteps.

"Hello, Cathrin, it's your father."

"Dad!" It was a miracle he got through. "Guess where I am? I'm in Ireland," I answered myself. "Wicklow County, where Mom came from."

"Isn't that something," Dad said, happy at the thought. "I walked the circumference of Ireland when I was young." This was fake news. Dad at ninety-four had begun to create memories, all of them happy.

"That must have been something too, Dad," I said. Tecca was leaning in as we walked into our village, to hear Dad's voice. The two of them loved to banter; they were both big believers in the value of a cheerful spirit.

"Now, Cathrin," Dad said, "I can't find my suit." He didn't sound worried, just eager to get into this suit and perplexed that he couldn't find it. This was a man who put on a suit and shone his shoes at the side door before he headed to work every day for fifty years.

"Which suit is that, Dad?"

"For the wedding. I need to get going, they're all waiting for me."

We chatted for a little while longer, but I failed to distract him from his desire to be at his dapper best for the big wedding.

"Huh," I said to Tecca when we hung up. "I hope it's not somewhere else he's getting ready for." But of course he was.

When I landed back in Toronto a few days later, after a loud farewell dinner around a big square table at a terrific restaurant in Dublin, after Ian put his old hiking boots in the garbage, after we bought many bottles of the best Irish whiskey at the airport and hugged goodbye, the first person who called me was Dad. He sounded nothing like the cheerful man on the phone in Ireland. He couldn't take a proper breath. "Cathrin, I need help. Help me, please."

It was time to get going, that part was true. But he wasn't going to need his suit.

16.

King of the Bright Side

I'LL BEGIN WITH THE STORY of the chocolate sundae. It was Wednesday at lunchtime and Dad wanted a chocolate sundae, so that's what he ordered. Not his usual fare, he was more of a hot-lunch kind of guy. But he was in high spirits. He didn't know that he would be gone by Sunday. None of us did.

"That chocolate sundae could have fed a family of twelve, and he ate every drop," said David.

"Tim and David killed him with that enormous chocolate sundae, that's all I know," I said.

"David and I weren't there when Dad ordered the chocolate sundae," said Tim.

"I don't know the details, except that it was a chocolate sundae," said Laura.

"If there is one fact that cannot be disputed, it's that it all started with a banana split," said Ann from Vancouver. "Possibly there was chocolate sauce on the split."

Our memories didn't match; keep that in mind. In *The Important Book*, Margaret Wise Brown looks at an apple, the sky, a plant from many sides before she gets to their essential truth. A spoon is like a little shovel. You hold it in your hand. It isn't flat, it's hollow . . . *But the important thing about a spoon is that you eat with it.* Dad's death was speedy. He was mostly cheerful, the siblings were there, it was warm for November. But the important thing about Dad's death happened when it was over.

A few hours after the chocolate sundae lunch, Dad phoned me on his speed dial. I'd just touched down from my Ireland trip, and it wasn't a good call. By the next morning, he was worse still, and the siblings sat with him while the good, kind doctor spoke to us. She had straight blonde hair to her shoulders and was tall and thin, and we'd immediately liked her when we'd moved Dad several months earlier into the Veterans Centre at Sunnybrook Hospital in north Toronto. She looked at each of us in turn as she spoke now and explained that he'd begun to fade in and out, and that this sometimes happened near the end of a life. Then she turned to Dad.

"Your body is giving up, Mr. Bradbury. It's done a good job for you." She paused and nodded at him, congratulating him for work well done. "But you're ninety-four, and it's slowly starting to shut down."

Dad smiled, muddled by the attention. "It's lovely to see you all," he said, like it was a party.

"Dad, you're dying," Tim said, leaning into his face to make sure he heard.

"Oh no." Dad started to cry a little. "I didn't know."

"What the hell, Tim," I said.

Have I mentioned that Tim has a side as blunt as a dull carving knife? When I made a toast to Mom that bordered on the profound the first Mother's Day after her death, he said, "Too long. Sit down and be quiet."

"People pay money to hear me talk, Tim," I lied. In that case, the siblings took Tim's side and applauded his shorter, better speech. Not this time.

"What?" Tim looked around the doctor's office for an ally he did not find. Nancy was glaring at him like there'd be trouble in his near future, but he was undaunted. "I want Dad to come to terms with it. When I die, I don't want to drift off to la-la land without a clue."

Note taken, Tim. There will be nothing but hard facts for you. But that wasn't Dad's style.

In all versions of the story of the chocolate sundae, it had a cherry on top. Of course it did. We're talking about the King of the Bright Side, after all.

Dad got happier as he got older, if that was possible. He said every decade was better than the one that went before it. "My thirties were better than my twenties, my forties were better than my thirties, my fifties were better than my forties." Dad was making a speech in my living room for his eighty-fifth birthday, and when he got to the eighties, he hesitated. "The eighties, I'm not so sure." Dad's idea that the future was always brighter sustained him throughout his life, until the facts couldn't keep up with the philosophy. His physical limitations meant his energy to keep going had to be balanced with a frequent need to sit still, and his dementia meant his forward pace had lost much of its purpose now that it had no link to where he was coming from. I mean that literally: he couldn't remember where he'd just been. And yet he held on to his optimism, or it held on to him. His insistence that everything be seen in the best light as we grew up meant that a lot was shut down. Sadness, contemplation, conversation. When he extolled a burnt husk of beef, my teenage self shot death rays at him across the dinner table, because this was his line in the sand—this good cheer over the unchewable burnt brisket meant you couldn't speak the truth about it, or anything else, without creating a ripple of unrest in his peaceable kingdom. Dad believed the unexamined life was the path to the bright side, and what an alluring idea that is. Also a false one. So said Socrates.

Dad's childhood was often precarious, which was perhaps why he was determined to give his children a steady upbringing, with a lot of singing. I used to keep the banality of my happy childhood a secret, although my grandparents had done their bit to add colour to my parents' formative years. Mom's alcoholic father didn't do her childhood any favours, except by furnishing the bleak stories that got funnier as she got older. Dad's erratic Irish mum, who'd begun work in the English cotton mills at thirteen (maybe this was why he so cheerfully waved me off to the egg factory; all in a day's work), packed off with her bags once a week, and when she was home, she often locked him in the basement. These stories he rarely told, or if he did, it was with mild surprise and not a lot of interest. "I don't know what she was thinking, really." I believed his basement days added dimension to my father. But if Dad had darkness, I didn't encounter it in the sixty years I knew him. He didn't linger or dwell, especially not on pain. "Suffer less" was Dad's dictum.

In the seven months he went on alone after Mom died, he did suffer, though. Each morning at Hazelton, he had to be reminded that Mom was dead, new grief at dawn. He began to fall, off-balance without his wife.

"How are you doing, Dad?" I said when I found him in a small curtained-off area at St. Michael's emergency after the tenth fall or so. They'd ordered brain scans and blood workups, as usual, so that was hours right there. "Are you sure you need the brain scan, Doctor? I mean, he's ninety-four." I'm not proud of it. Dad's forehead was oozing blood from under a makeshift bandage. "Stood up too fast, I guess." His bright-side kingdom never flourished more than when he was in the hospital. His cot posture was the same as his lounge-on-the-beach pose: legs crossed at the ankles, right hand under his head with elbow crooked. The only thing missing was the book in his left hand. And the beach.

"Anything I can get while you wait, Mr. Bradbury?" one of the nurses said as she took his blood pressure.

"Why, yes. I'll have a glass of white wine, please."

She thought he was cracking a joke, but he thought he was in his living room. When he did remember he was in the hospital, it was the best hospital in the galaxy. "You'll never meet a greater bunch of gals than these nurses." Or: "Warm apple juice isn't so bad. I'd never thought of trying it." His manners weren't a ploy but the way you behaved to strangers and family, both the same. His sense of right was tempered by respect to everyone around him. You saw it in the way he dressed, sharp in all circumstances; how his wallet stayed full, just in case.

He'd had plenty of opportunity to hone his hospital style. Philip Roth said getting old "isn't a battle, it's a massacre," and few knew this better than Dad. He'd spent his last thirty years battling cancer and heart disease. Laura and I counted at least six major surgeries in his sixties and seventies, although neither of us could recall much about his illnesses or recoveries, or even remember visiting him much in those years when he stopped being invincible. In our shoddy defence, he had the recovery speed of the Road Runner on an asphalt track. When Kelly and I walked into his room after a four-hour surgery for an aortic aneurysm that ripped him stem to stern, we caught him looking out at a grey concrete wall with a smile across his face. "I even have a window view," he said. Two months later, he was trying out a kayak for the first time. It didn't go so well. But still.

"Can you make a fist for me, Mr. Bradbury?" said the doctor, who appeared after two hours. "Strong," he said when he tried to push Dad's fist. I don't think he was faking it, though he was fit and young. Dad was strong. Most fathers are.

"Well, I was in the war, you know."

The doctor locked eyes with Dad. "Thank you for your service, sir," he said, and Dad nodded solemnly. The head wound needed stapling shut, with anaesthetic or without. "It's gonna hurt," the doctor said. "It's a four-staple gash."

"Without," said Dad, not looking away from the doctor.

"Tough guy, I get it."

He leaned into each staple with his shoulder, and it was loud—*bang, bang, bang, bang,* "*Ack. Ooch. Yeow. Stop.*" That was me, and I collapsed in a chair for the next few hours until the tests came back clear for concussion and my shift passed on to someone else. I'm not sure if it was this night or another when Dad ended up alone in front of St. Mike's emergency at 2 a.m.

"I walked for many, many, many miles," he repeated many, many, many times of his long trek north through the city from the hospital back home to Hazelton Place. "It was hard, but I kept going." We didn't know if the story was true—it was difficult to believe the hospital would have let him slip away like that. But history had shown that when he repeated something emotional, like wanting Mom's urn, he was on to something.

We did know that it was time to get him more care. Laura secured Dad a spot at the Sunnybrook Hospital Veterans Centre, in the city's north end, which had been set up to see out the last of the Second World War and Korean War veterans. Dad's mental incapacity meant he would live in a locked wing that not even he could escape. This hurt our hearts. We were proud of the way he busted out. The second blow was when we toured the common area for the locked-in veterans. Dad was excited on the way there. "We had a lot of fun in the war, you know. Singing and cards. They're a great bunch of guys." When we walked into the common room, most of the men were sunk down in their wheelchairs, and I saw the same look on Dad's face as I had on Mom's when she was wheeled into the palliative care unit at St. Mike's. The change from hope to despair registered quickly. Emotionally, though, the trek must have been terrifying, from the man he imagined he was—air force cap pushed back on his head, quick with the sums that made him unbeatable at cribbage—to the one he could become, one of the slack-jawed men he saw around him.

"I appreciate everything you kids have done for me," he said with his simple demeanour as he pushed his walker through the bunker-like hallways. "I believe I'm exactly where I need to be."

"We've got a happy one," said his nurse, Maria, when the doctor came by to see Dad in his new room. Maria was a twister of energy as she put slip-free socks on Dad's feet and stacked a mountain of adult Pampers in the bathroom next to a giant vat of Vaseline. ("Privacy is a privilege not granted to the aged or the young," said Margaret Laurence in *The Stone Angel*.) I avoided the terror of this bathroom on all subsequent visits.

"Your troubles are over, Mr. Bradbury," said the tall, thin doctor. "You'll never have to go to emergency again. We'll look after all your needs right here."

The good doctor was right: his troubles were over, for a while. Sometimes the conversations would turn to Mom, and sometimes she would be alive and sometimes she wouldn't be, but mostly he missed her less without her empty chair beside him. The locked ward didn't trouble him either; it wasn't a thing for him anymore, to escape. He got busy, putting his hand up for everything. The men's singing group didn't care if he remembered all the words; few of them did. Their songs dwindled chordlessly near the middle, until someone shouted, "'Four Leaf Clover'!" and they'd leap to the next tune for a fresh start. Dad even joined a bridge group, briefly. "They're past it, they can't bid," he said to Laura, a primo pot/kettle moment.

Mostly, though, our pleasures with Dad were small and private. David joined him for breakfasts in the central garden. One day a plane passed high up, a white chalk underline in the pale blue sky. "Most people wouldn't recognize it, but I know immediately that's a jet flying overhead," Dad said. Laura and Dad settled into a pattern of bust-out drives through nearby residential neighbourhoods, and became as close as they had ever been.

"How do you know all the words?" Dad asked when she sang along at the men's singing concerts. "Because I grew up with you." He liked the birds—I've never met anyone over ninety who didn't—and he and I sat by the feeders in front of the veterans' home. "I loved our friends, you know," Dad said as we watched sun-yellow finches land and then fly up and away. "Once Dale across the street came by when I was painting and said, 'Let me help you paint your house.'" Dad poked me in the arm to be sure I was paying attention. "Imagine that. That's the kind of friends we had our whole lives." I smiled at him smiling and realized I no longer felt oppressed by his optimism. Some people see the splash of stars, some see the black sky behind them—it's a disposition, not a choice. It wasn't Dad's fault, to be a happy man, any more than it would have been to be a depressed one. That was a big realization for me, sitting with Dad and the birds. He worried about the odd thing: if he had enough money, or if other people spent too much. Tim Hortons dropped off three massive coffee urns for the vets each day. "That must cost them a pretty penny," he said, frowning with concern, but only for a moment. "What a great thing for them to do that."

For a break from the routine of birds, singing, garden walks, and the one-minute repeating loop of conversation, there were outings. Tim and I took him to the air show at Exhibition Place by Lake Ontario, where pilots from around the world did aerobatics in the sky and afterward came and shook hands with the veterans in their front-row seats. "Tricky to land," said an American pilot when Dad told him he'd flown the de Havilland Mosquito. "A good landing was the one you walked away from," Dad said, and the airman gave him a heart-thumping grin. This pilot wore a zippered navy jumpsuit, looked like Tom Cruise in *Top Gun*, and had just flown a massive black jet at death-defying speed, so even though he was there to cheer my ancient father, I batted my eyes at him. Dad wasn't the only optimist. "The air show is way better in person!" I wrote on Facebook. The apex of the sunny day was when five women and one man from Normandy, each gloriously, beautifully young, gathered around Dad on his folding chair, in his straw fedora, navy blazer, and serious shades, and kissed him on both cheeks, twelve kisses total. "Dad heaven," said Tim. Dad smiled with his whole head. You could have seen it from the CF-18 Hornet in the sky.

The only outing Dad refused to join was the veterans' summer camp, a three-hour bus trip to a wide northern lake I knew well, where they would stay in a pleasant lodge for a week. But we wanted him to go, we siblings. I in particular would brook no resistance, behaviour I can only look back on as assholic. I thought it would be good for him, or maybe it was revenge for whatever I'd been made to do that I didn't want to when I was young, which was plenty. I wasn't just determined to get him to the camp, I was determined he'd be happy about it. Make new friends! Fresh lake air! "You love to swim, Dad." There were forms to be filled out and triple-signed. Laura circled the aisles of Honest Ed's discount store with the three-page list of camp necessities provided by nurse Maria. "Now, Cathrin, I don't want to go." Dad would call and say this mournfully. "You're going to like it, Dad." I needed a break; we all did. It had been a long year, with a lot of sickness from the parent camp and a lot of tending and caring from the children camp. Dad said he had a cold the day before the trip, but "No fever!" reported Laura, so camp it was.

When the big day came, Tim went and stood by the bus with Dad, his duffle bag at his feet, to be sure he didn't pull a fast one. "I don't want to go, Tim." My brother shoved (*helped*, says Tim) him up the bus steps, and Dad waved sadly from his window as they pulled away. I could say we felt bad for making our ancient father do this, but we were pleased as hell. It was nice all the same when Maria showed us the three framed pictures from the trip, Dad dancing with a different nurse in each one, smiling into her face. "I want you to know this was long after your mother passed away," he said to us.

Women liked Dad. He had a talent for quick banter that was dismissive and appreciative at the same time. On his ninetieth birthday, Mom read out cards in their living room from various widowed friends. Dad could still drive at night, or more accurately, Dad still *did* drive at night, taking women here and there. "Bertha says, 'You don't look a day over eighty.' Margaret says, 'Happy birthday to the life of the party.' Jean says, 'We love our Bill!'" Mom read each card in an even tone and stacked them on the coffee table beside her, for thank-you notes later. When Ann was visiting Number 9 from Vancouver earlier in the year, she made spaghetti and meatballs as Dad and I sat at the round white kitchen table. Ann cooked steadily for friends and family in her house on top of a hill, up in the trees; it was like being in a terrifically well-appointed bird's nest. In my kitchen, she cooked and talked at the same time, a skill I have not mastered.

"No one could kiss like the Italian women," Dad said.

"Which Italian women were those?" asked Ann, raising her eyebrow at me through the balloon of steam as she added the pasta to the boiling pot.

"During the war!" There was a pause.

"Weren't you married to Mom during the war, Dad?" I was getting the story straight, not judging.

"Was I? Yes, I suppose I was."

"Mom and Dad were having sex right through their eighties," said Ann later that night, as we discussed the veracity of the Italian woman and decided it was more fake news. "Mom said she didn't know too much about how it all worked, but Dad did, so that was good." It was hard to compute that buttoned-down Mom had had a satisfying sex life to the end, but as Dad lay dying, he smooched the air to all of us, alarming his grandsons, until we realized it was Mom he thought he was flirting with.

"I expect your father will be gone by Sunday," said the good doctor the Thursday before, and we gathered around for the second time that year. Dad had rarely had a more willing audience. ("Be quiet," Mom used to say, whenever he got going about anything.) "The day the war ended," he began one morning, "I stood on the balcony of Buckingham Place with the Queen. She was a lovely woman, by the way." He was sitting up in the bed he no longer left; he'd walked until four days before he died, but that part was over. "We couldn't believe the crowds. All of London was out to cheer." He smiled at each of us as he spoke. "When you're talking," he'd taught us, "be sure to include everyone." We nodded and smiled back, but the good times ended abruptly the next day.

"I've had enough," he said to Laura and David and Kristen, David's daughter.

"That's okay, Dad," said Laura, holding his hand.

"Everybody is waiting for you," said David. "Your brothers, sisters, friends. Mom."

Dad closed his eyes and all four of them held hands. "Goodbye, Daddy." "Goodbye, Granddad." "We love you, Dad." They were crying hard. "I can't find the path. I don't know where I'm supposed to go." ("You get why people believe in God, when the dying say things like this," Laura said later.) Dad got quieter and Laura texted for everyone to come quickly, and as we stood around his bed, he opened his eyes and picked up where he left off.

"As I was saying," he said, delighted to see that his audience had grown to include most of his children and grandchildren. "I flew hundreds of missions over the Atlantic." In truth, the war ended right before his first mission across the English Channel, but flying, and teaching other pilots to fly, was a lifelong joy. "Up there with the birds" was one of the last things he said.

Someone came by to ask if Dad wanted the last rites, or what the Catholic Church now calls the anointing of the sick. ("Even the Catholics don't say, 'You're gonna die,'" I hissed at Tim.) "I'd like that," Dad said, and sometime later a Catholic priest spoke some words over him as Ann and I stood on either side of the bed. "Would you like to take Holy Communion now?" the priest asked, and when Dad nodded yes like a schoolboy at the altar, the priest took a round gold container from his pocket and flipped the lid open to reveal a tiny stack of white Hosts.

"Do you carry that around with you?" I asked.

"Yes."

"Are they consecrated, those Hosts?"

"They are."

"So you just open that thing—"

"It's called a pyx," the priest interrupted.

"So you whip out your pyx whenever you need a consecrated Host?" I couldn't get over this portable Host idea, carrying around the body of Christ in your pants pocket.

"This is the body of Christ," the priest began, reciting the Eucharist prayer and doing the sign of the cross over Dad's forehead while Ann and I became solemn at the ritual.

"Amen," we said. It seemed to relax Dad, because he immediately fell into a soft snore, with the Host sitting like a round white toonie on top of his tongue.

"He's going to choke on that," I said. I'd had one too many panicked episodes of the white disc sticking in my throat on the way down when I was a child. It was dry as the desert sand, and about as appetizing to swallow. "You need to lift it off with a pair of tweezers," I said to Ann in my bossy tone, which worked less and less well on her.

"*You* lift it off with a pair of tweezers," Ann said, but neither of us was going to tweeze the body of Christ off our father's tongue, no matter how far we'd moved from the teachings of the church. And after a bit, a long bit, it dissolved.

Ann stayed on alone for the first shift that Saturday night. When Tim took over, Dad had begun to thrash. "It was a fight," said Tim. Dad had fought in the streets with the Protestants as a Catholic kid growing up in east-end Toronto, and Tim said he never lost his taste for a fight. "He kept it mostly hidden, but I saw him go for two cops once, when he thought they were wrong. I had to pull him off them. I got that fight from him; we all did." After four hours of tossing and kicking, Dad slowly stopped. "I couldn't say it happened then or then," Tim said. Laura arrived at 8 a.m. with a bag of warm croissants from an uptown French bakery and bustled around the room, finding napkins. Tim looked silently at her and then over at Dad. "He's gone," he said finally, and Laura dropped the croissants. "Oh, Daddy," she kissed him. At Number 9, Ann came into my bedroom and woke me up. "Dad's dead," she said, and we hurried to the hospital like we were late for an appointment.

There are several versions of what I said when I walked into Dad's room ("And that's that," "He's good and gone"), so we'll go with mine—"Classic Dad move, on to the next thing." If Mom's last room still held the idea of her presence, as if she might pop back in for some tea, Dad's seemed empty, as if he'd wiped his hands of all our sorrows. After a while, his caregivers carried in a Canadian flag, for what they called the flag ceremony. They draped it over Dad, and we bent our heads in prayer. I'm not sure what he would have thought. "I don't go in for the medals and parades," he'd said at the air show in his rebel fedora, but there in his room, it was also an ending. A statement that one thing was over, one life. And also one big part of our lives.

"We'll take the do-over," said David at the funeral home, slapping the table at the startled funeral director. "Mom times two." We chose the same urn, except in navy blue, the same church and hymns, and the same Father Vincent.

"All Saints' Day," he said knowingly when we told him Dad had died on November 1.

"What's that about?" I wanted to know.

"An auspicious day to die. The celebration of all the souls in heaven."

I didn't know about that, but as I stood at the pulpit to give Dad's eulogy, I noticed the way the cool winter light was warmed by the stained-glass windows as it flooded into the church. I noticed the pulpit's power and weight, too, the way Jeremiah described it. I felt like if I said something true up there, people would hear. I tried to capture Dad as best I could, although now I think just one word would have been enough, if I'd said it from the pulpit: DAD. DAD. DAD. Not to summon him. More to herald him.

Back at Number 9, we had the same small delicious sandwiches, made by the same friend who'd made small delicious sandwiches for Mom, and the same friends and family gathered with us. But one thing different was the singing. Mom's funeral had a lot of crying, Dad's a lot of singing. "Let's hear a war song," someone said, and the siblings rallied for "I've Got Sixpence," and our cousins joined in and the harmony could have been worse. Kelly took pictures of the grandkids in the backyard, all crowded panoramas. "I didn't realize, but the wide angle caught his family together. It felt like him." Kelly had his own arc around his grandfather's unstoppable optimism: "I thought he was putting on a good face for us." Except his positive outlook didn't change, which seemed impossible if it was a show. One fall day in the garden of the veterans' home, the brown leaves spinning to the ground around them, Dad told Kelly his secret. "It was simple," said Kelly. "Instead of making choices in pursuit of happiness, Granddad let his happiness dictate his choices." Dad had known darkness as a boy, locked in that basement.

He had known it growing up rough and poor in the Depression, and going to war, too, but he chose not to stay there. That would have felt like wallowing to him, but it was likely also the reason he chose to use his happiness as a guide, not a goal. As the most salient of his characteristics. I thought again about Socrates's "unexamined life is not worth living," and I guess he'd have included my dad in that, because it was true that Dad's trip to the bright side didn't include a slow and thoughtful excavation of who he was, where he was coming from, and where he was going. Few people have the luxury of time and space and education and class and money and comfort and ease to do that, but does that mean the unexamined life isn't worth examining, or even emulating? Dad taught himself to desire what he had, not what he aspired to. "I'll be lucky to hold on to Granddad's view when I stare at my own concrete walls," was how Kelly put it.

After more drinks and singing, Ian, one of the Ireland hikers, told the story of how he came to own Dad's portable powder-blue picnic table. When they were in their sixties and seventies, Mom and Dad went for drives and roadside picnics, often to take in the spring blossoms. It sounds modern now, a small COVID-times pleasure. Mom would make potato salad, and Dad would set up a hibachi to grill a bit of meat. They liked a warm lunch. Dad would get the portable powder-blue table from the trunk of the car and flip its latches open like a suitcase to create the perfect picnic table in miniature, just high enough off the ground so that it didn't diminish your dignity while you sat on its benches and enjoyed your lunch al fresco. They'd cover it with a tablecloth and eat their grilled chicken at the side of the road as the cars went by, blossom petals at their feet, or maybe pine needles. All five of us kids loved that picnic table almost as much as we loved our parents.

Ian came to own the picnic table the day a small group of us set off on a bicycle trip along the Niagara Parkway, from Queenston Heights to Niagara Falls. The kids were young and the bike trail was flat, and the other appealing part of the plan was that Mom and Dad could make us a picnic lunch at Queenston Heights Park, home of weekly family picnics when I was a kid. "You know they've been working on this picnic for two weeks," said Laura, not quite chastising me. "Great!" I said. "Be sure to make your potato salad, Mom, and the honey ham." Even though they were into their eighties, they could still do anything, as far as I was concerned. Dad carried the cooler from the parking lot, and then went back for the folding chairs and portable picnic table, and when we arrived on our bikes, we found them in the perfect place under a shady tree. The sunshine through the leaves made dancing spots on the picnic table, and it felt like a good time.

Before we ate, Mom and I walked to the statue of General Brock, and she twisted a Kleenex in her hand as she told me how worried she was about David's drinking. "Stop thinking about it, Mom," I said under Brock's outstretched arm, pointing to the invading Americans, not understanding that she was past the ability to stop worrying. "I can't. I can't stop," she said.

Back at the picnic table, John poured vodka from a silver flask into a plastic cup and held it to the light. "There's nothing I love more than an ice-cold glass of vodka," he said, and Mom stopped what she was doing to look full at him. "Really, John? Nothing you love more?" It was unusual for her to speak so boldly. I was sitting beside my husband when he said this, and the kids were playing around, and I don't know if he felt the sting that we'd let it come to this, but I did. We served ourselves ham and potato salad, and Mom had one bite of her couscous salad with currants, a modern picnic innovation to please me and my friends, when she began to choke. She didn't stop breathing, but she couldn't properly take a breath either, and Dad became panicked. "Do something, Cathrin!"

It occurred to me that they were both going to die, which of course they were, but not right there, not that day. You can see how everything that was to come was contained like the potential of a seed, or a virus, on that Queenston Heights picnic on a sunny July afternoon, though. Mom's terrible anxiety about David. The end of my marriage. Mom's choking death. Dad's panic to be without her. It was all laid out, like our picnic lunch. Even how Dad gave away the picnic table because that would be the last time they'd have a picnic, and maybe he knew that.

But this was meant to be a funny story. Back at Dad's wake, Ian was telling his version. "I'll tell you, those Bradburys really knew how to throw a picnic. And I didn't get the picnic table only because I saved Mrs. Bradbury's life." As Mom kept choking, Ian gave her the Heimlich manoeuvre behind a large tree, hidden from us because she was embarrassed, and after one push against her frail solar plexus, a small black currant flew out. "My knight in shining armour," Mom said.

"I didn't get the picnic table only because I saved your mother's life," Ian reminded the room again, because the hostility over the way he had absconded with our picnic table was as thick as two planks, "but also because I'd admired the way it suggested that to be a perfect father was to have such a table as this." Ian looked around the unfriendly room. "And that's when your father said, 'I want you to have my picnic table.'"

"Booo," Ann said from the corner near the piano. "Give it back," said Laura, possibly calculating legal recourse. "It's *my* picnic table," Tim said. As a journalist, Ian was familiar with the sensation of a growing mob disagreeing with something he'd said. "Don't get between a clan from St. Catharines and their portable picnic table," he jabbed, and sidled to safety through the kitchen to the back door.

He still has the picnic table, by the way, and refuses to return it.

Back in January, at the beginning of this year of many confusing changes, Dad and I chatted in his sauna living room at Hazelton Place as steam dripped down the windows. My divorce had just come through, Number 9 was a mess of crossed wires, and the thin membrane between all is well and all is lost had never felt more fragile. I asked Dad how he'd been able to stand it when he watched his children make mistakes with their lives: married to the wrong people, lost in alcohol, beaten down by work. Kelly and Mary were just starting out, their adult lives ahead of them, and I wanted to get it right. But I was also angry that Dad hadn't protected me from my own fateful choices. "Why didn't you say, 'Look out. Do this, don't do that'?"

Dad seemed surprised by the question. "You were launched," he said. "My job was done."

Now the year was almost over and Dad had followed Mom. It was sad, and I'd miss having them in my life. But there was something else as well. Underneath the grief we all experience at the death of aged parents, I felt a sense of relief. The burden of their example had been lifted. The model was gone, their authority was gone, even their expectations and the possibility of disappointing them. My parents were launched. My job with them was done.

And that's when *the most important thing* about Dad's death came to me, and I think he would have agreed. Because it wasn't only Mom and Dad who were launched. It was me too. My future was without my parents, and without their idea of me and who I was. It wasn't a full future—I was sixty years old, after all. But the time left was *my* time. There was no one ahead of me. No parent to conform to. Dad was the last to go, and I let that thought roll over me to see how it felt. Mom had left out how she felt when she'd seen the last of her own older generation out. "Well, that was the last of them," she'd said in her sixties, after the death of some dimly remembered aunt, and I'd imagined her fear that she'd just moved closer to the grave herself. But now I was pretty sure that I'd had that wrong. It wasn't frightening to have no one on the road ahead. It was freeing.

I could feel myself moving closer to something. Not an abyss but the warm and open water's edge. It felt like a place with a lot of potential.

17.

Ho

DECEMBER BROKE ALL PREVIOUS RECORDS for warmth. "Scorching. Balmy. Or just plain mild. However you want to describe it, 2015 ended on an extraordinarily mild note," reported Environment Canada, adding that it was the warmest wrap-up for a year in Toronto since 1840. I'm not above thinking the weather will bend to my will. Two years earlier, during the great ice storm of 2013, which turned the city into a crime scene of taped-off fallen trees, many of them on my street—glorious, huge old trees—I was pretty sure the big freeze was brought on by my fury at having to host another fuming fractured faux family Christmas with John and the kids. A few hundred thousand people went without power for days, but the important thing about the ice storm of 2013 was that I didn't have to do Christmas at Number 9. So this extraordinarily mild and hopeful December that ended 2015? I wouldn't put it past my superpowers (weatherwise, is all I'm saying) because a new weather system had landed on me too, a calm and thoughtful lull. The view outside the broad casement windows at Number 9 was mostly bright as the sun rode high in the sky and the temperatures rose to 15°C, but as the year came to a close, I was more interested in the inner landscape.

"What do you want to do for Christmas?" I asked the kids. This was a loaded question, and we all knew it. I loved Christmas, or I had as a kid growing up. The decorating, not just of the tree but of every available surface in our house in Grimsby. Reading and sorting the dozens of cards that came in the mail. The frenzy of ripping open presents in the morning, then running wild while our parents and aunts and uncles collapsed in armchairs after dinner. The singing, of course the singing. My own family Christmases with my kids had a lot to live up to, and to my surprise, more and more often they did not. Which didn't stop me from trying to drag us into a happy holiday. The harder it got to do that, as my marriage slowly unravelled, the harder I pulled. I was the family tugboat, after all, and never more than at Christmas.

But not this year. This year, it was time to pay attention instead to what was right in front of me in my living room at Number 9. This year, I really wanted to hear Kelly's and Mary's answers when I asked them what they wanted to do for Christmas.

"Please just no pressure, Mom." This was Mary, head down as she edited her photographs on her phone. She knew a line when she heard one, and she didn't think for a second that I was going to listen to anything she said.

"Let's just hang out," said Kelly, also not looking at me as he wrote coding formulas in a black notebook. We were scattered around the room, distanced in our own chairs, on this strangely spring-like and breezy afternoon for December, and their heads-down, monotone uninterest in our family Christmas was normally the kind of thing that would send me. The ingratitude. The indifference to everything I had done all these years to keep us going, no matter what. To keep us happy and on track. I wouldn't have said any of this out loud, but Kelly and Mary would have seen it in my tight smile, which was likely why they kept their heads down now. They'd have heard it in the needle prick of my voice too. Christmas happiness was as non-elective in my household as surgery for a burst appendix.

Except that if they had looked up, the kids would have seen my demented grin. Ebenezer woke up to the joy of Christmas after his night of transformation. I woke up to the joy of letting mine go. "I'm as light as a feather!" said Alastair Sim, the best Scrooge of all, as he danced around the room in his nightshirt. "I don't know anything. I never did know anything. But now I know that I don't know anything." I didn't stand on my head or do a jig, but what I was thinking as I grinned at my children's bent and silent heads was how gorgeous they were, even or especially in their defiant pissiness. What a good job John and I had done to get them this far. And how they were pretty much launched. I'd done my job.

It was a lot of launching for one year. Ordinary events in any life had crowded together so densely in the past twelve months that time had become a kind of place, a place where something happened, like Alice Munro had said. And somewhere in that place—that year that crashed together and smashed apart—a new track, or three or four, began to open up. Number 9 had stopped locking me out, for one thing. The holes in the walls were of my own making, to hang the modest art I had begun to collect, which required a surprising amount of self-examination, which in turn brought on a nervous collapse over what I liked and didn't like—because who knew what my style and image were. Me least of all, but I'm getting there. But the big lift-off was more personal than my house. These days, looking for, even waiting for, moments of grace had become my new modus operandi. Like my kids sitting here with me.

This is what we did for Christmas on December 25, 2015: we hopped on the subway to the Eglinton SilverCity movie theatre in midtown Toronto to watch the opening of the new *Star Wars*. I took a picture of Kelly's and Mary's backs as they leaned too close to the tracks on the empty St. George subway platform and managed not to tell them to step back. We joined a mismatched group of their friends and mine—Laura and David were there too—and we took up an entire row of prime seats, which stretched out into almost prone positions. Someone took another picture of all of us, reclining. I was wearing a red sweater, my flag to Christmas cheer, and everyone looked relaxed and happy, unlike Christmases past, when my children could look exhausted. By me, I now realized. Not by my cheerfulness but by my constant fear of letting in the sadness just the other side of it. The Japanese have a word for it, *kintsukuroi*. It refers to the art of repairing broken pottery with gold or silver lacquer, understanding that a piece is more beautiful for having been broken.

Star Wars was enjoyed by all, except Kelly. You'll never recreate the joy of Star Wars for a generation of kids who *were* Luke Skywalker, who sliced the air with their lightsabers when the Force was with them. I wouldn't recreate the Christmas of my childhood, and I didn't want to anymore. I wasn't who I had been growing up. I wasn't even who I had been a year ago.

Back at Number 9, we opened the last of our Christmas presents from under our tiny Grinch tree. A small package had my name, a gift from a friend. I unwrapped it quickly, an old habit, to find a wooden rabbit with pink ears and black spots. "*Reculer pour mieux sauter*—Draw back to make a better jump," said the card. I sat for a moment, looking into the rabbit's uncertain face, and then put it on the bookshelf, where I could keep an eye on it, until we were ready.

EPILOGUE

WHEN KELLY WAS LITTLE and I'd finish reading him a book, he'd say, "What's the epilogue, Mom?" Because at the end of *Matilda*, when her parents disappeared to Spain, blithely leaving their daughter behind, he was not pleased.

"That's it? That's the end?"

"Not at all," I said. "Matilda grows up and buys a bookstore, where her run of bestsellers are displayed in the window for all to admire. Everyone but her old, crippled, and ugly parents, who go by one day and say, 'Huh,' and keep walking." The epilogue did the trick, and from then on, we agreed I'd tell him what went on after all the books were done, which was satisfying for both of us.

So here's *The Bright Side* a few years on.

David found love and grows tomatoes, peppers, and peas in his small backyard, like Dad used to when we were young. Tim lives one town over from David and not far from Grimsby, where we all grew up. Tim and David renovate houses together, still, in their seventies, and recently built me a new bathroom. "You okay, Tim?" I'd hear David over the hammering. "I'm okay. You okay, Dave?"

Ann and her family holiday on remote Hornby Island, a three-ferry trip into the Pacific Ocean, off the coast of British Columbia. I had the honour of joining them one recent summer, and Ann's minimalist shopping habits were nowhere evident as we processed daily along the ocean beach with chairs and bright umbrellas and beach toys and inflatable orange settees and bamboo mats and blankets and towels and wine and beer and food to last for days. It reminded me exactly of our picnics as kids, except that instead of running wildly, I was the one sitting under an umbrella with a blanket to keep me warm from the ocean air while my niece rubbed my hands.

Laura bought a zippy car and an off-grid cabin—as a family, we tend to go off-grid ourselves in our sixties and seventies, one way or another. She had a sign made in honour of Dad, Bill's Perch, which she attached to a wooden bench with a high view of the dark and silent northern lake. "Have you ever seen a more beautiful view?" she says as we sit over our morning coffee.

Mom and Dad are buried under a rose of Sharon, side by side in their urns, in a pretty setting near mom's sisters and parents. I woke up to a loud banging on Number 9's big wooden front door with the lion's head knocker—knock! knock! knock!—for three nights in a row, three knocks each night. "Didn't your mother die a year ago this week?" said Tim the Jungian, who was not opposed to ghosts, and she had, and sometimes since then, I do feel her ghost nearby at Number 9. She's never fully left, Mom. No surprise there.

All the siblings took a trip to Ireland the year after our parents died. "Five of us are going in. We don't know how many will come out," I wrote in the *Toronto Star* of the trip, and we did re-enact the brutal tribalism of our childhood in terrifyingly infantile ways over things as small as bag of potato chips, mint jelly, and recycling systems; the minuscule scale of the stakes was what made them compelling. But mostly we moved past our childhood and learned to be with each other without our parents.

My other travel companions, the hikers, are grounded for now. Ireland was the first of many annual hikes, we stuck to that. We were set to hike the Coleridge Way in the west of England, before the pandemic sent us home, but we hope to get back there before our muscles atrophy.

Meryl and I often discover we are reading the same chapter of a book, or watching the same episode of a TV show, at the exact same time. It doesn't surprise us; we're connected. She and her husband have closed up their yellow house and moved west, for now. "We're mulling and deciding what to do next," she texted the other day.

John also bought a house near water, where he lives with his crazy-eyed poodle, Roxy, who I'm pretty sure he loves more than he ever did me. John hasn't had a drink in many years.

Mary and Kelly have both found love and work. Mary has bought a telescope and takes haunting pictures off her balcony of the huge grey moon at night. Kelly and Vonnie left Guatemala and moved into Number 9, where there's plenty of room. They are going to have a baby soon. His middle name will be William, after Dad.

ACKNOWLEDGMENTS

This book isn't only about my year, it's about family and friends who agreed to let me write parts of their own stories, and to use their names. My siblings didn't have a choice but to appear as themselves and were endlessly good sports about it. Laura Bradbury was with me every step, reading and fact-checking countless drafts of chapters and the completed manuscript. I am immensely grateful for her love and encouragement. When I asked David Bradbury if I could tell his story, not only of his return but of the years when he wasn't at his best, he was silent for a number of minutes. "Anything you write is fine by me, Sis," he finally said, and in an act of remarkable generosity, he asked me to change just one word in the chapter about him. Tim Bradbury and his wife, Nancy Keenan, were continuously interested, curious, and supportive; Tim would like everyone to know he will never talk about that commune, by the way—a mystery he feels is one of most compelling parts of the book. Ann Bradbury laughed at her own depiction, the most thrilling response of all. "I feel I don't come off so well in the Mom chapter," she said. "I'm okay with that."

Meryl, who changed her name for this book, had her own arc thinking and talking about her past. I don't like to say I tortured Meryl, but her memory was so supremely excellent that I texted her all night long for months. "Did your mom like Tom Jones or Elvis Presley best?" I'd ask. "Engelbert Humperdinck," she'd reply at 4 a.m.

I'm grateful to the friends who helped me with their own memories of that year and let me share them: Ellen Vanstone, Johanna Schneller, Tecca Crosby, Gillian Graham, Ron Graham, Shane Mackay, Jason Logan, Elizabeth Renzetti, Matt Hart. The people who saw me as a writer before I was one have a special place in my heart. Carol Toller and I continue to have illuminating conversations about writing, which began when my own writing was a baby of an idea. Lesley Harrison put books in my mailbox with encouraging notes based on very little evidence. Tim Pilgrim said one day, "So what are you writing?" a deceptively simple question that launched me on this book, and I thank him for his counsel, intelligence, and insight at every stage. Ian Brown, long-time friend and colleague, paid me the compliment of telling me I was a writer before I'd written a word and gave me the benefit of his writerly brain, and the book is better for it.

It's a pleasure to thank my editors, agents, and readers. Dianne de Fenoyl, a top-notch editor, published my stories in the *Toronto Star* (parts of which make their way into some chapters), and those stories led to this book, which Dianne then also read, adding her wise and encouraging notes. Jen Knoch was the first person to ask what a book from me might look like, and *The Bright Side* wouldn't exist without our long and thoughtful conversations over coffee. Jen also read the manuscript, and her notes were smart, warm, and helpful. Rosie Westwood, friend and colleague, was another reader who steered me right with her always-useful insights. It was Lesley Harrison, a film agent herself, who introduced me to literary agent Jackie Kaiser, who became my wonderful, present, world-expanding agent. Diane Turbide is my editor at Penguin. Those vastly irritating words I sprinkle liberally as an editor myself—dig deeper; less; more; unclear; awkward; CUT!—under Diane's pen were buoys tossed out to a drowning woman on a rough sea. Diane followed the long rope of a thought to where it needed to go, and urged me to cut what was superfluous along the way. Janice Weaver copy-edited the manuscript with patience and humour, and more than one of her side notes made their way into the text. Nicole Winstanley, the publisher of Penguin, saw this book from the beginning, and her encouragement was energizing.

It's not happenstance that some of the people quoted are Margaret Laurence, Carol Shields, Margaret Atwood, and Alice Munro, that quadrumvirate of Canadian talent and my first loves as a reader. This is what Laurence said about her writing and her kids: "If I hadn't had my children, I wouldn't have written more and better, I would have written less and worse." Kelly and Mary, my last and biggest thanks are to you, my dear children, my lights and joy. You were as interesting, challenging, and unexpected to write about as you were to raise, and remember what your mom says about your raising: I did the best I could with the information available to me at the time.

Thank you all.

© Mary Barber

CATHRIN BRADBURY is a Senior News Director at CBC News. She has worked as a leader and top editor at *The Globe and Mail, Metro News,* and *Maclean's* magazine. Her writing often appears in the *Toronto Star,* where she is a regular contributor. She lives in Toronto.